UNDERSTANDING THE
TEACHING OF JESUS

Understanding
the Teaching of Jesus

DAVID ABERNATHY

Based on the Lecture Series of

NORMAN PERRIN

"The Teaching of Jesus"

THE SEABURY PRESS | NEW YORK

1983
The Seabury Press
815 Second Avenue
New York, N.Y. 10017

Except where noted, scripture quotations contained in the text
are from the *Revised Standard Version of the Bible*, copyright
©1946, 1952, New Testament Section, second edition, copyright
©1971, by the Division of Christian Education of the National
Council of the Churches of Christ in the United States of America.

Library of Congress Cataloging in Publication Data

Abernathy, David.
Understanding the teaching of Jesus.

Includes bibliographies and index.
1. Jesus Christ—Teachings.   2. Bible.   N.T. Gospels
—Criticism, interpretation, etc.   I. Perrin, Norman.
II. Title.
BS2415.A43   1983   226'.06   82-19183
ISBN 0-8164-2438-1

Audio cassettes with a study guide on the contents of
this book are available from:
The Protestant Radio and Television Center
1727 Clifton Road, N.E.
Atlanta, GA 30329

A NOTE TO THE READER

Understanding the Teaching of Jesus is based on a series of lectures which Norman Perrin recorded privately in 1962. In these lectures, Prof. Perrin tried to present the findings of New Testament scholarship about the teaching of the historical Jesus, as he then understood them, in a way that would be accessible to the non-expert. Thus, references were explained, background materials were given, and other concessions to the lay audience were made.

In the years since the lectures were recorded, New Testament scholarship has not stood still. It became more and more clear that the lectures could not be published, if they were now to fulfill their original purpose, without change. In order to carry out the original intent, David Abernathy, a student and associate of Norman Perrin, labored for a number of years to update, adapt, and make even more accessible the materials in the original lectures, and to turn them into book form. This book, which includes some of the latest conclusions of New Testament scholarship, is the result.

It must be stressed that Norman Perrin, who died in 1976, did not read this book in anything like its current shape. He did not have a chance to approve it, and therefore he cannot be held responsible for its final form. Nevertheless, it incorporates substantially the materials from his 1962 lectures, and we are proud to make this work available to a wider public.

THE PUBLISHERS

To Those Whose Lives
May Be Enriched
By the Teaching of Jesus

CONTENTS

PREFACE

Faith consists not in ignorance, but in knowledge.
John Calvin

A T some point while reading this book, you will find it helpful to read a portion of the New Testament for a basic orientation to this study. Use a good, easy-to-read translation of the first four gospels and rapidly read the narrative accounts about Jesus, preferably in this order: Mark, Luke, Matthew, then John. You will be able to see the numerous similarities and differences in the various treatments by the evangelists, especially when reading all four accounts at one sitting. If you can set aside any preconceptions about Jesus and his teaching, it will help you in perceiving the variations in these narratives.

There are several helpful references available to aid the beginning student of the Bible. Two of the most important for a study of the teaching of Jesus are a good translation of the Bible and a parallel text of the synoptic gospels. Clearly the best Bible for study purposes is *The New Oxford Annotated Bible with the Apocrypha*. Recommended for use by Protestant, Catholic, and Orthodox authorities, it is the best one-volume annotated edition of the Bible available today.

Another resource book is the *Gospel Parallels*, edited by Burton Throckmorton. This helpful publication of the synoptics places the gospels of Matthew, Mark, and Luke in parallel columns, thus making it easy to see the similarities and variations in the different narrative accounts about Jesus. The gospel of Thomas parallels are also included in the footnotes, revealing in a convenient way all significant and related materials on one page. The introduction to the *Gospel Parallels* is an authoritative and concise discussion of the various manuscripts and types of texts in the gospel accounts of Jesus.

One of the many commentaries available is *The Interpreter's One-Volume Commentary on the Bible*. This volume would be a good addition to one's library, especially if seeking good commentary and cross-references between the Old Testament and New Testament, essential to studies about the Jesus materials beyond the scope of this book.

The Interpreter's Dictionary of the Bible is an excellent reference source for biblical studies. Originally issued in 1962 in four volumes, it was updated in 1976 with a supplementary volume to make it more current. The numerous articles written by various scholars present a variety of viewpoints, each of them a sound treatment of the topic covered.

A larger reference source, available in many public libraries and church libraries, is the twelve-volume *Interpreter's Bible*. This reference source is actually an encyclopedia of biblical information on numerous topics.

For the advanced student with a working knowledge of Greek and Hebrew, the *Theological Dictionary of the New Testament* in ten volumes is a reference source used by professionals. An English translation of the editorship of Gerhard Kittel and Gerhard Friedrich, these two volumes are a classic and a standard for biblical studies.

In addition to those printed works, the authors of this book have recorded a set of six audio cassettes presenting this material in lecture form. These twelve lectures include a synopsis, glossary of terms, and generally follow the outline of the twelve chapters of this book. The cassettes have been produced by the Protestant Radio and Television Center and may be purchased by writing to the Center at 1727 Clifton Road, NE, Atlanta, GA 30329.

The contents of this book have been arranged so as to meet the needs of two types of readers: those who are looking for general information and readers who wish to study the teaching of Jesus in detail.

For the convenience of the general reader, the resource materials can be easily skipped over without losing the continuity of movement from beginning to end. For those readers using this book for study purposes, the resource materials at the end of each chapter will be helpful. The glossary attempts to provide for a clear understanding of terminology; scripture references are listed in the order they are used in the chapter and are provided for those who wish to refer to them before reading the chapter itself. The bibliography shows the source of some of the conclusions drawn in each chapter as well as indicating books with other viewpoints and books with additional information about the subject of each chapter. The questions have been designed primarily for testing comprehension of the subject matter with answers in the back of the book. It has been our intention to make this book easy to read, include as much information as possible and create a valuable reference and resource book.

So much for resources for a study of the teaching of Jesus. Before beginning the study itself, we would like to say an introductory word about New Testament studies in general.

References

Abernathy, David, and Perrin, Norman. *Understanding the Teaching of Jesus Audio Cassettes.* PRTVC, 1727 Clifton Road, NE, Atlanta, GA 30329. Twelve lectures recorded on six audio cassettes in vinyl folder with study guide (1982 price, $49.95).

Bruce, F. F. *History of the Bible in English.* New York: Oxford University Press, 1978. Third edition; available in paperback (1982 price, $3.95).

Buttrick, George Arthur, ed. *The Interpreter's Dictionary of the Bible.* Nashville: Abingdon Press, four volumes, 1962. Supplementary volume, 1976. These five volumes are more like a brief encyclopedia than a dictionary (1982 price, $95.00).

Good News New Testament: The New Testament in Today's English Version. New York: The American Bible Society, 1976. This fourth-edition rendering is a highly readable translation in a convenient format, available in paperback. Synoptic parallels are listed under each topic heading.

The Interpreter's Bible. New York and Nashville: Abingdon Press, 1952–57. A twelve-volume encyclopedia available in many public libraries (1982 price, $199.50).

Kittel, Gerhard, and Friedrich, Gerhard, eds. *Theological Dictionary of the New Testament.* Grand Rapids: Eerdmans Publishing Company, 1968. This classic work is a ten-volume translation by Geoffrey W. Bromily of the *Theologisches Wörterbuch zum Neuen Testament.* For advanced work in biblical studies, use of Kittel requires at least a cursory knowledge of Greek and Hebrew (1982 price, $269.95).

Lattimore, Richmond. *The Four Gospels and the Revelation.* New York: Farrar, Straus & Giroux, 1979. A stiff and literal translation by a classical Greek scholar.

Laymon, Charles M., ed. *The Interpreter's One-Volume Commentary on the Bible.* Nashville: Abingdon Press, 1971 (1982 price, $22.95).

May, Herbert G., and Metzger, Bruce M., eds. *The New Oxford Annotated Bible with the Apocrypha.* New York: Oxford University Press, 1977. Without a doubt, the best study Bible in existence today (1982 price, $21.95).

Throckmorton, Burton H., Jr., ed. *Gospel Parallels: A Synopsis of the First Three Gospels.* Nashville: Thomas Nelson & Sons, 4th revised edition, 1979. Indispensable for the reader of the gospels who wishes to see at a glance the variables in the synoptic gospels and the gospel of Thomas (1982 price, $8.95).

INTRODUCTION

New Testament Studies

NEW Testament studies consist of research and teaching. Through research, scholars attempt to push forward the frontier of human knowledge and understanding. Through teaching, they seek to interpret the results of research and harness the results to the service of the Christian faith and its ministry. Because any New Testament professor is both a research scholar and a teacher, the inevitable tension between these two responsibilities is important.

Without research, teaching becomes the reiteration of the insights and understanding of yesterday, as valueless in New Testament scholarship as it would be in the field of medicine. Yesterday's work is important; it is the basis on which scholars build further, but only in this way can one pay true homage to it. Without teaching, research rapidly becomes too esoteric. In isolation, the pure research scholar could find himself/herself busily engaged in some modern equivalent to the medieval concern for the number of angels that could dance on a pinhead. Therefore research and teaching belong together. The tension between the two is necessary to the proper function of both.

The student normally plunges into the world of New Testament studies at the level of introduction. In this context there is a natural emphasis on literary and historical questions concerning the New Testament as a whole and, more specifically, on individual works. A great deal of solid achievement in this respect has now allowed scholars to understand the process by which the New Testament came into being. One can answer most of the questions that arise about authorship, dates, sources, and the like.

The interest and emphasis today is toward acceptance of the results of literary and historical criticism, giving attention now to more theologically oriented questions. Thus, scholars accept the findings of literary and historical research regarding the synoptic gospels. Then one can deal with the theological significance of why the early Christian community chose to present Jesus in the number of ways it did as well as dealing with the relationship between the gospels and the preaching of the early church. One important question is why the church did not simply reiterate the preaching and teaching of Jesus in the gospels. Also, the church proclaimed Jesus as the Messiah of God, but Jesus himself had primarily proclaimed the kingdom and the will of God.

In examining Luke-Acts and accepting the results of literary and historical research, one sees the theological significance of Luke's connection between the history of the early church and the history of Jesus. This opens for study Luke's understanding of history and the significance of Jesus and the Spirit active in Christian experience.

Then too, scholars today accept the results of the work already done on the Pauline epistles, rejoicing in the way one can now understand, present, and expound the work and theology of Paul. These results comprise a great achievement. Paul seems to quote from the liturgy of the early church, material that antedates his epistles. Scholars pay careful attention to his work in the light of questions raised in connection with the synoptic gospels, such as what Paul means by "word of the Lord."

In addition, New Testament scholars have been able to assimilate and use some of the more spectacular achievements and discoveries of modern times—the flood of papyri and inscriptions written in the language of the New Testament; the reconstruction of Galilean Aramaic, the mother tongue of Jesus and the language in which he taught; the treasure of Jewish apocalyptic and rabbinical literature; the Dead Sea Scrolls and the Nag Hammadi finds along with the continuing contributions of archaeological exploration. The results of all of this discovery have been truly spectacular, especially helpful in the field of exegesis. We can now understand constructions, interpret words, catch allusions, and see things in their context in a way impossible a generation ago. The modern exegete has at his disposal a wealth of material almost embarrassing in its richness. The production of commentaries that assimilate and use this material is now and will continue to be a major preoccupation of modern New Testament scholarship.

In the wider world of theological studies, perhaps the most important achievement of modern scholarship has been the theological word study. Using the resources available to modern exegesis, scholars can make a careful study of theologically significant words to determine their exact theological meaning and usage. *Redemption, sin, faith, Lord, Christ, Holy Spirit*—whatever the word, New Testament scholars have studied it. Today there can be no acceptable theology nor adequate preaching that does not take the results of these word studies into account.

Many modern scholars have concerned themselves with the quest of the historical Jesus. Accounts of the life and teaching of Jesus appear with ever-increasing frequency, and it is difficult to make positive statements about Jesus of Nazareth and his teaching. However, there are six things one can claim to demonstrate about Jesus of Nazareth using the canons proper to historical research: (1) there was a Jesus of Nazareth; (2) he had some connection with John the Baptist and was baptized by him; (3) he proclaimed the kingdom of God and interpreted the will of God in a markedly independent manner; (4) he cast out demons in a way considered remarkable by his contemporaries; (5) he gathered about himself a group of disciples that included some people considered to be outcasts by the Judaism of his day; (6) he was crucified by the Romans. In addition to these statements, there is much that we can believe on the basis of the testimony of the early church and from our own personal Christian experience.

The true object of Christian faith is the Christ of Christianity's proclamation, the risen Lord of Christian experience—not the historical Jesus. The gospels proclaim this Christ, just as did the preaching of the apostles and just as Christians do today. The gospels are not merely historical records of a Galilean peasant named Jesus barJoseph. But the gospels do identify the risen Lord with this Jesus. For the early church, the Christ who speaks in Christian experience is the Jesus who spoke in Galilee and Judaea.

Knowing what the gospels have said about Jesus, we seek to go further and determine what he said about himself. Knowing that the early church proclaimed his earthly ministry as revealing God active in human experience and in historical events, we seek to determine the nature of that experience and the features of that event. We already know that the early Christian community and Jesus were at one in understanding his teaching as "the last word of God before the End" (Rudolf Bultmann). Therefore, we are impelled to seek to reconstruct that teaching to the best of our ability. There have been some significant efforts made in this regard—Joachim Jeremias's work on the parables, the post-Bultmannian work on the "indirect Christology" of Jesus, Tödt's work on the Son of man sayings, materials on the kingdom of God in the teaching of Jesus, and many others.

But for all these advances, we have to say that any report on contemporary New Testament scholarship must be simply a report of work in progress. Fortunately, research is built on the premise that questions are asked in order to be answered and that problems are formulated in order to be solved.

Bibliography

Henry, Patrick. *New Directions in New Testament Study*. Philadelphia: Westminster, 1979.

Perrin, Norman. *The New Testament: An Introduction*. New York: Harcourt Brace Jovanovich, 1974. See especially the section on "Techniques and Methods of New Testament Scholarship," pp. 6–15.

_____. *What is Redaction Criticism?* Rev. ed. Philadelphia: Fortress, 1971. The foreword to this helpful volume on methodology (pp. vii–x), written by Dan O. Via, Jr., is especially descriptive.

_____. *Rediscovering the Teaching of Jesus*. New York: Harper & Row, 1967. See especially chapter 1, "The Reconstruction and Interpretation of the Teaching of Jesus," pp. 15–53.

Part I

SOURCES,
METHODOLOGY, AND
BACKGROUND

Chapter 1

SOURCES AND METHODOLOGY

THIS chapter presents a discussion of the sources available for a knowledge of the teaching of Jesus. It includes discussion of the methodology of this book, showing how the sources are used in determining what Jesus taught. The chapter also includes a discussion of the difficulties involved in a study of the teaching of Jesus.

The teaching of Jesus is important to many different persons. It is important to the Christian, for whom Jesus was the Messiah of God and is the Lord of life. To the Jew, Jesus was an important teacher from the period of the second Temple. To the humanist, Jesus is one of the most important representatives of the spirit of humankind at its best. The teaching of Jesus is important to anyone who stands in the tradition of Western civilization and culture, because Jesus and his tradition have been influential in the formation and development of Western culture.

A. Sources for the Teaching of Jesus

The importance of the study of the teaching of Jesus is matched by the difficulty of the study. The difficulty lies in the nature of the sources of our knowledge of this teaching. The gospels of Matthew, Mark, Luke, and John are secondary sources, not eyewitness accounts. The gospels are more like a painting than a photograph. We do not have a snapshot of Jesus, but an interpretation of his teaching. Unfortunately, Jesus did not write a single word of his teaching, so we approach the gospels as theological sources, not historical ones. The evangelists who wrote the gospels molded the sayings of Jesus from the perspective of their theological tradition and put it into a continuous story about Jesus.

3

There are three sources for our knowledge of the teaching of Jesus: the four gospels in the New Testament, the noncanonical sayings of Jesus (recorded outside the gospel tradition), and the Coptic gospel of Thomas.

1. MATTHEW, MARK, AND LUKE

Matthew, Mark, and Luke are called the synoptic gospels because they can be put side by side and read together. They present very much the same story and the same kind of teaching, and they are at one in their differences from the fourth gospel. The synoptic gospels have long been understood as the "historical" gospels as compared with John, the so-called spiritual gospel. In the past, some people have assumed that the synoptic gospels were concerned with presenting the ministry and teaching of the historical Jesus, that the synoptics were first-class historical records. However, we need to examine these gospels a little more closely to see what they actually are like.

First of all, let us note their close relationship to one another. We know from a study of them as literature that Mark's gospel has served as a source for both Matthew and Luke. In fact, the writers of Matthew and Luke used Mark extensively. Further, we know that Matthew and Luke have a second source in common with one another, a collection of the sayings of Jesus. We have no knowledge of the source except insofar as we may assume its use by both Matthew and Luke. Scholars refer to the source as Q, the first letter of the German word Quelle, which simply means "a source."

Further, each gospel has its own original material, which is not taken from Mark and is not shared with the other. They have therefore not taken this material from Q. We call these sources M for Matthew and L for Luke. Matthew, therefore, uses Mark, Q, and M. Luke, likewise, uses Mark, Q, and L.

Therefore, Mark's gospel is a primary source for Matthew and Luke. Matthew's gospel is based on Mark. Also, Matthew has expanded Mark by adding material he has taken from Q and material of his own we call M. Luke has used Mark together with material from Q and material of his own, which we call L.

Keeping these sources in mind, let us look at two passages from the gospels themselves in order to illustrate this interrelationship of gospel materials. The first is Mark 9:1 with its parallels in Matthew 16:28 and Luke 9:27: "Truly I say to you, there are some standing here who will not taste death before they see the kingdom of God come with power" (RSV). This is a saying about the consummation, the end time. It makes two points: first, the consummation is imminent; second, the end will take the form of the coming of the kingdom with power.

On the basis of the literary evidence, we know that both Matthew and Luke are following Mark at this point. Notice what both of them do with this saying. Matthew 16:28 reads: "Truly I say to you, there are some standing here who will not taste death before they see the Son of man coming in his kingdom." Here we see exactly the same note of imminence as in Mark 9:1, but a real difference in the form that the consummation will take. The "coming of the kingdom with power" has been reinterpreted to mean the coming of the Son of man in his kingdom, by which Matthew certainly understands the so-called second coming of the Lord.

The version in Luke 9:27 reads: "But I tell you truly, there are some standing here who will not taste death before they see the kingdom of God." Again there is the same note of imminence but a form of expectation different from both Matthew and Mark. For Luke, the phrase to "see the kingdom of God" means to experience the era of Pentecost—the day the Christian church was empowered to perform its mission to the world. He is the first of many to interpret Mark 9:1 in this way.

What we have in Matthew 16:28 and Luke 9:27 are interpretations of the Marcan version, Mark 9:1, which is itself most likely an interpretation by Mark. Matthew 16:28 interprets the saying to mean the Second Coming, and Luke 9:27 interprets the saying to mean Pentecost and the era of the Christian church. There is nothing particularly remarkable about the different interpretations. The remarkable thing is that both of these interpretations are read back on to the lips of the Jesus of the gospel record. Neither Matthew nor Luke quotes Mark and then goes on to indicate that he is interpreting the saying. They rewrite it, ascribing their own interpretation to the Jesus of the gospel record.

Now, for purposes of illustration, let us look at another passage from the gospels, the parable of the great supper, found in two forms in Matthew 22:1–10 and Luke 14:16–40. It has also been found in the gospel of Thomas, Logion (or "saying") 64. The three versions of the parable of the great supper represent three independent traditions. In this parable Matthew and Luke have written independently of each other and Thomas is independent of both. In each tradition the parable has been preserved and reinterpreted. As Jesus most likely originally told it, the parable was a simple story of a man who arranged a dinner and invited guests to this dinner. The custom in the East during the first century was for the occasion to be scheduled, except for the actual time for the event. When the dinner was ready, the guests were invited. These would be guests who had already indicated their willingness to accept the invitation. In this parable the guests were being told that "the time for the dinner is now."

In Jesus' story the guests back out. All reject the invitation they had previously accepted. So the host invites other people who had not been previously invited to the dinner. Such a situation would be wholly familiar to the people hearing this parable in the first century. The narration by Jesus invites his hearers to pass judgment on the hosts and the guests in the story. Their reaction would certainly be "it serves them right; quite right and proper." But as his hearers pass judgment on the characters and situation in the story, they find themselves passing judgment on themselves and upon this particular situation in the ministry of Jesus. Thus, the hearers pass judgment on the religious Jews who rejected the challenge of the ministry of Jesus. But they are also passing judgment on Jesus' apparent acceptance of those outcasts among the Jews who did respond to the dinner invitation and to his challenge.

In Matthew, the story has been developed, changed, and reinterpreted. It has become a story about all of the following things: God's dealings with people through servants, the prophets and the Messiah; people's rejection of them all; their killing some of them; and God's subsequent judgment on the Jews through the destruction of Jerusalem by the Romans in A.D. 70.

In Luke the story has been developed and changed to a lesser extent than in Matthew. It has become a story about the gospel being preached to the orthodox Jews, then to the outcasts among the Jews, and finally to the Samaritans and gentiles.

In the gospel of Thomas, the story has been developed and changed to a lesser extent than in either Matthew or Luke. It has become a story about the inability of worldly persons to accept the truth of the gospel.

A close reading of all three versions reveals that the story has been developed and changed. The final, reinterpreted form has been read back on to the lips of the Jesus of the gospel tradition. Matthew clearly presupposes the situation subsequent to the fall of Jerusalem; Luke clearly presupposes the ministry of the early church to the gentiles. Both Matthew and Luke have reached an understanding of the parable in terms of their own particular situation. They have turned the parable into an allegory and have read this allegorical interpretation back to the lips of the Jesus of the gospel tradition.

In such a situation you can see how an understanding of the material in the synoptic gospels presents a problem. The material presents a tradition about the teaching of Jesus. And this tradition has been modified and interpreted with insights, understanding, situation, and faith from a latter time. The synoptic gospels present the teaching of Jesus as each of the evangelists understood it. In other words, we cannot depend on the evangelists to present the teaching of Jesus just as he gave it. Rather, they present that teaching in an interpreted form, modified by their own times and circumstances. Their presentation of Jesus' teaching may be an accurate reflection of the application of that teaching to their situation and circumstances. But their situation is not necessarily the same as the setting and circumstances of Jesus.

2. THE GOSPEL OF JOHN

The fourth gospel is the gospel of John, generally regarded as the "spiritual" gospel, a designation given to it as early as the third century A.D. by Clement of Alexandria. This gospel of John is a presentation of Jesus as the Christ of Christian faith, designed to bring out the significance of Jesus for the believer. In it, the presentation of the ministry of Jesus and the record of his teaching have been filtered through the highly personal interpretation and understanding of the evangelist who wrote it. John is a supremely important gospel as devotional literature for the Christian believer. But it does not offer very much direct help in the task of reconstructing the actual teaching of the historical Jesus. Following are some illustrations that will make this become apparent to the careful reader of the New Testament.

Style

In the fourth gospel, because everyone speaks in the same way, we can conclude that the author presents his material at the expense of historical accuracy. It is obvious that whether the statements are the words of the evangelist himself, of John the Baptist, or of Jesus, each person uses the same vocabulary and linguistic style. For example, there is a long discourse that begins on the lips of Jesus in John 3:10–11: "Jesus answered him (Nicodemus) 'Are you a teacher of Israel and yet you do not understand this? Truly, truly, I say to you, we speak of what we know and bear witness to what we have seen!...'"

The *we* in this statement indicates that this is not just a recording of the teaching of Jesus. As the discourse continues, it becomes obvious that we are hearing the comment of the evangelist himself. We read in verse 18: "He who believes in him is not condemned; he who does not believe is condemned already, because he has not believed in the name of the only Son of God." This is almost certainly a comment by the evangelist. The discourse begins on the lips of Jesus and moves on to become a comment by the evangelist. But where does the one end and the other begin? One simply cannot decide, because Jesus and the evangelist have exactly the same linguistic style. In addition, we can see that this linguistic style is very different from that attributed to Jesus in the synoptic gospels.

Vocabulary

The vocabulary of the teaching of Jesus is also very different in the fourth gospel from that presented in the other three. In the first three gospels, a central concept is the kingdom of God. But in the fourth gospel, the central concept is that of eternal life. We read about the kingdom of God scarcely at all in John, just as in the first three gospels we read nothing about eternal life.

Form

The form of the teaching of Jesus in the gospel of John is very different from that presented in the other three. In the first three gospels there are parables and short, pithy sayings. In the fourth gospel these sayings are replaced by allegories and long, involved discourses.

The difference between a parable and an allegory is important; understanding the difference is crucial to understanding the teaching of Jesus. A parable is a story, like the parable of the good Samaritan in Luke 10, in which the individuals are characters in a story and no more than that. The man who went down the road to Jericho, the priest, the Levite, the man from Samaria—these are characters in the story. These characters are present in order to tell a story that has one general point.

An allegory is an involved presentation in which the characters or elements are important not only in themselves but also because they represent something else. One example of an allegory is the story of the vine and the branches in John 15:1–8, where heavy symbolism is used.

A parable makes one general point, illustrates one general teaching, drives home one specific lesson—the total story is what is important. In an allegory, the involved picture makes a series of points. Each element in the allegory represents something other than itself, and one needs the clue in order to understand the whole message.

The parables of Jesus were misunderstood very early in the tradition. They were taken to be allegories, a curious feature in the history of the interpretation of the teaching of Jesus. One example of the danger inherent in the making of a parable into an allegory is found in the parable of the sower. In the teaching of Jesus, the parable of the sower is a story of a man who sowed a field (Mark 4:3). The parable was designed to make one specific point: the man who sowed should have confidence in the outcome; from small beginnings, great endings can and do come.

But to the evangelist Mark, this has become an involved allegory: the sower, the seed, the birds, the heat of the sun, the depth of the ground—all these things have come to represent something other than themselves. In his book *The Parables of Jesus*, Professor Joachim Jeremias explains how this misunderstanding developed (pp. 52–70). He shows that we must take this misunderstanding into account to arrive at the original meaning of the teaching of Jesus.

To summarize, there is difficulty in using the gospel of John to reconstruct the teaching of Jesus. The form of the sayings is different. The parables and pithy sayings of the first three gospels have been replaced by the allegories and long, involved discourses. The Jesus of the first three gospels is very reluctant to make any claims. But in the fourth gospel, Jesus is consistently quoted as saying things like "I am the resurrection and the life," and "I am the way, the truth, and the life." The reticence of the Jesus of the first three gospels has been replaced in the gospel of John by a Jesus who makes sweeping claims the historical Jesus likely did not make for himself.

3. OTHER SAYINGS OF JESUS

In addition to the gospels as a source for the teaching of Jesus, we also have nonsynoptic sayings. One of these is located at the end of Paul's speech to the elders at Miletus in Acts 20:35: "In all things I have shown you that by so toiling one must help the weak, remembering *the words of the Lord Jesus*, how he said 'It is more blessed to give than to receive.' "

There are also a number of other sayings, such as those recorded in the writings of the church fathers. There are still others in surprising places; one important saying is in the Muhammadan tradition. In the *Unknown Sayings of Jesus*, Joachim Jeremias has collected these sayings, discussed them in detail, and offered an interpretation of them.

4. THE GOSPEL OF THOMAS

Another source for the teaching of Jesus is the Coptic gospel of Thomas, which is part of an archaeological discovery made at Nag Hammadi, Egypt, in 1945. At that time a chest containing a number of pottery jars was found buried in the ground. In these jars were rolled scrolls containing various works written in Coptic, the language of Egypt in the first century and still spoken by some people in Egypt today. These writings seem to have been the library of a Gnostic Christian church, probably dating from the third century A.D.

The gospel of Thomas is a collection of the sayings of Jesus. The gospel has no narrative, no stories, no miracles, no account of the passion—it is simply a collection of sayings introduced by a phrase such as "Jesus said ..." or "Peter said ..." or "Peter asked ..." or "Jesus replied ..." For the most part, these sayings are interesting to us only as instances of Gnostic Christian teaching. They are obviously Gnostic sayings read back on to the lips of Jesus.

An example of this Gnostic method is found in the last saying, Logion 114: "Simon Peter said to them, 'Let many go out from among us because women are not worthy of the life.' Jesus said, 'See, I shall lead her so that I will make her male that she too may become a living spirit resembling you males, for every woman who makes herself male will enter the kingdom of Heaven.' " This saying represents the Gnostic understanding of creation as a mistake. The Gnostics believed that creation was not the act of the true God but of a false god, an enemy of the true God. Their ideal and hope was to retrace the steps of creation. In the face of the creation story in Genesis where women were made from Adam's rib, the Gnostics wanted to retrace this step so that the women might again become part of the male, Adam. We find this understanding and hope reflected in this saying from the gospel of Thomas.

There are other sayings in the gospel of Thomas significant for insight into the teaching of Jesus. In Thomas, Logion 2, we read, "Let him who seeks not cease seeking until he finds, and when he finds he will be troubled, and when he has been troubled, he will marvel and he will reign over the all." This statement is a Gnostic version of the saying in Matthew 7:7, 8: "Ask, and it will be given you; seek, and you will find; knock, and it will be opened to you." A parallel saying from *Q* is also found in Luke 11:9. These provide a contrast with the gospel of Thomas, where this saying has obviously been interpreted in terms of Gnostic myth. However, some of the Thomas sayings that are variations or versions of sayings in the canonical tradition do provide insights for us. One such example is the parable of the great supper (Logion 64).

Some sayings in Thomas had never been seen before 1945 by scholars, but they bear the marks of authenticity. Two parables in Thomas are worthy of mention here, located in Logia 97 and 98. In Logion 97 we read: "Jesus said, 'The kingdom is like a woman who was carrying a jar full of meal. While she was walking on a road, the handle of the jar broke, the meal streamed out behind her on the road; she did not know it. She had noticed no accident. After she came into her house, she put the jar down. She found it empty.' " This parable teaches the lesson that one should be aware of what is going on. One should be responsive to a crisis, although one is unprepared for it. This is a characteristic feature of the teaching in the parables of Jesus that we see in the synoptic gospels.

The other parable in Logion 98 is perhaps even more interesting: "Jesus said, 'The kingdom of the Father is like a man who wishes to kill a powerful man. He drew the sword in his house, he stuck it into the wall in order to know whether his hand would carry through. Then he slew the powerful man.' " Here we have a most unsavory character, a murderer, being used as a vehicle for teaching. It is likely that no one other than Jesus would have chosen such an unsavory person as the central figure of a parable. Jesus used the character of the so-called unjust steward as a central feature in one of the canonical parables (Luke 16:1–13). But here in Logion 98 we find a murderer. Through him, Jesus is teaching that one should be prepared to stay with whatever commitment one makes. A similar message is expressed in the canonical saying "No one who puts his hand to the plow and looks back is fit for the kingdom of God" (Luke 9:62).

The gospel of Thomas is a most interesting discovery because it offers us new versions of sayings we had known before. These versions have been influenced by Gnosticism, but they are independent of the canonical versions of these sayings and parables. The gospel of Thomas also contains some sayings and parables that had never been seen before, but that may well have claims to authenticity.

Identification of these sources for our knowledge of the teaching of Jesus leads us now to a discussion of methodology, that is, the way we use the sources to reconstruct and interpret the teaching of Jesus. Several processes serve us in this essential task. They are comparison, examination of changes, retranslation, variations from Judaism, and dissimilarity. They can be combined, but for purposes of discussion we shall separate them to show the distinctive features of each.

B. The Method of Interpretation

1. COMPARISON

First, by careful comparison of the various forms of a saying, we seek to determine the earliest form of that saying. A good example is the Lord's Prayer because there are two versions: one in Matthew 6:9–13 and one in Luke 11:2–4. It is necessary to read a modern translation such as the Revised Standard Version to see this comparison clearly. In the King James version the two forms of the prayer have been made to conform to each other, but in the earliest manuscripts the Lukan form is different. The two different versions of this prayer make it extraordinarily useful for study and comparison.

Reading the Matthean and Lukan versions of the prayer calls attention to the differences between them immediately. Matthew says, "Our Father who art in heaven," whereas Luke simply says, "Father." Matthew has "hallowed be thy name, thy kingdom come, thy will be done on earth as it is in heaven," but Luke has only "hallowed be thy name, thy kingdom come." It becomes apparent by comparison that the Matthean "thy will be done on earth as it is in heaven" is an expansion of the original. This kind of expansion shows up frequently in a study of liturgical texts and texts of prayers. At the end of the prayer, Luke has "lead us not into temptation," and Matthew has ". . . and lead us not into temptation, but deliver us from evil." The phrase "deliver us from evil" is likely a liturgical expansion. Thus, by comparison of these two forms of the prayer we are able to determine the earlier form—the one in Luke. A thorough explanation of this liturgical expansion is located in Joachim Jeremias's *The Lord's Prayer*.

2. EXAMINATION OF CHANGES

The second part of the methodology of comparison is to seek to understand the kind of changes or modifications that have been made. These changes were introduced into the tradition of the teaching as it was transmitted in the early church. We saw earlier that Mark 9:1 was reinterpreted by both Matthew and Luke. What Matthew did was to introduce the idea of the second coming, an identifying characteristic of Matthew.

Likewise, an identical saying takes two different forms in Mark 13:33 and Matthew 24:42. Mark says, "Take heed, watch; for you do not know when the time will come." Matthew says, "Watch therefore, for you do not know on what day your Lord is coming." Matthew introduces the statement about the second coming, even though the source, Mark, did not use it.

There are many characteristic changes and modifications of this kind introduced by the evangelists, especially Matthew and Luke. When we compare them with their sources and take the variations into account, we can work back to a more nearly original form of the sayings.

3. RETRANSLATION

A third method of using the sources to interpret the teaching of Jesus is to retranslate his teaching into Aramaic. Jesus taught in the language spoken by the people of his day, Palestinian Aramaic, a language derived from Hebrew. But for the most part, the early church used the Greek language, which is very different from Aramaic. When we translate the teaching from Greek back to Aramaic, this step puts us behind many of the changes and modifications introduced during the transmission of the sayings in the early church.

An example of this retranslation process can be demonstrated using the Lord's Prayer. Luke 11:1 uses the simple word *Father* and Matthew 6:9 reads "Our Father who art in heaven." In Aramaic, "Father" would be the word *abba*. We already know from Mark 14:36, in the description of the scene in the garden of Gethsemane, that Jesus said, "Abba, Father." The term *abba* is also used in Galatians 4:6 and Romans 8:16 where Paul talks about the spirit of sonship, also preserving the Aramaic *abba* instead of using the Greek. Thus, it is apparent that Jesus characteristically used *abba* as the word for "Father." Because this use of *abba* is highly significant in understanding the teaching of Jesus, we will discuss it in detail later. For the moment, our point is that by retranslation into Aramaic, we have learned from the studies by Joachim Jeremias that the original form of the address in the Lord's Prayer is "*Abba* (Father)" and not "Our Father who art in heaven."

4. VARIATIONS FROM JUDAISM AND THE EARLY CHURCH

A fourth method used in understanding the teaching of Jesus is to look for places where the teaching is different from the Judaism of Jesus' day and where the teaching does not represent characteristic interests or emphases of the early church. The use of *abba* in the Lord's Prayer is a good example. A Jew would never have said *abba*, but instead would have said it as Matthew puts it, "Our Father who art in heaven." Matthew has therefore modified the teaching of Jesus at this point. He was a conservative Jew, and the use of *abba* was too informal for him.

The criterion for authenticity is that where it is not likely that the teaching came from Judaism or that it was introduced by the early church, it likely comes from Jesus himself. This assertion may not appear to be extremely significant, but it has helped scholars come to see some of the most important aspects of the teaching of Jesus.

5. DISSIMILARITY

The method of dissimilarity concentrates attention on those elements that we have good cause to believe are the actual teaching of the historical Jesus, such as the Lord's Prayer. We know that it was characteristic of religious teachers of Jesus' day to teach prayers to their followers. For Jesus not to have taught a prayer would have been most unusual.

Also, the Lord's Prayer, especially in its Lukan form, is easily translatable back into Aramaic. In Matthew, the Lord's Prayer reads: "Forgive us our debts as we also have forgiven our debtors." In Luke: "Forgive us our sins as we ourselves forgive every one who is indebted to us." This curious difference can be explained. The word *hobha* in Aramaic means both "debt" and "sin." The tradition Luke represents has translated the noun as "sin" and the verb as "to be indebted." These differences in the Lord's Prayer show up solely because the one Aramaic word *hobha* was behind both traditions. We may take the Lord's Prayer largely in its Lukan form as being representative of the teaching of Jesus. It gives us insights into the things Jesus felt important enough to become the subject of the prayer of his disciples.

Some parables of Jesus were also modified in the early church by being interpreted as allegories. These modifications, for the most part, took place in Greek, although the original parable was in Aramaic. In most cases we can reconstruct the original form of the parable with a very high degree of probability. Joachim Jermias, in *The Parables of Jesus*, has traced these parables to their original form.

Another focus for study is the kingdom of God in the teaching of Jesus. Jesus used the term "kingdom of God" frequently, but the term is not widely used in the early church. When "kingdom" is used in such places as in Acts 20:25, it has a meaning quite different from the teaching of Jesus.

Thus we have points at which we may be fairly sure of the authentic teaching of Jesus. A major part of the work of New Testament scholars today is to take these points and use them to construct an overall picture of the teaching of Jesus that has a high degree of authenticity. The reconstruction of a total picture of his teaching thereby becomes a context in which to understand and interpret the teaching of Jesus, or ways in which this teaching appears to have been modified.

C. Summary

In summary, the sources for our knowledge of the teaching of Jesus are the four gospels in the New Testament and the noncanonical sayings of Jesus, including the gospel of Thomas. Of these four gospels in the New Testament, the gospel of John has limited value for the study of the teaching of Jesus. It is such a radically reinterpreted version of the teaching of Jesus that it presents too many difficulties for use in reconstructing the actual teaching of Jesus. Of course, the synoptic gospels of Matthew, Mark, and Luke also interpret the material they present. But the fact that there are three of them to compare with each other helps us learn something of the way the teaching has been handled by each evangelist.

The noncanonical sayings of Jesus are few in number. However, some of the sayings are important, especially the gospel of Thomas, which contains some parables and sayings parallel to materials in the synoptic gospels. Thomas also contains some sayings that had been previously unknown, but that may be authentic sayings of Jesus.

The method is to compare the sayings as they exist in the various sources in order not only to see the differences, but also to find the earliest form of the saying which is most likely to be authentic. Since the forms of the sayings differ, an attempt is made to understand the kinds of changes and to take these changes into account. The changes are usually consistent with the sources of the tradition. For example, Matthew is consistent in presenting a Jewish interpretation of the teaching of Jesus. Thus, it is easy to recognize what is called a "Matthean" or a "Lukan" emphasis.

The sayings of Jesus are also retranslated back into Aramaic, the language he used in teaching, a process that is highly revealing. For the most part, the teaching of Jesus after his death was passed from one person to another at first instead of being written down. The sayings were spoken in Greek as one person taught another. When the gospels were later written, it was natural that they should be written in Greek and not in Aramaic, as Jesus spoke them. Therefore, when we translate the Greek back into Aramaic, we may be on the way to getting to the actual teaching of the historical Jesus.

It is difficult to determine what Jesus actually said, since no record was written down as Jesus taught. Therefore translation, not only of language, but also of cultural idiom, plays a major part in understanding what Jesus taught. New Testament scholars must study Greek, Hebrew and Aramaic in order to be able to work with the ancient manuscripts themselves. It is also helpful to have a knowledge of Syriac and Coptic. Jesus spoke in Aramaic, the evangelists wrote in Greek a generation later, and we ourselves are accustomed to modern languages nearly two thousand years later in a Western culture. The language problem is complex, yet essential to our understanding Jesus' message.

We must remember that Jesus was a Jew, and therefore we could expect him to embrace Judaism's tenets, as indeed he does. Some care needs to be taken in using the criterion of dissimilarity. In studying the teaching of Jesus, we look carefully at the difference between the concepts of first-century Judaism and a saying of Jesus, looking for particular emphases of the early church of the first and second centuries. Because Christianity developed from a subsect of Judaism, the distinctive elements become important. But the radical differences between Judaism and Christianity of the first century must not be overstated. Without clear evidence, the differences cannot be supported. The criterion of dissimilarity can be supportive in examining a saying. It may be stated thus: If the saying is not characteristic of first-century Judaism or of the early church, it may be a genuine saying. And that kind of identification leads, then, toward the actual teaching of the historical Jesus. Our goal and purpose is to understand that teaching.

D. Resource Material

GLOSSARY

ALLEGORY   A complicated story, the characteristic of which is that the people, incidents, or things in the story represent something else. The allegory makes a whole series of points by means of the people, incidents, and things in it. An allegory is not to be confused with a parable, which makes only one point by means of the whole story.

ARAMAIC   The language of the Jews who lived in Palestine at the time of Jesus, derived from the Hebrew language. It was in use from about the third century B.C. to the second century A.D., when it died out after about five hundred years of usage.

CANON   The word *canon* means "a rule." It is also used in the sense of a "list of books"—a list of essential books. There is a biblical canon—the list of books that officially make up the Bible. There is the Old Testament canon (the list of books that make up the Old Testament) and a New Testament canon (the list of books that make up the New Testament). A book is called "canonical" if it is included as one of the books of the Old Testament or the New Testament.

COPTIC   The language of the common people in Egypt in the early church at the time of Jesus. It is the Egyptian language written with the Greek alphabet. The ruling class and the more educated people in Egypt, as everywhere else, spoke Greek at the time.

CRITICISM   Several phrases using the word *criticism* refer to biblical studies. Some of these refer to methods of interpreting and understanding events leading to oral tradition and expression in literary form. The word *criticism* in English frequently implies something negative. But when used in literary or biblical studies, one could substitute the word *analysis*, because it refers to a method of studying oral tradition and literary materials. Terms frequently used in referring to biblical studies are *literary criticism, form criticism*, and *redaction criticism*.

GNOSTIC   From the Greek word *gnosis*, which means "knowledge." Gnostic Christianity attempted to improve on orthodox Christianity by adding the Greek idea of salvation through a special kind of knowledge.

GOSPEL   The first four books of the New Testament are called gospels. The word *gospel* comes from the Anglo-Saxon *godspel*, which means "good news," derived from the Greek *evangelion*, which also means "good news." The first four books of the New Testament are called *gospels* because of the first verse of the gospel of Mark, which reads "The beginning of the *gospel* of Jesus Christ, the Son of God." The term is unique to literary products of New Testament Christianity; only the early Christians produced gospels.

GOSPEL OF THOMAS   A gospel found in Egypt in 1945 written in Coptic. It contains teaching with no narrative, and is a collection of the sayings of Jesus, usually introduced by such a phrase as ". . . and Jesus said. . . ."

LOGION   The Greek word for "a saying." Scholars use it academically with this same meaning. For example, there are 114 *logia* in the gospel of Thomas. We could just as simply say, "there are 114 sayings in the gospel of Thomas."

PARABLE   A simple story designed to illustrate one main point, to teach one lesson. The distinguishing characteristic of a parable is that the people and incidents in the story are intended to represent real people and real incidents, credible because they are what Aristotle would call "probable." The total story itself (not the characters in the story) is what illustrates the point or makes the lesson. Not to be confused with an allegory.

Q   *Q* is the first letter of the German word *Quelle*, which means "a source." It is used to designate the preaching material that Matthew and Luke have in common. The writers of Matthew and Luke obviously took their preaching material from a common source, simply called *Q*.

SYNOPTIC   A term made up from two Greek words, *syn* and *opsis*, which mean "together" and "looking." The word *synoptic* means "those books that can be *looked at together*." The first three gospels (Matthew, Mark, and Luke) are called synoptic gospels because they can be put side by side and looked at together. They tell the same story in much the same way. For this reason, the synoptic gospels can be distinguished from the gospel of John in both form and content.

TRADITION A word derived from Latin meaning "to hand down." In references to sources for the teaching of Jesus, it means material handed down—passed on—in the church. Much of what we read in the New Testament was used by the church before it came into its present form. The texts, therefore, have been "handed down" in the tradition of the church. The tradition of the teaching of Jesus is preserved in various forms by the evangelists and other authors of the New Testament.

SCRIPTURE REFERENCES

John 3:10
John 3:18
Mark 4:13–20
John 3:17f.
Mark 9:1f.
Mark 16:28
Luke 9:27
Matthew 22:1–10
Luke 14:16–40
Thomas, Log. 64

Acts 20:35
Thomas, Log. 114
Thomas, Log. 2
Matthew 7:7,8
Luke 11:9
Thomas, Log. 97
Thomas, Log. 98
Luke 16:1–13
Matthew 6:9–13
Luke 11:1–4

Mark 13:33
Matthew 24:42
Matthew 6:9–13
Luke 11:1–4
Mark 14:36
Galatians 4:6
Romans 8:16
Matthew 6:12
Luke 11:4

BIBLIOGRAPHY

Beardslee, William A. *Literary Criticism of the New Testament.* Philadelphia: Fortress, 1975.

Bornkamm, Günther. *The New Testament: A Guide to Its Writings.* Philadelphia: Fortress, 1973.

Bultmann, Rudolf, *The History of the Synoptic Tradition.* New York: Harper & Row, 1963.

Cartlidge, David R., and Dungan, David L. *Documents for the Study of the Gospels.* Philadelphia: Fortress Press, 1980.

Crossan, John Dominic. *In Parables.* New York: Harper & Row, 1973.

Detwiler, Robert. *Story, Sign and Self: Phenomenology and Structuralism as Literary-Critical Methods.* Philadelphia: Fortress Press, 1978.

Drane, John. *Jesus and the Four Gospels.* New York: Harper & Row, 1979.

Fuller, Reginald H. *A Critical Introduction to the New Testament.* Naperville, Illinois: Allenson, 1966.

Gerhardsson, Birger. *The Origins of the Gospel Traditions.* Philadelphia: Fortress, 1979.

Harner, Philip B. *Understanding the Lord's Prayer.* Philadelphia: Fortress, 1975.

Henry, Patrick. *New Directions in New Testament Study.* Philadelphia: Westminster, 1980.

Jeremias, Joachim. *The Lord's Prayer*. Philadelphia: Fortress, 1964.

_____. *New Testament Theology: The Proclamation of Jesus*. New York: Scribner, 1971.

_____. *The Parables of Jesus*. Rev. ed. New York: Scribner, 1963.

_____. *Unknown Sayings of Jesus*. New York: Scribner, 1959.

Jonas, Hans. *The Gnostic Religion*. 2d ed. Boston: Beacon Press, 1963.

McKnight, Edgar V. *What Is Form Criticism*. Philadelphia: Fortress, 1965.

Manson, T. W. *The Teaching of Jesus: Studies of Its Form and Content*. 2d ed. Cambridge: Cambridge University Press, 1959.

Marxsen, Willi. *Introduction to the New Testament: An Approach to Its Problems*. Philadelphia: Fortress, 1968.

_____. *Mark, the Evangelist*. Nashville: Abingdon, 1969.

May, Herbert G., and Metzger, Bruce M. *The New Oxford Annotated Bible with the Apocrypha*. New York: Oxford University Press, 1977 (esp. pp. 1167ff., 1519ff., and 1551ff.).

Metzger, Bruce M. *The Early Versions of the New Testament*. Oxford: Clarendon Press, 1977.

Nickle, Keith F. *The Synoptic Gospels*. Atlanta: John Knox, 1980.

Pagels, Elaine. *The Gnostic Gospels*. New York: Random, 1979.

Patte, Daniel. *What Is Structural Exegesis?* Philadelphia: Fortress, 1976.

Perrin, Norman. *The New Testament: An Introduction*. New York: Harcourt Brace Jovanovich, 1974 (esp. pp. 41–42, 72–74).

_____. *Rediscovering the Teaching of Jesus*. New York: Harper & Row, 1967 (esp. pp. 15–49).

_____. *What Is Redaction Criticism?* Rev. ed. Philadelphia: Fortress, 1971.

Reumann, John. *Jesus in the Church's Gospels*. Philadelphia: Fortress, 1977.

Robinson, James M., ed. *The Nag Hammadi Library*. New York: Harper & Row, 1977.

Russell, D. S. *The Method and Message of Jewish Apocalyptic*. Philadelphia: Westminster, 1964.

Smith, Morton. *Jesus the Magician*. New York: Harper and Row, 1978.

Spivey, Robert A., and Smith, D. Moody, Jr. *Anatomy of the New Testament*. New York: Macmillan, 1969.

Stoldt, Hans-Herbert. *History and Criticism of the Marcan Hypothesis*. Macon: Mercer University Press, 1980.

Throckmorton, Burton H., Jr., ed. *Gospel Parallels: A Synopsis of the First Three Gospels*. 4th ed. New York: Nelson, 1979.

QUESTIONS

1. Why is it important to study sources other than the gospels for the teaching of Jesus?
2. What are three sources of knowledge about the teaching of Jesus?
3. How would you describe the gospel of John?
4. What are some difficulties in using the gospel of John as a source for the teaching of Jesus?
5. What is the difference between a parable and an allegory?

6. What important point is made about the misinterpretation of parables?
7. What are the differences in the way Jesus is characterized in the fourth gospel as compared to the first three?
8. What three parts of the synoptic gospels include the actual teachings of Jesus?
9. What are the first three gospels called?
10. Why are the first three gospels referred to in this way?
11. Which of the three synoptic gospels is used by the other two as a source?
12. What is a source common to both Matthew and Luke?
13. What is a source that only Matthew has?
14. What is a source that only Luke has?
15. Do the synoptic gospels present only the teaching of the historical Jesus?
16. What is a source for our knowledge of the teaching of Jesus other than the synoptics?
17. What is still another source of our knowledge of the teaching of Jesus?
18. What is the value of the gospel of Thomas for the Christian?
19. What are the methods in using the sources of the teaching of Jesus to help decide what the historical Jesus actually said?

Chapter 2

FIRST-CENTURY JUDAISM

THIS chapter contains a discussion of the necessity for knowing first-century Judaism in order to understand the teaching of Jesus. It includes demonstrations of how this knowledge helps to interpret the teaching of Jesus. Also included are the sources for a knowledge of Jews and Judaism of the first century and a discussion of how these sources relate to a study of the teaching of Jesus.

It should be noted that the discussion that follows describes historical Judaism of the first century. Most twentieth-century persons will recognize at once that Jews of the first century held attitudes and had adopted practices that are not characteristic of contemporary Judaism.

A. The Need to Know About First-Century Judaism

If we are to understand the teaching of Jesus, it is mandatory to study his teaching in its setting. That is, we need to know the times, places, and circumstances in which he taught. In the first chapter we discussed the sources for our knowledge of the teaching of Jesus and the methodology for reconstructing that teaching from the sources. Now we turn to the way we interpret and understand the teaching of Jesus once we have reconstructed it.

1. INTERPRETING SAYINGS

As an example, Matthew 12:28 contains material useful for interpreting a saying. Here we read, "But if it is by the spirit of God that

I cast out demons, then the kingdom of God has come upon you." A parallel to this saying is found in Luke 11:20: "If it is by the finger of God that I cast out demons, then the kingdom of God has come upon you." This most likely represents an authentic saying of Jesus (see Perrin, *The Kingdom of God in the Teaching of Jesus*).

But we need to understand what it means to say "If I by the spirit [or finger] of God cast out demons." What, for example, did the Jews of the first century think about demon possession? To what were they referring when it was mentioned? What exactly does "kingdom of God" mean in this saying? These questions illustrate that a proper understanding of this saying in Matthew and Luke depends upon knowledge of demon possession at the time of Jesus, that is, we need to know how demon possession was understood by Jesus and his contemporaries. And we need to know what was meant by the phrase "kingdom of God." Because Jesus uses the phrase here without further explanation, we assume that he is using "kingdom of God" with a commonly accepted and understood meaning.

2. UNDERSTANDING THE TEACHING

A second example is in Mark 8:38: "For whoever is ashamed of me and my words in this adulterous and sinful generation, of him will the Son of man also be ashamed when he comes in the glory of his Father with the holy angels." Most scholars agree that Jesus did say something very much like this, although the agreement in this instance is not so widespread as in the previous example.

A pertinent question here is what Jesus meant by "Son of man." He uses the phrase without explanation, apparently in a way commonly understood by his hearers. What did this phrase mean to him and to his hearers? Jesus also talks about the "coming of the Son of man in the glory of his Father with the holy angels." How did the Jews at the time of Jesus understand this coming of the Son of man? To answer questions like these we need to be grounded in the knowledge of Jews and Judaism at the time of Jesus. Therefore, as we reconstruct and interpret the teaching of Jesus, we need to know the background in order to interpret and understand his teaching properly.

B. Sources of Knowledge about First-Century Judaism

At the time of Jesus there were two kinds of Judaism, Palestinian and Hellenistic. Palestinian Judaism means the kind of life, thought, belief, and practice of the Jews who lived in Palestine, who spoke Aramaic and read an Aramaic translation of their Hebrew scriptures. Hellenistic Judaism means the life, work, thought, and practices of the Jews who lived outside Palestine in the empire called Hellenistic because it spoke Greek. Hellenistic Jews spoke Greek, read their scriptures in Greek, and were influenced by Greek practices and Greek concepts—the Greek way of life of their neighbors and friends. In a sense, Palestinian Judaism could be characterized by the symbols of the sacred, theology and faith, whereas the Hellenistic culture could be symbolized by the secular, detachment and the power of reason.

We are primarily concerned with Palestinian Judaism because the teaching and ministry of Jesus took place in first-century Palestine. His teaching therefore presupposes the world of thought of Palestine and the Palestinian Jew rather than that of Hellenism and the Hellenistic Jew.

The six major sources for knowing about first-century Palestinian Judaism are the Old Testament, the Apocrypha, apocalyptic literature, the Dead Sea Scrolls, the writings of Flavius Josephus, and rabbinical literature of the period.

1. THE OLD TESTAMENT

The Old Testament is important for any understanding of Jews and Judaism at the time of Jesus or at any other time. Indeed, there is a sense in which the Old Testament *is* Judaism. The Jews are the people of the Old Testament; the Old Testament was the basis for their faith, the foundation of their beliefs, and the medium from which they drew instruction for their practices. Thus, the Old Testament, essential to an understanding of Jews and Judaism in the first century, is also important for an understanding of the teaching of Jesus. The writings now included in the Old Testament end, however, about 167 B.C.

Between the writings of the Old Testament and the New Testament there is a time gap of more than two centuries. This period of time was extremely important to the Jews as the era when their country was conquered by the Greeks, the Egyptians, the Syrians, and the Romans. These were the centuries in which the Jews developed many new ideas and many new practices. In the light of such influences, as important as the Old Testament is in itself, we cannot move directly from it to the New Testament. We have to know about the intermediate period, the period between the second century B.C. and the ministry of Jesus.

2. THE APOCRYPHA AND PSEUDEPIGRAPHA

The Apocrypha is a selection of the sacred literature of the Jews from the period between the Old Testament and the New Testament, written probably between 200 B.C. and A.D. 100. At the time of Jesus this literature was regarded as sacred, but it did not find its way into the canon of the Old Testament. The canon, decided after the time of Jesus, is the definitive selection of the books that made up the sacred scriptures of the Jews (the Council of Jamnia, A.D. 100 or thereabouts).

The Apocrypha is a necessary part of our study because it offers us literature from the period between the close of the Old Testament and the ministry of Jesus, books that were read and were regarded as having authority at the time of Jesus. The books of the Apocrypha are varied in form. There are historical books such as 1 Maccabees, an account of the Maccabean Revolt of the second century B.C., written by someone who had participated in the revolt, a first-class piece of historical writing. There is also wisdom literature, similar to the book of Proverbs in the Old Testament. Two examples of apocryphal wisdom literature are The Wisdom of Solomon and Ecclesiasticus, sometimes called The Wisdom of Sirach. A third form of literature is novels: The Book of Judith and Additions to the Book of Esther. The fourth major category of writings in the Apocrypha is apocalyptic literature.

The Apocrypha is still printed in many Bibles. For many centuries it was regarded as important enough to be included among Jewish scriptures. But the Reformers and the Puritans, revolting against the practice of the Roman Catholic church, tended to follow the canon of the Jews. The canon of the earliest Christians, however, did include these books; but the canon of the Jews at the Council of Jamnia did not include the Apocrypha. The books are not always printed in the

Bible, but several good translations are available. One lively translation is by E. J. Goodspeed; it includes a helpful introduction to the Apocrypha and to each of the various books therein.

3. APOCALYPTIC LITERATURE

The word *apocalyptic* means "to uncover, to reveal." Literature called apocalyptic claims to uncover, to reveal the secrets and purposes of God. It is a rather strange kind of literature to us, yet it was very important to the Palestinian Jews at the time of Jesus. In many ways, it is the most important of all our sources used to interpret the teaching of Jesus. There are two examples of this kind of literature in the Bible: the book of Daniel in the Old Testament and the Christian Apocalypse, known as the book of Revelation, in the New Testament.

The book of Daniel was the first really important apocalyptic work. It was written at the time of the Maccabean revolt when the Jews were engaged in a war against Syria. By Syria, we mean the Seleucid Empire, the eastern part of the division of Alexander's empire in 323 B.C. at his death. Palestine fell to Syria (Seleucid) in 198 B.C. when Antiochus the Great defeated the Egyptians. The Jews lived in an occupied country and could carry on war only by means of what we would call today an underground movement and guerrilla warfare. Their fighting forces hid out in the hills and attacked the Syrians at every opportunity. They resisted valiantly, fighting bravely and well. In this situation of oppression and suffering the book of Daniel was produced to encourage the Jews and to improve their morale. Its purpose was to show them that God was at work in their circumstances, active in their history. The book of Daniel predicted that God would soon act in a decisive manner and intervene in their circumstances to visit them, redeem them, destroy the Syrians for them, and bring them to a life of glory. This was a very important message to bring to the people, but very difficult to communicate because of the Syrian occupation. The Jews therefore had to circulate this book under what we would call Syrian censorship.

In order to circulate the book, they decided to write it under the name of a person from the past—the person of Daniel from the time of the Babylonian captivity of the Jews. The writers cast its message in the form of symbols—dreams, beasts, and the like, so that any Syrian reading it would not catch its significance, but a Jew would. The Jews did. The book of Daniel was tremendously effective and became very popular. As only one example of apocalyptic literature,

Daniel is not a prototype, but an illustration of a successful piece of writing.

For the next three hundred years there was a great deal of literature of this type. The Jews wrote apocalyptic literature and so did the Christians. In the second century of our era, this type of literature passed into disrepute among both Jews and the Christians, finally dying out. Most of it did not find its way into the canon; the books that did—Daniel and Revelation—were largely misunderstood. Its symbols were regarded as mysteries and there was a period of time when people interpreted the Beast as almost every figure of any significance—Napoleon, Hitler, and so on.

Apocalyptic literature always follows the same form. Usually it is written in the name of a person of the past, such as Daniel; its message is always presented in the form of symbols. As noncanonical examples, we have the book of Enoch, the Assumption of Moses, the Apocalypse of Baruch, the Psalms of Solomon, and many others. Much of this literature is still not readily available to the general reader; but there is Daniel in the Old Testament, 2 Esdras in the Apocrypha, and Revelation in the New Testament.

Several themes characterize apocalyptic literature, such as the concept of a general resurrection. We read, for example, in Daniel 12:1, 2: "At that time [when God will intervene] shall Michael stand up, the great Prince who has charge of your people. And there shall be a time of trouble, such as never has been since there was a nation till that time; but at that time your people shall be delivered, every one whose name shall be found written in the book. And many of those who sleep in the dust of the earth shall awake, some to everlasting life, and some to shame and everlasting contempt." This concept of a general resurrection is one of the major themes to be found in most apocalyptic literature. Other important ideas include the final judgment, the kingdom of God and its coming, and the Son of man and his coming.

4. THE DEAD SEA SCROLLS

Scholars refer to the Dead Sea Scrolls as the Qumran Texts. Qumran is the name of the place where the monastery was found with which these texts are connected. The discovery of these scrolls in 1947 is one of the most fascinating stories of modern biblical studies. Frank M. Cross, Jr., has described the discovery and the nature of the scrolls in *Ancient Library of Qumran*; also there is another good discussion of them in A. Dupont-Sommer's *The Essene Writings from Qumran*.

Briefly, these scrolls are the remains of a library from a monastic community of Jews existing at the time of Jesus and destroyed during the Jewish War in A.D. 68 or 69. The texts come to us, therefore, directly from the time of Jesus, and thus they offer us valid information about the way in which one important community of contemporary Jews lived, thought, believed, and worked.

The writings are of several different kinds. There are Old Testament texts and church "orders," or manuals of instruction for the beliefs and practices of the group; devotional literature, hymns and prayers; apocalyptic literature, especially the War Scroll, which is a description of a war between the children of light—the people of the scrolls—and the children of darkness—their enemies; and commentaries on Old Testament books or on selected Old Testament passages. In these commentaries, the people of the scrolls apply these passages to their own experience as they seek to understand and interpret their situation.

There are some interesting parallels between the people of the scrolls and early Christianity. For example, the office of the bishop in the early Christian church is remarkably parallel to the office of the "Overseer of the Camp" in the community of Qumran. The Christian Eucharist seems to have parallels in the sacred meal of the people of Qumran. And Christian baptism appears to have parallels in the washings of the Qumran people. The Dead Sea Scrolls are an important source because they offer direct information from the period.

5. FLAVIUS JOSEPHUS

Flavius Josephus was a younger contemporary of Jesus, living through the period of the Jewish War from A.D. 66 to 70. After that war he went to Rome, where he acted as a lobbyist for the Jewish people. He lived in Rome and sought to influence the Roman Senate on behalf of his fellow Jews, in a manner similar to that of modern-day lobbyists. Josephus wrote two important works, *The Wars of the Jews* and *The Antiquities of the Jews*. In *The Wars of the Jews*, he tells the story of the period immediately preceding the war of A.D. 66–70 and the story of the war itself. In *The Antiquities of the Jews* he tells the story of the Jewish people from the very beginning down to his own day. He therefore describes for us the Jews of Palestine at the time of Jesus.

Josephus was also the main source, together with Pliny the Elder, for an understanding of the Essenes prior to the discovery of the scrolls in 1947. He tells us, for example, about Pharisees, Sadducees, and Essenes; he describes John the Baptist and his ministry, and he even says something about Jesus and James, the brother of Jesus.

But there are two drawbacks to our use of this source. First of all, because Josephus was a lobbyist he has presented his story in a particular way. He has written, consequently, of the events in a way best suited to influence the Romans favorably toward the Jews; therefore he is not always accurate. Second, his works were edited at a later date. His description of Jesus, for example, has been edited by a later Christian hand—a great disappointment.

New Testament scholars would be greatly excited to have a picture of Jesus drawn by one of his contemporaries who was not a Christian. But, unfortunately, some unidentified Christian has written what he thinks Josephus ought to have said. In his book *The New Testament Background: Selected Documents*, C. K. Barrett talks about Josephus and gives extracts from his writings, including his descriptions of John the Baptist, Jesus, and James, the brother of Jesus (pp. 190–207).

6. RABBINICAL LITERATURE

The rabbinical literature important for our study comes from the period after A.D. 70. As a matter of fact, it is the religious literature of the Jews from after A.D. 70 down to about the fifth century of our era. There are three types: the Talmud (exposition of the Law), Midrashim (commentaries), and Targums (scriptures in Aramaic).

Included in the exposition of the Law are the Mishnah, an interpretation and application of the teaching of the first five books of the Old Testament—the Law of Moses, or the Torah, as the Jews call it. In the Mishnah, the teaching is applied to the circumstances of the Jews of their day. In the Talmud, the teaching of the Mishnah is interpreted and further applied.

The second type of rabbinical literature is commentaries on scripture, or Midrashim. These are commentaries on Old Testament books in which teaching about scripture is expounded and applied.

The third type of rabbinical literature is Targums, translations of the Hebrew scriptures into Aramaic. These are important, because these interpretative translations show us how the Jews understood the Old Testament at the time of Jesus. There is a great deal of free expression, for example, in the translation of Isaiah 53 concerning the suffering servant. In these Targums, all the references to the suffering of the servant are taken away from the servant and applied to his enemies. This interpretation is interesting because it shows how difficult it was for a Jew to conceive of the representative of God suffering. Students of early Christianity already know how difficult it was for Paul and the early Christians to persuade the Jews that the Messiah had been crucified. C. K. Barrett, in *New Testament Background*, elaborates upon this literature, presenting it and discussing it in detail (pp. 139–72).

In the New Testament, at least one particular passage is greatly illuminated by the rabbinical literature of the period. Mark 10:2ff. tells of the incident in which Jesus is questioned about marriage and divorce: "And Pharisees came up and in order to test him asked, 'Is it lawful for a man to divorce his wife?' He answered them, 'What did Moses command you?' They said, 'Moses allowed a man to write a certificate of divorce, and to put her away.'"

This is the kind of question that was asked among the rabbis, and answered in various ways. For example, the school of Shammai used to say a husband shall not put away his wife, unless he has found in her something shameful: their interpretation of Deuteronomy 24:1 was that he had found some unseemly thing in her. A group of Jews almost contemporary with Jesus said in effect that divorce is possible only if the wife has done something shameful, usually understood to mean adultery or fornication. Their basis for this opinion is also Deuteronomy 24:1. The school of Hillel, contemporary with Shammai and almost contemporary with Jesus, took a broader view than that. Hillel allowed divorce for anything that a husband found "unseemly," even letting his dinner burn. Rabbi Akiba, martyred in A.D. 135, said that a husband could divorce his wife simply because he found another woman more beautiful than her, for it is said in Deuteronomy 24:1: "It shall be if she find no favor in his eyes." Akiba, interpreting the same Deuteronomy passage, has arrived at a very liberal ruling on the question.

When Jesus was asked the question about marriage and divorce, what he is being asked in effect is "How do you interpret Deuteronomy 24:1?" In response he sweeps away the Mosaic Law (the Torah) of the Deuteronomy passage in Mark 10:5–8: "But Jesus said to them, 'For your hardness of heart he wrote you this commandment. But from the beginning of creation, "God made them male and female. For this reason a man shall leave his father and mother and be joined to his wife, and the two shall become one flesh."'"

What Jesus does, in effect, is to refuse to discuss the question of divorce. He insists on a new view of marriage, which does not rest on the Law of Moses, but on the setting of the garden of Eden and the paradise will of God. He can do this, because he believes that men and women are now in a new paradise-type of relationship with God; in one sense the kingdom of God has come.

These sources and examples show how a knowledge of the ways Jews discussed divorce at the time of Jesus enables us to understand better this particular teaching of Jesus in Mark.

C. Interpreting the Teaching of Jesus

Let us give another example of the way we use knowledge of Jews and Judaism at the time of Jesus as we interpret his teaching. This process can be illustrated by the parable of the prodigal son (Luke 15:11–32).

1. THE PARABLE OF THE PRODIGAL SON

In the parable of the prodigal son, notice what the younger son does. He says to his father, "Give me the share of property that falls to me." This was the son's right. He could ask his father for his share of an inheritance while his father was still alive. If he did so, he had the right to use this property but not to dispose of it. The right of disposal came to him only at his father's death. Therefore, when the son sells the property and takes the money with him into the far country, he is treating his father as if he were already dead.

In the far country the son squanders his living and eventually becomes a swineherd. At this point in the telling of the parable, a shudder would have run through the audience of Jesus. For a Jew to become a swineherd meant to become as a gentile. There were some professions that no Jew could enter and still remain a Jew—tax collecting, for example. A Jew also could not become a swineherd, because that meant he would associate himself with unclean animals. If a Jew became as a gentile, he put himself beyond the scope of the mercy of God.

Jews at the time of Jesus—and certainly official Judaism—divided the world into two groups—the Jews and the gentiles. The Jews could hope for the mercy of God, but for the gentiles there was no hope. Some Jews transcended this way of thinking, but not many of them. The Jew who had thus put himself beyond the scope of the mercy of God could not expect forgiveness. If he wished for the forgiveness of God, the only thing he could do would be to go through the whole process of making himself once more a Jew.

The son who is in this position in the parable comes to himself in the far country and decides to return to his father: "He will say to his father, 'I have sinned against heaven and before you.'" In the first century the Jews, reluctant to pronounce the name of God or even to use the word for God, used alternative expressions. One way was to speak of "heaven"; therefore, here the son is saying in effect, "Father, I have sinned against God and against you." He sinned against his father in breaking the law—in treating his father as though he were dead by selling his property. He has sinned against God, because the Law he broke is God's Law.

When the father welcomes the son, he does three things. First he says, "Bring quickly the best robe and put it on him." Bringing the best robe and putting it on the son means that the son would be treated as the guest of honor at the feast to be given to celebrate his return. Second, "Put a ring on his hand." This is a signet ring, used for stamping and sealing contracts in a day before the use of signatures as we now use them. Thus the son is now given authority to enter into contracts on his father's behalf. Third, "And shoes on his feet." Because shoes were the mark of a free man, not a slave, the son is to be treated as a free man. The importance of this act is that some Jews believed that one who had made himself as a gentile might be spared by the mercy of God. But if he were spared, he would be spared only to serve as a slave to the Jews in the perfect blessed state of the kingdom of God.

Jesus is saying that the father welcomes the son, makes him the guest of honor, gives him full authority, and makes him a free man and not a slave. This story is important, because it is designed to illustrate the way God acts toward the penitent sinner. The Jew of Jesus' day said that God will accept the penitent Jew, but will not accept the penitent gentile. Neither will God accept the penitent Jew who has made himself as a gentile.

Jesus tells this story to defend and explain his own action as he, in the name of God, invites tax collectors, swineherds, and other Jews who had made themselves as gentiles to enter into the fellowship of the kingdom of God. The one major point made by this parable is God's mercy and forgiveness. This was a bone of contention between Jesus and his contemporaries. Jesus envisioned the love of God reaching out beyond the barriers that his contemporaries were quite sure were there. This is certainly one reason they rejected him.

D. Summary

As illustrated in the discussion of the parable of the prodigal son, a knowledge of first-century Judaism is helpful for interpreting this story. In the same way, knowledge of first-century Palestine gives us an opportunity to interpret and understand other elements in the teaching of Jesus.

E. Resource Material

GLOSSARY

AKIBA, RABBI   An important rabbi of the early second century A.D., slightly later than Shammai and Hillel.

APOCALYPTIC   Apocalyptic means "to uncover, to reveal." The term is used to designate the literature of the Jews from the time before the book of Daniel (written during the Maccabean Revolt) through 150 A.D. The literature was designed to reveal the purpose of God. Among Christian apocalyptic literature, a canonical example is the book of Revelation.

APOCRYPHA   The Apocrypha is the list of books connected with the Old Testament, written probably between 200 B.C. and A.D. 100. They were not accepted as canonical by the Jews when they made their official list of Old Testament books. Their list was made after the time of Jesus at the Council of Jamnia, A.D. 100 or thereabouts.

DEAD SEA SCROLLS   The literature, scrolls, and fragments found in a series of caves near the Dead Sea, thus called the Dead Sea Scrolls and sometimes the Qumran Texts. The literature comes from the time of Jesus and seems to have been the library of a monastic community. The remains of the monastery were found in a place called Qumran, on the shores of the Dead Sea.

GENTILE   The Jews considered all non-Jews "gentile." A gentile is any person who is not a Jew.

HEAVEN   In the Jewish understanding the world was a three-story universe: (1) a flat earth with (2) *Sheol* (the abode of the dead) beneath it, and (3) the heavens above the earth. The heavens were separated from the earth by the firmament. There were "holes" in the firmament through which the glory of the heavens shone. We call these "holes" the stars. The Jews believed that when the End came, the firmament would break up, the glory of the heavens (God and the angels) would descend to earth and transform it. For the Jew, the final blessed state was envisaged as taking place on a transformed earth, not in the heavens. The word *heaven* is also important because the Jews used the word as a way of avoiding the name of God. They tended to avoid the name of God or the word *God*, using *heaven* instead. Thus, the phrases "kingdom of God" and "kingdom of heaven" mean exactly the same thing.

HELLENISTIC JUDAISM   The life, work, thought, beliefs, and practices of the Jews who lived outside of Palestine. The area outside Palestine at the time of Jesus consisted of the Greek-speaking Roman Empire. *Hellenistic* essentially means "Greek." The Hellenistic Jews spoke Greek and read their scriptures in Greek. Hellenistic Judaism refers to the post-Alexandrian experience of the Near Eastern nations, although there had been a diaspora community of Judaism since the sixth century B.C. (See *Palestinian Judaism*)

HILLEL   An important teacher among the Jews in the first century A.D. Shammai and Hillel, contemporaries of Jesus, were the two leading teachers of their day. In rabbinical literature, their opinions are often quoted. Frequently they disagreed with each other.

JOSEPHUS, FLAVIUS   Josephus was a Jew, a younger contemporary of Jesus who lived through the war of the Jews against Rome (A.D. 66–70). After the war, he went to Rome, where he acted as a kind of "lobbyist" at the Roman Senate on behalf of the Jews in Rome. He wrote a number of works, two of which are very important: (1) *The Wars of the Jews*, an account of the Jewish Revolt of A.D. 66–70 and the events that led up to it; and (2) *The Antiquities of the Jews*, an account of the history of the Jewish people from earliest times to his own times.

MACCABEAN REVOLT   The revolt of the Jews against the Syrians in the second century B.C. (around 167 B.C.). The revolt was led by Judas, who was nicknamed "the Maccabea"—so called because of his success against the Syrians. The revolt is called the Maccabean Revolt because it was led by Judas the Maccabea. Maccabeus means "hammerer."

MIDRASHIM The plural form of the word *Midrash*. It designates a part of the rabbinical literature. It is a series of commentaries on books of the Old Testament.

MISHNAH A part of the rabbinical literature. The Mishnah is a commentary on the five books of Moses (the Torah, or Law, as they were called), the first five books of our Bible. The Mishnah is instruction, a commentary on the Law, designed to relate their teachings to the circumstances of the commentator.

MOSAIC LAW (The Book of the Law) A general term designating what the Jews understood as the teaching of Moses, the Law of the Old Testament. It is roughly equivalent to the first five books of our Old Testament.

PALESTINIAN JUDAISM The life, work, thought, beliefs, and practices of the Jews who lived in Palestine at the time of Jesus. It refers to the Jews who spoke Aramaic. Palestinian Judaism is a major concern in a study of the teaching of Jesus. (See *Hellenistic Judaism*)

PSEUDEPIGRAPHA A body of Jewish religious texts written between 200 B.C. and A.D. 100 and spuriously ascribed to various prophets and kings of Hebrew scriptures.

RABBINICAL LITERATURE The literature of the Jews dating from the time after the Jewish Revolt—after A.D. 70 to about the sixth century A.D. It is called rabbinical literature because it was produced by the rabbis who became important in Judaism at that time. They have remained important to the present time. (See definitions of *Midrashim, Mishnah,* and *Talmud*)

SHAMMAI An important teacher among the Jews in the first century A.D.

TALMUD A part of the rabbinical literature. There are two Talmudim—a Palestinian Talmud and the Babylonian Talmud. The two Talmudim are designed to relate the teaching of the Mishnah to the circumstances of the teacher and his hearers.

TARGUM A translation of the Hebrew Old Testament into Aramaic. There are several Targums that were used by the Palestinian Jews at the time of Jesus.

TORAH   The first five books of the Old Testament, which contained the Law. Also referred to as the Pentateuch.

SCRIPTURE REFERENCES

Matthew 12:28
(Luke 11:20)
Mark 8:38
1 Maccabees
The Wisdom of
Solomon
Ecclesiasticus
Judith

Esther (including
the Additions)
Enoch
Assumption of Moses
Apocalypse of Baruch
Psalms of Solomon
Daniel

2 Esdras
Revelation
Isaiah 53
Mark 10:1–12
(Matthew 12:1–12)
Deuteronomy 24:1
Luke 15:11–32

BIBLIOGRAPHY

Barrett, C. K. *The New Testament Background: Selected Documents.* New York: Harper & Row, Torchbooks, 1961.

Braun, Herbert. *Jesus of Nazareth: The Man and His Time.* Philadelphia: Fortress, 1979.

Cross, Frank M., Jr. *Ancient Library of Qumran and Modern Biblical Studies.* New York: Doubleday, Anchor, 1961.

De Lange, Nicholas. *Apocrypha: Jewish Literature of the Hellenistic Age.* New York: Viking Press, 1978.

Dupont-Sommer, André. *The Essene Writings from Qumran.* New York: World, 1967.

Farmer, William R. *Jesus and the Gospel.* Philadelphia: Fortress, 1982.

Gaster, Theodor H., trans. *The Dead Sea Scriptures.* New York: Doubleday, Anchor, 1964.

Goodspeed, E. J. *The Apocrypha.* New York: Modern Library, 1959.

Grant, Robert M. *Early Christianity and Society.* New York: Harper & Row, 1977.

Guillamont, A. et al. *The Gospel according to Thomas.* New York: Harper & Row, 1959.

Hultgren, Arland J. *Jesus and His Adversaries: The Form and Function of the Conflict Stories in the Synoptic Tradition.* Minneapolis: Augsburg, 1979.

Jeremias, Joachim. *The Eucharistic Words of Jesus.* New York: Scribner, 1966.

_____. *Jerusalem in the Time of Jesus.* Philadelphia: Fortress, 1978.

_____. *Jesus' Promise to the Nations.* London: SCM, 1958.

_____. *New Testament Theology: The Proclamation of Jesus.* New York: Scribner, 1971.

Josephus, Flavius. *The Great Roman-Jewish War.* New York: Harper, 1960.

Kee, Howard Clark. *The Origins of Christianity: Sources and Documents.* Englewood Cliffs, N.J.: Prentice-Hall, 1973.

Keller, Werner. *The Bible as History.* New York: Morrow, 1981.

Lapide, Pinchas. *Israelis, Jews and Jesus.* New York: Doubleday, 1979.

Lipman, Eugene J., ed. and trans. *The Mishnah: Oral Traditions of Judaism.* New York: Schocken, 1974.

Lohse, Eduard. *The New Testament Environment.* Nashville: Abingdon, 1976.

Mowry, Lucetta. *The Dead Sea Scrolls and the Early Christian Church.* Notre Dame: University of Notre Dame Press, 1966.

Perrin, Norman. *Rediscovering the Teaching of Jesus.* New York: Harper & Row, 1967 (chap. 1, esp. pp. 49–53).

Rabin, Chaim. *Qumran Studies.* New York: Schocken, 1975.

Reicke, Bo. *The New Testament Era: The World of the Bible from 500 B.C. to A.D. 100.* Philadelphia: Fortress, 1979.

Robinson, James M., ed. *The Nag Hammadi Library.* New York: Harper & Row, 1977.

Simon, Marcel. *Jewish Sects at the Time of Jesus.* Philadelphia: Fortress, 1980.

Vermes, Geza. *The Dead Sea Scrolls in English.* 2d ed. New York: Penguin, 1977.

_____. *Jesus the Jew: A Historian's Reading of the Gospels.* New York: Macmillan, 1974.

QUESTIONS

1. What is the main benefit of understanding Jews and Judaism at the time of Jesus?
2. What were the two kinds of Judaism in Jesus' time?
3. Of which kind of Judaism was Jesus a part?
4. What are our sources of knowledge about Palestinian Judaism?
5. What Judaic writings do we have that give us information about the period of two centuries between the Old and the New Testaments?
6. Did the canon of the early Christian church include the Apocrypha?
7. What church still includes the Apocrypha in its Bible?
8. What is the nature of the Apocrypha?
9. What does *apocalyptic* mean?
10. What are two examples of apocalyptic literature in the Bible?
11. What is an extremely difficult problem in interpreting the book of Daniel?
12. What is another name for the Dead Sea Scrolls?
13. What do the Dead Sea Scrolls contain?
14. What did the people of the Dead Sea Scrolls call themselves?
15. What did they call their enemies?
16. What were two important works that Flavius Josephus wrote?
17. What are the three general types of rabbinical literature?

18. What are two types of exposition on the Torah?
19. What are the Jewish commentaries on the scriptures called?
20. What are translations of the Hebrew scriptures into Aramaic called?
21. What are the three rabbinical schools mentioned that give opinions on divorce?
22. In the parable of the prodigal son, the son has the right to ask for his share of the property. Does he have the right to dispose of it?
23. The son squanders his living and becomes a swineherd. What are the implications of becoming a swineherd for a Jew?
24. What is the meaning of the phrase "sinned against heaven"?
25. In the parable of the prodigal son, what three things does the father do when the son returns?
26. What is the significance of the robe?
27. What is the significance of the ring?
28. What is the significance of the shoes?
29. What three things did the Jews in Jesus' day think about penitent sinners, both Jews and gentiles?
30. What was the significance of the parable of the prodigal son as Jesus taught it?

Part II

THE ACTIVITY OF GOD

Chapter 3

THE KINGDOM OF GOD

THIS chapter offers a look at the different ways the term "kingdom of God" is used in the Bible, especially in the teaching of Jesus. It includes a presentation of the varied meanings of the term and an interpretation of what Jesus meant when he referred to the kingdom of God.

In the first two chapters of this book, we discussed the sources for reconstructing the teaching of Jesus and an appropriate methodology for understanding that teaching. We also talked about the importance of a knowledge of Jews and Judaism at the time of Jesus in interpreting this teaching. Now we move on to a discussion of the teaching itself.

The most predominant teaching recorded in the synoptic gospels is the kingdom of God. The evangelists report that Jesus came proclaiming the kingdom, the most dominant motif recorded in the gospels.

A. Kingdom of God in the New Testament

Any concordance to the New Testament reveals that the term kingdom of God is used nearly one hundred times in the synoptic gospels and only about twelve times in the remainder of the New Testament. Moreover, in the New Testament outside the synoptic gospels, the term has a meaning rather different from what it has in the synoptic gospels. For example, in Acts 19:8, "And he [Paul] entered the synagogue and for three months spoke boldly, arguing and pleading about the kingdom of God." Here the term kingdom of God obviously means the totality of the Christian message; it is a synonym for the Christian gospel.

Similarly, in Acts 28:23, "And he [Paul] expounded the matter to them from morning till evening, testifying to the kingdom of God and trying to convince them about Jesus both from the Law of Moses and from the Prophets." Here again, the phrase is practically synonymous with the Christian gospel. Paul also uses the phrase in this way in 1 Corinthians 4:20: "For the kingdom of God does not consist in talk but in power [of the Spirit]."

Paul even uses the phrase to mean the Christian way of life in Romans 14:17: "For the kingdom of God does not mean food and drink but righteousness and peace and joy in the Holy Spirit." In addition, Paul uses the phrase to mean the Christian church, as in Colossians 4:11: "And Jesus who is called Justus. These are the only men of the circumcision among my fellow workers for the kingdom of God, and they have been a comfort to me." These meanings—the totality of the Christian gospel, the Christian way of life, the Christian church—are not the meanings the phrase has in the synoptic gospels.

1. RECONSTRUCTING

The phrase "kingdom of God" in the teaching of Jesus is comparatively easy to decipher as the evangelists use it. Notice how "kingdom of God" is used in Mark 1:15: "The time is fulfilled, and the kingdom of God is at hand; repent, and believe in the gospel. . . ." and in Matthew 12:28: "But if it is by the Spirit of God that I cast out demons then the kingdom of God has come upon you." In these passages, "kingdom of God" does not mean the Christian message, the Christian church, or the Christian gospel, as it does when used by Paul.

The use of "kingdom of God" is characteristic of the teaching of Jesus rather than its use by the early church. When we approach the kingdom-of-God teaching as recorded in the synoptic gospels, we have a clue to help us determine where the modifying hand of the early church has been at work and where it has not. Where we find "kingdom of God" being used as it is in Acts or in the Epistles, we have to reckon with the possibility of the influence of the early church. For example, Matthew 4:23: "And he went about all Galilee, teaching in their synagogues and preaching the gospel of the kingdom. . . ."

Again, in Luke 9:27: "But I tell you truly, there are some standing here who will not taste death before they see the kingdom of God."

Here, and in a few other places in the gospels comparatively easy to recognize, we have the influence of the usage of the early church. But in the vast majority of the cases in the synoptic gospels, the use is characteristic of Jesus. And where this is the case, it is comparatively easy to decipher the actual teaching of Jesus. Our problem is not to determine what Jesus said about the kingdom of God—that is relatively easy to do. Our problem is to determine what he meant by what he said, and this has turned out to be extraordinarily difficult.

2. UNDERSTANDING

In his book, *The Kingdom of God in the Teaching of Jesus*, Norman Perrin traces the discussion of the teaching of Jesus about the kingdom of God through the first half of the twentieth century. As the book demonstrates, scholars have used the phrase "kingdom of God" in many different ways. To some, the term means the era of the beginnings of the Christian church; to others, it means the moral reformation of society. To still others, it means the rule of God to be established by moral and spiritual reform. To yet others, it means the catastrophic activity of God breaking into history, moving the stars, transforming the earth, and destroying evil.

There have been many different interpretations of the kingdom of God in the teaching of Jesus. Since there are so many different interpretations, there is only one thing we can do: that is, to go back again to the sources, to Palestinian Judaism at the time of Jesus. Jesus used the phrase "kingdom of God" without explaining what he meant by it. It is therefore a fair assumption that his hearers would have understood his use of it. If we can understand the use of the "kingdom of God" in Palestinian Judaism at the time of Jesus, we shall have taken a long step toward understanding that teaching.

B. Kingdom of God in Palestinian Judaism

1. KINGDOM OF HEAVEN

In the synoptic gospels, sometimes we read "kingdom of God" and sometimes "kingdom of heaven." As a matter of fact, careful reading of the gospels calls attention to Matthew's almost exclusive use of "kingdom of heaven" in his record of the teaching of Jesus. Luke uses "kingdom of God" almost exclusively, and Mark uses both. !There is absolutely no distinction in meaning between the phrases "kingdom of God" and "kingdom of heaven." They are parallel phrases and mean exactly the same thing. The fact that these different phrases are used has led some scholars to see a different meaning between the two, to emphasize perhaps that "kingdom of heaven" has a more transcendent reference than "kingdom of God." But because of our knowledge of Jews and Judaism at the time of Jesus, we know that there is absolutely no distinction between these two phrases. A Jew at the time of Jesus would have been very reluctant to use the word for God. And being reluctant to use the word for *God*, most Jews would tend to use other words or phrases to avoid it.

We have seen this Judaistic attitude reflected in discussing the parable of the prodigal son (Luke 15:11–32). We noted that when the son comes to himself in the far country, he says, "I will go to my father and I will say 'Father, I have sinned against heaven and against you.' " The phrase "against heaven" stands for "against God"—in the mind of the Jew who is reluctant to use *God*.

It is characteristic of Matthew, very much a Jew with a strong prejudice against using the word *God*, to use "kingdom of heaven" almost exclusively. Luke, who is almost certainly a gentile, has no such prejudice and therefore uses "kingdom of God" almost exclusively. Mark, a Jew who has lived for a long time in the gentile world, has partly lost his prejudices and thus uses both phrases.

2. THE OLD TESTAMENT

In the Old Testament, the expression "kingdom of God" does not occur very frequently. What does occur is a variety of phrases that mean the same thing: God reigns, God is King, and so on. What is important to us is the meaning of the Old Testament phrase "kingdom of God." There is an interesting piece of Jewish parallelism in Psalm 145:11ff. Here, as in much Jewish poetry, two successive lines express the same thought in different words. The lines are parallel in thought but different in expression: "They shall *speak* of the glory of thy [God's] *kingdom* and *tell* of thy *power*." Here the kingdom of God is the power of God. Continuing in verse 12: "To make known to the sons of men thy *mighty deeds*, and the glorious splendor of thy *kingdom*." The parallel here is between *mighty deeds* and *kingdom*: the kingdom of God is what God does through mighty deeds.

The most important thing to notice about "kingdom of God" here is the meaning of the Hebrew and Aramaic word being translated, *malkuth*. This does not mean a place where a king rules, nor does it mean the idea of kingship. The phrase can be misleading in English because we have a tendency to think of a place ruled by a king or of a community where the king rules, the idea of kingship. The Hebrew and Aramaic word *malkuth* means what a king does, or the "kingly activity." Therefore, in the Psalm 145 passage, "kingdom of God" means the kingly activity of God.

Now let us look at the way in which the phrase "kingdom of God" or its equivalent is used in the Old Testament, especially in the Prophets. One of the distinctive characteristics of the Old Testament prophets was that they looked toward the future. They looked forward to a moment in history when God would act decisively to visit and redeem the faithful community. They looked forward to the moment when God would act in such a manner that everything would be changed—evil would be destroyed, sins would be forgiven, and the glorious blessing of the End Time would be established.

In connection with this eschatological hope, the Prophets used phrases like "kingdom of God." There is a good example in Isaiah 24:21–23 where the kingdom is expressed as that moment when God acts to punish the host of heaven, to imprison the kings of the earth, and to destroy evil. Another illustration is located in Isaiah 33:22: "For the Lord is our judge, the Lord is our ruler, the Lord is our king; he will save us." In other words, the Lord will act as king in that particular moment, acting to bring about salvation. Another example is found in Isaiah 52:7–10: "How beautiful upon the mountains are the feet of him who brings good tidings, who publishes peace, who brings good tidings of good, who publishes salvation, who says to Zion 'Your God reigns.'" God will reign and will act as king. The kingdom will come in that moment when God acts to establish peace, to bring salvation.

Similar expressions of this hope are to be found in Micah 2:12ff., Micah 4:1–7, Obadiah v. 21. In each of these passages, the same concept is being expressed—God acting decisively. The kingdom of God comes when the kingly activity of God is known in human experience, destroying evil, forgiving sins, establishing good, bringing salvation. In the Old Testament the phrase "kingdom of God" generally means that moment in the future when the kingly activity of God will be known.

3. THE KADDISH PRAYER

The Kaddish prayer, used in the synagogue at the time of Jesus, is pertinent to our discussion at this point. It was a popular prayer and was used in the synagogue service very much as we use the Lord's Prayer today. Certainly every Jew at the time of Jesus knew it by heart.

Gustaf Dalman was able to reconstruct the text of the Kaddish prayer as it was most likely used in the synagogue at the time of Jesus. According to Professor Jeremias, this version is most likely the oldest: "Magnified and sanctified be his great name in the world which he has created according to his purpose. May he establish his kingdom in your days and in your lifetime and in the lifetime of all the house of Israel, even speedily and at a near time. And say ye, Amen" (Perrin translation). At the end of the prayer, the congregation collectively said "Amen" and so made the prayer their own.

Here you can see how "kingdom of God" was used frequently in the time of Jesus by the Jews in their prayers, very much in the same way that we say "thy kingdom come." The references to the kingdom of God in the Kaddish prayer and the Lord's Prayer are a reference to this activity of God. It is a prayer that God may act as king speedily, now; that God may act to visit and redeem—to destroy evil, to forgive sins, to bring salvation, to establish the perfect relationship that will last forever. The relationship with God is to be one that death cannot end and sin cannot harm.

4. THE DEAD SEA SCROLLS AND APOCALYPTIC LITERATURE

Apocalyptic literature and the Dead Sea Scrolls represent an important aspect of Judaism at the time of Jesus. In this literature we find the concept of the kingdom of God being used with two different emphases. First, there is an emphasis on God's intervention in human history and human experience. Second, there is an emphasis on the final blessed state to which that intervention is designed to lead.

A series of references to the intervention of God is fully discussed in the book *The Kingdom of God in the Teaching of Jesus* by Norman Perrin (pp. 168ff.). For example, there is a passage in the apocalyptic Assumption of Moses 10:1: "And then his kingdom shall appear throughout all his creation, and then Satan shall be no more and sorrow shall depart with him." Here the reference clearly is to that intervention of God into human history and human experience where Satan is destroyed and sorrow banished. Similar references are located in other apocalyptic works—Psalms of Solomon 17:3, in the Sybilline Oracles 3, ll. 46ff., and in the War Scroll of the Dead Sea Scrolls 1QM, col. 6, l. 6: "And to the God of Israel shall be the kingdom, and among his people will he display might." This is a reference to God's activity, intervening in the holy war against the sons of darkness. A similar usage also occurs in the War Scroll, 1QM, col. 12, l. 7.

The use of "kingdom of God" also points to the final blessed state that God's decisive intervention is designed to secure. There was a tendency in apocalyptic literature to place the emphasis either on the activity of God or on the blessed state which the activity was designed to establish. A series of references illustrates these two emphases (p. 178ff.). For example, in the Sybilline Oracles 3, ll. 767–71: "And then indeed he will raise up his kingdom for all ages over men, he who once gave a holy law to godly men, to all of whom he promised to open out the earth and the world, and the portals of the blessed, and all joys, and everlasting sense and eternal gladness." The reference is to that glorious kingdom that the redeemed will enter, that perfect blessed state in which they will enjoy communion with God.

Similar references are to be found in the Psalms of Solomon 5:18ff. and in the Dead Sea Scrolls, in the so-called Formulary of Blessing 1QSb, col. 4, ll. 25ff.: "Thou art as an angel of the Presence in the dwelling of sanctity. Mayest thou serve forever to the glory of the God of Hosts; mayest thou be surrounding as one who serves in the palace of the kingdom." This is a promise of the priests to the community. It promises them a place in the perfect, blessed state here envisaged in the imagery of a sanctuary, the palace of the kingdom. Another similar reference is located in 1QSb, col. 3, l. 5.

In apocalyptic literature and in the Dead Sea Scrolls, "kingdom of God" is used either about the activity of God or about the End Time, which the activity of God is designed to secure.

C. Kingdom of God in the Teaching of Jesus

Jesus uses the phrase "kingdom of God" just as it is used in the Kaddish prayer—a general reference to the coming of God's kingly activity. One such reference is in Mark 1:15: "The time is fulfilled, the kingdom of God is at hand." Here Jesus is proclaiming the coming of that for which people prayed in their Kaddish prayer. This same emphasis appears also when Jesus sends out his disciples, commissioned to give the same message. One example is in Matthew 10:7: "And preach as you go, saying 'The kingdom of heaven is at hand.'" Also in Luke 9:2: "And he sent them out to preach the kingdom of God." Likewise, in Luke 10:9–11: "Heal the sick . . . and say to them, 'The kingdom of God has come near to you.'"

So in the teaching of Jesus, we have a usage remarkably parallel to the usage in the Kaddish prayer. The parallel can be no accident. Jesus began his ministry by challenging people to recognize that what they had been praying for was now at hand. He sent out his disciples with the same message. When we move from this general challenge to a more specific teaching, we find that there is an emphasis on God's activity in personal experience.

1. GOD'S DECISIVE INTERVENTION

In the teaching of Jesus, the emphasis on God's intervention appears in Matthew 12:28: "But if it is by the spirit of God that I cast out demons, then the kingdom of God has come upon you." The parallel saying is in Luke 11:20: "But if it is by the finger of God that I cast out demons, then the kingdom of God has come upon you." (See Exodus 8:19.) Here the statements are similar to those references in the War Scroll at Qumran—to the kingdom of God as God's intervention in a struggle against evil.

Whereas the Qumran people envisaged the struggle against evil in terms of a war fought with weapons and armies, Jesus sees it in terms of human experience. The exorcisms are an intervention of God in the experience of the individual, a conflict against evil in which the personal experience of the individual has become the arena of that conflict. It is one of the basic emphases of the message of Jesus that God is now intervening in the experience of individuals in their personal struggle against evil. Through Jesus and his ministry, the kingly activity of God is now manifest in this personal, individual experience.

There is an interesting and difficult saying in Matthew 11:12ff.: "From the days of John the Baptist until now the kingdom of heaven has suffered violence, and men of violence take it by force. For all the prophets and the law prophesied until John; and if you are willing to accept it, he is Elijah who is to come." Here is a brief summary from the discussion in Perrin's *The Kingdom of God in the Teaching of Jesus* (pp. 171ff.). The meaning of the first part of the saying is fairly clear: "From the days of John the Baptist until now the kingdom of heaven has suffered violence. . . ." Here we have a conflict; God's kingly activity is manifest in an intervention in this struggle between good and evil.

This reference almost certainly points to the ministry of John the Baptist, here identified with Elijah, and to the ministry of Jesus. The reference to Elijah is understandable: He was the Old Testament prophet who was caught up to heaven. Some Jews believed that just before God intervened in this decisive manner, Elijah would prepare the way. This led the Jews to speculate on Elijah's return and to view his return as the beginning of the End. Jesus is claiming in Matthew 11:12 that in the person of John the Baptist, Elijah has returned, that the End is indeed here—the kingdom of God has come. In the preparatory ministry of John the Baptist and in the fulfillment in the ministry of Jesus, God is intervening. This part of the passage is relatively easy to interpret.

In contrast, we come to the second part of verse 12, translated in the Revised Standard Version as "men of violence take it by force." This portion of the passage may be interpreted differently, because the verb translated as "take" also means "to plunder." A better translation would be "and men of violence *plunder* it." The reference clearly points to the conflict situation. God is intervening in the struggle against evil and the forces of evil are counterattacking.

The Dead Sea Scroll people maintained a similar view. They felt that when the great war against evil began there would be moments when evil would triumph temporarily. In Jesus' teaching, there is a similar reference—a phase of the struggle against evil in which evil triumphs temporarily. It is an attractive hypothesis to suppose that the reference to violence is to the imprisonment and death of John the Baptist. In his imprisonment and death, evil is counterattacking. Whether the reference is specifically to John the Baptist or whether it is more generally to the experience of Christian people whose heightened conscience leads them to know that evil does indeed counterattack, we cannot be certain. The only thing of which we can be certain is that this saying does teach that the kingdom is present in the ministry of Jesus. The kingdom thereby takes the form of an activity of God in the struggle against evil. That struggle in which God is victorious is not, however, bought without a price.

Another important saying about God's decisive intervention is found in Luke 17:20ff.: "Being asked by the Pharisees when the kingdom of God was coming, he answered them, 'The kingdom of God is not coming with signs to be observed; nor will they say, "Lo, here it is!" or "There!" for behold, the kingdom of God is in the midst of you.' " The Jews believed that the decisive intervention of God would be accompanied by recognizable signs. There would be astrophenomena—stars would appear to fall. There would be terrestrial phenomena—earthquakes and the like. There would be all kinds of signs and wonders accompanying the kingly activity of God. In this saying, the Pharisees are asking Jesus, "How about these signs and wonders? Is it true, as you say, that the kingdom of God is now present? Where are the signs and wonders to accompany it?"

But Jesus is teaching that the kingdom of God does not come like that. The kingdom of God is not something accompanied by signs to be observed—the falling of stars, earthquakes, wars, and the like. No. It is something known in the experience of individuals. "Behold, the kingdom of God is in the midst of you"—to paraphrase the words of Jesus, "it confronts you in my ministry, in the experience of my disciples and those who respond to the challenge of my ministry. It is there for those who have eyes to see. It is in your midst, if only you have the eyes to see it." Thus in the teaching of Jesus, "kingdom of God" is being used with the emphasis on God's intervention. The kingdom of God is present in the experience of the individual who is confronted by the ministry of Jesus and its challenge.

2. THE FINAL BLESSED STATE

The emphasis on the final blessed state of the kingdom of God in the teaching of Jesus is similar to the emphasis in apocalytpic literature. We can see this in the beatitudes, Matthew 5:3–12 (and the parallel in Luke 6:20–23): "Blessed are the poor in spirit for theirs is the kingdom of heaven. Blessed are those who mourn for they siall re comforted. Blessed are tie meek, for they shall inherit the earth," and so on.

The reference here is to that finalstate of the redeemed to which the agtivity of god as king will lead. It is a final state in which the values of this world may well be reversed and the values of God will be established. In such a situation, "the poor will become rich, the mourners will be comforted, the meek will inherit the earth"—in other words, the values of God will be established.

Another reference to the future aspect of the kingdom of God is located in Matthew 8:11: "I tell you, many will come from east and west and sit at the table with Abraham, Isaac, and Jacob in the kingdom of heaven." This is called the "Messianic Banquet" by most scholars. The Jews believed that when the final blessed state came they would enjoy the blessings of God forever. They described this event in the imagery of a banquet. Of course, they did not take this imagery literally, but they believed that the redeemed persons would know the blessings of God forever. Therefore they spoke of this situation in terms of a banquet—eating and drinking—as a metaphor, probably symbolic, for sharing the eternal blessings of God.

A reference to the kingdom of God in the present is found in Mark 2:19, where the Pharisees ask Jesus why his disciples do not fast: "And Jesus said to them, 'Can the wedding guests fast while the bridegroom is with them? As long as they have the bridegroom with them, they cannot fast.' " The fellowship between Jesus and his disciples is being pictured as the fellowship of a wedding feast—the fellowship of the Messianic Banquet. It is a fellowship in which the blessings of God are known, the fellowship in which the disciples partake in these blessings by eating and drinking. So Jesus uses this imagery of the perfect blessed state with a future meaning (Matthew 8:11), as well as with a reference to the present (Mark 2:19).

A further aspect of the teaching of Jesus concerning the kingdom of God is his speaking of persons "entering" or "receiving" the kingdom. Examples of this emphasis are in Matthew 5:20, Mark 10:14ff. (and parallels), Matthew 7:21, Mark 10:23–25, Matthew 21:31, Mark 9:47 (and parallels). In all of these references, the kingdom of God is expressed as the final blessed state of the redeemed into which persons will enter, which they will inherit, and which they will receive at some point in the future.

D. Summary

Jesus uses the phrase "kingdom of God" in two ways. First, he uses it to mean God's intervention into human history and human experience. Second, he employs it as a reference to the final blessed state of the redeemed to which God's intervention leads.

Jesus teaches that God's intervention is present in his ministry. Persons may know that intervention in their own experience, as they respond to his challenge. Jesus teaches that this final blessed state is in some sense present, and persons may know it in fellowship with him.

He also teaches that the kingdom of God is future. In both the Lord's Prayer and the beatitudes we find references to the future. And there is a future sense in the sayings about entering and receiving the kingdom.

Thus, in the teaching of Jesus about the kingdom of God, there is a tension between present and future. This dual emphasis of Jesus is the critical key to an understanding of "kingdom of God" as he used it in his teaching.

E. Resource Material

GLOSSARY

ESCHATOLOGICAL   From the Greek word *eschaton* which means "end," and from the Greek word *logia*, which means "teaching." Eschatological means "pertaining to the End" or "the teaching concerning the End." It is used particularly of the teaching understood by the Jews as referring to the moment when God would intervene in history and human experience to visit and redeem faithful individuals.

KADDISH PRAYER   A prayer from the Jewish synagogue at the time of Jesus. A form of it is still used by the Jews today. The form that it had in the first century has been reconstructed. The Kaddish prayer was frequently used in first-century Judaism, and its use is similar to the use of the Lord's Prayer in Christianity.

MALKUTH   The word in Hebrew and Aramaic translated in our Bible as "kingdom." Sometimes it is spelled *Malchuth*. As Jesus used it (*Malkuth Shamayim*), the term means "kingly activity" of God.

MANUAL OF DISCIPLINE (1QSb)   From cave number 1 at Qumran there is a Manual of Discipline, a kind of church "order." It is called 1QS, from the first letter *S* of its Hebrew title. There are two other documents that formed appendices to 1QS: 1QSa is a description of the community as it will be after the war; 1QSb is a formulary of blessings—blessings that certain members of the Jewish community will enjoy after the war is over and won.

PSALMS OF SOLOMON   A collection of psalms written slightly before the time of Jesus. A part of the apocalyptic literature.

SYBILLINE ORACLES   A part of the apocalyptic literature.

WAR SCROLL (1QM)   Qumran literature is designated by the number of the cave in which it was discovered, the caves being numbered in order of their discovery. The alphabetical designation comes from the first letter of their Hebrew title. Thus, 1QM means it was discovered in cave number 1 at Qumran; the *M* is from the Jewish word for "war." The official title of 1QM is "The Scroll of the War of the Children of Light Against the Children of Darkness."

SCRIPTURE REFERENCES

Acts 19:8
Acts 28:23
1 Corinthians 4:20
Romans 14:17
Colossians 4:11
Mark 1:15
Matthew 12:28
Matthew 4:23
Luke 9:27
   (Luke 15:11–32)
Psalms 145:11f.
Isaiah 24:21–23
Isaiah 33:22
Isaiah 52:7–10
Micah 2:12f.
Micah 4:1–7
Obadiah v. 21
Assumption of
   Moses 10:1

Psalms of Solomon
   17:3
Sybilline Oracles
   III, 1, 46f.
War Scroll, 1QM,
   col. 6, l. 6
War Scroll,1QM,
   col. 12, l. 7
Sybilline Oracles
   III, 767f.
Psalms of Solomon
   5:18f.
1QSb IV col. 4, l. 25f.
1QSb III, 5
Mark 1:15
Matthew 10:7
Luke 10:9–11
Matthew 12:38
   (Luke 11:20)

Exodus 8:19
   (Matthew 11:12f.)
Luke 17:20f.
Matthew 5:3–12
   (Luke 6:20–23)
Psalm 37:9–29
Matthew 8:11
Mark 2:19f.
Mark 14:25
   (Luke 22:16)
Matthew 5:20
Mark 10:14
Matthew 19:13–15
   (Luke 18:15–17)
Matthew 7:21
Mark 10:23–25
Matthew 21:31 (43)
Mark 9:47

BIBLIOGRAPHY

Crossan, John Dominic. *Cliffs of Fall: Paradox and Polyvalence in the Parables of Jesus.* New York: Seabury, 1980.

Frye, Northrop. *The Great Code: The Bible and Literature.* New York: Harcourt Brace Jovanovich, 1982.

Perrin, Norman. *Jesus and the Language of the Kingdom.* Philadelphia: Fortress, 1976.

_____. *The Kingdom of God in the Teaching of Jesus.* Philadelphia: Westminster, 1963.

_____. *Rediscovering the Teaching of Jesus.* New York: Harper & Row, 1967 (esp. chap. 2).

Wilder, Amos N. *Early Christian Rhetoric: The Language of the Gospel.* Rev. ed. Cambridge: Harvard University Press, 1978.

QUESTIONS

1. How many times is the phrase "kingdom of God" used in the synoptic gospels?
2. How many times is the phrase "kingdom of God" used in the remainder of the New Testament?
3. Outside the synoptic gospels, what are the three different meanings of "kingdom of God?"
4. Is the meaning of "kingdom of God" the same in the synoptic gospels as when it is used outside the synoptic gospels?
5. Did Jesus use "kingdom of God" in the same manner as the early church?
6. What two examples are exceptions to the general meaning of "kingdom of God" as it is normally used in the synoptic gospels?
7. Which is the harder: discovering what Jesus *said* about the kingdom of God or discovering what Jesus *meant* by the phrase "kingdom of God"?
8. What are four interpretations of "kingdom of God" as interpreted by liberal scholars?
9. To which source do we return to gain an understanding of "kingdom of God" as Jesus used it?
10. Why would this be a legitimate way of reaching an understanding of the phrase "kingdom of God" as Jesus used it?
11. What is the difference between the two phrases "kingdom of God" and "kingdom of heaven"?
12. Why did the Jews use both "kingdom of God" and "kingdom of heaven"?
13. Which of the two phrases does Matthew use and why?
14. Which of the two phrases does Luke use and why?
15. Which of the two phrases does Mark use and why?
16. What are the two variations of meaning given to the phrase "kingdom of God" in Psalm 145:11, 12?
17. What are the two things which the phrase "kingdom of God" means in English that never occur in Hebrew?
18. What is the word in both Hebrew and Aramaic that means "kingdom"?

19. What is the precise meaning of the word *malkuth* as it was used by the Jews?
20. What was the one distinctive characteristic of the prophets of the Old Testament?
21. What are the three things to which the prophets looked forward?
22. What is the term that in general referred to the future?
23. What is the relevance of the phrase "kingdom of God" when the prophets refer to its futuristic aspects?
24. What does the phrase "kingdom of God" mean as used in the Old Testament?
25. What is the meaning of the phrase "kingdom of God" in the Kaddish prayer and in the Lord's Prayer?
26. What are two general things that the phrase "kingdom of God" means in apocalyptic literature and the Dead Sea Scrolls?
27. Is the phrase "kingdom of God" used to refer to a final blessed state in the Old Testament?
28. How does Jesus himself use the phrase "kingdom of God"?
29. How does Jesus use the phrase "kingdom of God" in Mark 1:15, Matthew 10:7, Luke 9:2, Luke 10:9–11?
30. What does Jesus mean by "kingdom of God" in Matthew 12:28 and Luke 11:20?
31. What does Jesus intend "kingdom of God" to mean for the individual?
32. How is the term "kingdom of God" used in Matthew 11:12ff.?
33. Whom does Jesus indicate as fulfilling the role of Elijah as the forerunner of the coming kingdom of God?
34. What is the meaning of the following phrases in Matthew 11:12: "They will take it by force" or "they will plunder it"?
35. What did the Jews believe about the signs of the intervention of God into human history?
36. What does Jesus say about this belief in Luke 17:20?
37. What is the interpretation of "kingdom of God" in the beatitudes?
38. How is the image of the Messianic Banquet used in Matthew 8:11?
39. How is the image of the Messianic Banquet used in Mark 2:19 in reference to the wedding feast?
40. To what period in time does Jesus imply that "kingdom of God" has reference?
41. How does Jesus speak of the future aspects of the kingdom?

Chapter 4

THE FORGIVENESS OF SINS

IN order to understand the teaching of Jesus, we must know something about the understanding of sin and forgiveness among the
people whom he taught. We can then proceed to a discussion of the
forgiveness of sins in the ministry of Jesus and the teaching of Jesus
about sin and forgiveness.

In the first century, the Jews were very conscious of the fact of sin.
They were convinced that sin had its consequences for their everyday
life. They believed that sin and its consequences applied not only to
the individual but also to the nation.

A. The Jewish Understanding of Sin

1. SIN AND ITS CONSEQUENCES

The Jews were convinced that they were truly the people of God
and that they were living in the world that God had created. They
believed that as God's people they should live well in this world;
things should go well for them. But the very opposite was the case.
In their history, they had continually been subjected to foreign inva-
sions; godless people had conquered them. At the time of Jesus, the
godless Romans controlled them in almost every aspect of their lives,
and they hated this. Not only did they hate it, they also wondered
how they—the people of God living in the world that God had
created—could be subject to a godless power. The only answer could
be because of their sin, which must have made them as a people
subject to the power of godless Rome.

In their personal life the same kind of considerations held as in the
national life. If a person was ill or if he had bad luck, it was considered

56

the result of his sin. The rabbis had a saying: "The sick man shall not arise from his bed until all his sins are forgiven him." The Jews were sure that there was an intimate and direct connection between the sufferings of any individual and the status of that person's life, hopes, and standing with God. If a person was a sinner in the eyes of God, this would show up in that person's everyday life. If things went well, that person was not a sinner in the eyes of God. Now, of course, they had all sorts of problems here. For example, if a rabbi who was known to be a pious man suffered illness, how could this be explained? The answer normally was that he had committed some small sin without knowing it. Or, if there were notorious sinners for whom things went well, how could this be explained? The answer usually was that the notorious sinner must have done something good. There are many stories in Jewish literature illustrating this attitude.

But the important point is that the Jews did conceive of sin having its consequences in their lives collectively as a people and in their lives as individuals. Therefore they were concerned with removing these sins. They were intensely concerned with the possibility of atonement for sin and the possibility of forgiveness for sin.

2. THE MEANS OF REDEMPTION

Granted that the Jews were sinners, how could they atone for their sin? Granted that they were—so to speak—in God's disfavor, how could they change this condition? There were a number of things they believed they could do to atone for their sins.

a. Temple Sacrifices

Many Jews believed that they could atone for their sins as a people and as individuals by means of various sacrifices and offerings. These were made during the Temple year, with special attention given to the Festival of the Great Day of Atonement. Because they felt they could earn their redemption in this way, they were eager and conscientious in the performance of these sacrifices. They believed that they were taking the right steps to turn God's disfavor into favor and that things would begin to go well for them as individuals and as a people.

b. Works of Special Virtue

Most Jews believed that they were responsible for keeping the Law. To many Jews, keeping the Torah was living in God's grace, according to God's word. It was a means of grace, because if they kept the

Law, they stood well in the sight of God. The Law was part of God's goodness toward them, given as a means whereby they could earn God's favor.

Of course, no one could keep anything so complex as the Jewish Law completely and perfectly. And the Jews recognized this. They recognized that any individual Jew has a responsibility for keeping the Law, but not absolutely. Their responsibility to God was such that there was a kind of breakage allowance built into it. It was as if they were allowed about 10 percent for margin of error. If they kept 90 percent of the Law conscientiously, they stood well with God. Also, if they kept the Law even more perfectly than expected of them and did certain things beyond what God expected of them, such as alms-giving, they could earn favor. Then they would pay off part of the debt of sin that they owed to God.

So most Jews were concerned with keeping the Law perfectly. And they were concerned with things that God did not really expect of them but for which God would reward them. They believed that in this way they would be able to earn God's favor, to earn redemption from sin. Indeed, the rabbis had a saying that if all Israel were to keep the Sabbath perfectly for three consecutive sabbaths, the kingdom of God would come—all sins would be forgiven and evil vanquished.

c. Righteous Individuals

Some Jews had come to believe that the suffering and death of righteous individuals could serve as a means of atonement. They were led to this belief partly by chapters in the Old Testament like Isaiah 53, where the righteous servant suffers for the sins of many. The key phrases are found in Isaiah 53:11, 12: ". . . the righteous one, my servant [shall] make many to be accounted righteous; and he shall break their iniquities . . . he bore the sin of many and made interces-sion for the transgressors." It is difficult to know how great a part this scripture played in Judaism at the time of Jesus and it would be easy to exaggerate it or, on the other hand, to underestimate it.

Perhaps more immediately influential was the experience of the Jews at the time of the Maccabean Revolt. When the Jews revolted against the Syrians under Judas Maccabeus about 167 B.C., all Jews were subject to persecution. They were subject to torture and even death as a means of making them break the Law, to abandon their faith. A large number of them did suffer torture and death rather than break the Law. These people were called the Maccabean Martyrs, and their example meant a great deal to the Jews. They thought about them a great deal and concerned themselves with keeping their memory alive. They gradually came to the conviction that the suffering and death of a righteous person for a good cause helped their faith, helped to atone for the sins of the people.

d. The High Priest

The High Priest, too, played a prominent role in the Jewish understanding of sin and forgiveness. He was the Great Man of God—the man who, on the Day of Atonement, entered into the Holy of Holies—the most sacred place in the Temple, which no one else could enter. Even he could enter only on one day of each year, on the Day of Atonement. Therefore, this was a great day and a great moment.

The High Priest came to have a special sanctity attached to him because of his special role. It was believed that the sanctity of that place dwelt with him when he came out of the Holy of Holies. His garments had efficacy; if a Jew could touch them, sins could be forgiven—even the garments of the High Priest were a means of atonement. But still more prominent was the High Priest himself. In the first century the High Priests were also called upon to suffer, and it was believed that the death of a High Priest atoned for sin. As a matter of fact, we have reason to believe that at the death of a High Priest all murderers were set free—his death had atoned for their sin.

Certainly the Jews had a very lively sense of sin and its consequences, and they also had great hopes about the means of redemption. But from their past experience, they knew that these means were not enough. Despite the Temple sacrifices, the works of special virtue, the efficacy of the suffering and death of righteous individuals, there still were sinners in their midst. There still were the consequences of sin. The gentiles still occupied the holy land; individual Jews still fell ill and suffered in this world. So despite the means of atonement, sin and its consequences had to be reckoned with. Thus, the Jews turned their thoughts and hopes to the messianic forgiveness.

3. THE MESSIAH

Many Jews believed that when the End came, God would intervene in human history and experience by sending the Messiah. They dreamed of this day, and they associated every kind of possible hope with it. One hope, perhaps above all others, was the hope for the forgiveness of sins. There is a saying in rabbinical literature about the Messiah—that he will come "with grace and pardon on his lips." In other words, he would come bringing forgiveness of sins.

This hope is expressed vividly in apocalyptic literature. In the book of Enoch, the Jews looked for the coming of the Messiah. They looked for his coming as one who would bring with him the final, decisive forgiveness of sins, as one who would destroy all evil. He would forgive the sins of the people of God and so work among the people that never again would they sin.

4. THE EXCLUSION OF THE GENTILES

To the Jew, the gentile was a sinner. The term *sinner* is used here in a rather technical sense. It means one who lived outside the Law, who defied God with every breath because of not observing the Law of God. The gentiles were simply not members of the chosen people of God. A gentile was one who was beyond the reach of the Law and therefore beyond God's forgiveness.

First-century Judaism designated two kinds of sinners. First, there were the gentiles—people who lived beyond the Law and therefore beyond the scope of the mercy of God. Then there were sinners among the Jews—people who lived within the Law yet failed at certain points and at certain times. For those who lived within the Law yet failed—the Jews who had fallen away morally or spiritually—for them there was hope. They could look for the forgiveness of sins when the Messiah came. On the other hand, for the gentiles there was no hope: they could expect nothing at the hand of the Messiah except destruction. If they were spared destruction, they would be spared only to serve as slaves to the Jews in the blessed End Time.

We can see something of this distinction in Galatians 2:15: "We ourselves, who are Jews by birth and not gentile sinners." To be a gentile sinner was to be without hope. But to be a Jew by birth, even if one fell away, was to have hope for God's forgiveness. The same thought is expressed in Enoch 5:6, 7. In this passage, the forgiveness of sins is promised to the Jews who are sinners: "There shall be salvation unto them. . . ." They have lived within the Law and broken the Law. The other kind of sinners, however—the gentile sinners—have no hope: "And for all you sinners there shall be no solution. . . ." They have lived totally beyond the Law and therefore are totally beyond the scope and mercy of God.

An important point to notice in this connection is that a Jew could make himself as a gentile. A Jew who lived within the Law but broke it could still hope for the forgiveness of God. However, there were some things that would make him as a gentile—would put him permanently in the same position as the gentiles.

For example, he could become a swineherd, as in the parable of the prodigal son, discussed earlier (Luke 15:15). Swine not only were unclean animals, but they had also been the means for persecution at the time of the Maccabean Revolt. To force a Jew to sacrifice a pig upon the altar was the favorite way the Syrians had of forcing a Jew to deny his faith. Anyone who had anything to do with swine became unclean—became as a gentile, like the prodigal son. By becoming a swineherd, the prodigal son puts himself beyond the scope of the mercy of God. Up to that point he could hope for forgiveness. He could even be penitent and hope for the forgiveness of God for treating his father as if he were dead (for selling the property). But to become a swineherd was to go past the point of no return. From then on, so far as the Jews were concerned, there was no hope for him.

Similarly, a Jew could not become a tax collector. In the first century, a tax collector was one who not only collected taxes, but also used his office to extort money from people. It was an office open to every kind of abuse, and every kind of abuse was practiced within it. But even this was not the real reason tax collectors were hated so bitterly. They were hated bitterly because they collected taxes from their fellow Jews on behalf of the godless—the gentile, occupying power. Thus they betrayed the Jews, and in serving the gentiles they made themselves as gentiles. For them there was no hope.

Another example is prostitution. A Jewess who became a prostitute and accepted only Jewish clients was considered to be a sinner. But there was hope for her; she could be penitent and hope for the mercy of God. However, if she accepted a gentile as a client, such as one of the mercenary soldiers, she became as a gentile. She had passed the point of no return. For her there was no further hope for the mercy of God.

In the gospels we read again and again the phrase "tax collectors and sinners." This phrase really means "tax collectors and other Jews who have made themselves as gentiles." In other words, they were the Jews who had put themselves beyond the scope of the mercy of God.

Among the Jews at the time of Jesus, the lively hope for the coming of the Messiah and of the messianic forgiveness of sins applied only within bounds. It did not apply to the gentiles or to those Jews who made themselves as gentiles—the tax collectors and sinners.

B. Forgiveness of Sins in the Ministry of Jesus

1. MESSIANIC FORGIVENESS

In several scripture passages, the evangelists highlight Jesus' claim about bringing forgiveness. One such illustration is the scene at Capernaum. A crowd gathers around the house where Jesus is reported to be; four men come bringing a paralytic person. They let the paralytic down through the roof of the house. "And when Jesus saw their faith he said to the paralytic 'My son, your sins are forgiven.' Now some of the scribes were sitting there, questioning in their hearts 'Why does this man speak thus? It is blasphemy. Who can forgive sins but God alone?' " (Mark 2:5–7). What the scribes are saying is that no one can forgive sins except God and God's special representative, the Messiah.

You will notice that healing accompanies this claim to forgive the sins of the paralytic. The Jews would understand this man's paralysis to be the consequence of his sin. If Jesus claimed to forgive the man's sin, he would also be able to heal his paralysis. The incident continues: "And immediately Jesus, perceiving in his spirit that they thus questioned within themselves, said to them, 'Why do you question thus in your hearts? Which is easier, to say to the paralytic "Your sins are forgiven," or to say, "Rise, take up your pallet and walk?" ' " (vv. 8, 9). Both utterances, in essence, have the same meaning. To forgive the sin is to remove the consequences of the sin—the paralysis. This is the key to understanding the healing ministry of Jesus. He heals because he forgives sins. Healing is the consequence of the forgiveness of sins.

The incident continues: " 'But that you may know that the Son of man has authority on earth to forgive sins,'—he said to the paralytic—'I say to you, rise, take up your pallet and go home.' And he rose, and immediately took up the pallet and went out before them all; so they were all amazed and glorified God, saying, 'We never saw anything like this!' " (vv. 10–12). This incident points up a major aspect of the ministry of Jesus. Jesus was claiming to bring the messianic forgiveness of sins. We also see the accompanying healing ministry that is to be understood in this context. Professor Joachim Jeremias discusses this type of ministry thoroughly in *The Parables of Jesus* (pp. 99–120).

Let us look at another account of an incident in the ministry of Jesus, Luke 15:3–10, where we have two important parables about forgiveness. First, let us look at the parable of the lost sheep in which the man with 100 sheep loses one and leaves the 99 to go out after the one. "And when he has found it, he lays it on his shoulders, rejoicing. And when he comes home, he calls together his friends and his neighbors saying to them 'Rejoice with me, for I have found my sheep which was lost.' Just so, I tell you, there will be more joy in heaven over one sinner who repents than over ninety-nine righteous persons who need no repentance" (vv. 5–7).

Then follows the story about the woman who has ten silver coins and loses one. It is likely that the "ten silver coins" means a wedding headdress the woman wore to her wedding and kept as a symbol of her marriage vows. One can easily understand her concern for losing the headdress and the frantic nature of her search. "And when she has found it, she calls together her friends and neighbors, saying, 'Rejoice with me, for I have found the coin which I had lost.' Just so, I tell you, there is joy before the angels of God over one sinner who repents!" (Luke 15:9, 10).

Both of these parables end with a summary of their intent, the lesson they teach. "More joy in heaven" in verse 7 is a roundabout way of saying that God will rejoice; to talk about what goes on in heaven is to talk about God. Similarly, "joy before the angels of God" in verse 10 is a roundabout way of talking about God's rejoicing. So Jesus is teaching that in his ministry there is forgiveness of sins. In these parables, he is explaining the main thrust of his ministry and defending that ministry against its critics.

As a further illustration of the forgiveness of sins in the ministry of Jesus, there are two other parables—the parable of the hidden treasure and the pearl of great price. In Matthew 13:44–47: "The kingdom of heaven is like treasure hidden in a field, which a man found and covered up; then in his joy, he goes and sells all that he has and buys that field." Legally, this was a sound practice. Because Palestine was a country that had been fought over many times, people had buried their treasures to hide them from the marching armies. The law concerning treasures was similar to the British law of "treasure trove." When people find buried treasures in Britain today, there is a law to cover such circumstances. Similarly, in Palestine in the first century the law decreed that the treasure belonged to the owner of the land where it was found. No Jew would object to a man's finding a treasure, hiding it again, then going and buying the land to possess the treasure. He would be thought of as a shrewd man and would be envied, not thought of as doing anything wrong.

In the parable about the pearl of great price, there is "a merchant in search of fine pearls, who, on finding one pearl of great value, went and sold all that he had and bought it." A person who had spent his whole life looking for pearls would be tempted to spend everything for the supreme pearl of great price.

In both of these parables, Jesus is talking about ordinary persons who have a stroke of great fortune and make every effort to own that fortune. Jesus is claiming that in his ministry he is now offering the supreme gift—the gift of the forgiveness of sins. It is up to individuals to respond to the challenge of that forgiveness so they may make it their own. This is a major aspect of the teaching of Jesus: that in his ministry, the messianic forgiveness of sins is now offered. Jesus is saying that persons should recognize this and respond to it. Of course, they might not recognize that forgiveness is being offered—but this is the challenge. Those people in Capernaum could look at Jesus proclaiming the forgiveness of sins to the paralytic and say "He's blaspheming. He has no right to do what he says he is doing." To take this attitude was to shut oneself out from the forgiveness of sins. But one could also turn to this same Jesus and to this same proclamation with faith. One could say "Jesus does have the right to forgive sins." One could accept the challenge being offered and respond to it, thereby entering into the experience of the forgiveness of sins. This was the great gift, the great treasure—the pearl of great price that Jesus offered.

2. BOUNDARIES TO FORGIVENESS

Obviously, the ministry of Jesus caused a great stir because he was forgiving sins and thereby implying a claim to be the Messiah. Many of his contemporaries refused to accept him because he claimed that God forgave the sins of those Jews who had made themselves as gentiles if they would respond to the challenge of that forgiveness. This caused immense offense to his contemporaries. He was challenging their presuppositions, their conviction that they knew what God was like.

a. The Call of Levi

Jesus' calling of Levi offers an example of the commotion caused by his ministry. It is described in Mark 2:13–17: "He went out again beside the sea; and all the crowd gathered about him, and he taught them. And as he passed on, he saw Levi the son of Alphaeus sitting at the tax office, and he said to him, 'Follow me.' " As a tax collector,

Levi was a Jew who had made himself as a gentile—he had put himself beyond the scope of the mercy of God.

Yet Jesus offered Levi forgiveness, offered him the challenge to become part of the redeemed community of his disciples—and this action caused great offense. "And as he sat at table in his house, many tax collectors and sinners (that is, many Jews who had made themselves as gentiles) were sitting with Jesus and his disciples; for there were many who followed him. And the scribes of the Pharisees, when they saw that he was eating with sinners and tax collectors, said to his disciples, 'Why does he eat with tax collectors and sinners?' " Table fellowship for the Jews was the most intimate kind of personal relationship. For a man of God—especially for one implying a claim to be the Messiah—to eat with Jews who had made themselves as gentiles was blasphemy. Even as the Messiah Jesus would have had no right to do this because to the scribes and the Pharisees, God would not forgive these people. "And when Jesus heard it, he said to them, 'Those who are well have no need of a physician, but those who are sick.' "

b. The Woman Who Was a Sinner

A similar example occurs in the incident of the woman who was a sinner in Luke 7:36–40: "One of the Pharisees asked him to eat with him, and he went into the Pharisee's house and sat at table. And behold, a woman of the city, who was a sinner, when she learned that he was at table in the Pharisee's house, brought an alabaster flask of ointment, and standing behind him at his feet weeping, she began to wet his feet with her tears, and wiped them with the hair of her head, and kissed his feet, and anointed them with the ointment. Now when the Pharisee who had invited him saw it, he said to himself, 'If this man were a prophet, he would have known who and what sort of woman this is touching him, for she is a sinner.' "

Jesus has been invited to this house for a formal meal. The probability is that the Pharisees in this district, meeting together for a formal meal, had invited Jesus to join them. No doubt they wanted to get to know him and judge for themselves the validity of his implicit claim to be the Messiah. And then comes a woman from the streets, a sinner—a Jewess who has made herself as a gentile, perhaps a prostitute or the wife of a tax collector, who anoints the feet of Jesus. Her action is the supreme way of expressing thankfulness. At this time, the Jews had no word for "thank you" in their language, so one did something to express thankfulness. The greatest thing one could do was to kiss the feet of the person to whom one was thankful. It was proper to do this, for example, to a person who had saved one's life.

This woman is thanking Jesus for the supreme gift he has brought her (or perhaps to her household)—the forgiveness of sins. The Pharisees object to it. They were prepared to consider the possibility that Jesus is a prophet. But the moment they see him allowing this woman to kiss his feet, they know he is not a prophet. By their presuppositions, if Jesus were a man of God, he would know what kind of a woman she was. And if he knew this, he would certainly never allow her to have anything to do with him—the love of God did not extend to such people.

Then we have the story that Jesus tells in response to their doubts (Luke 7:40ff.). He paints a little picture for Simon about the creditor who had two debtors and the thankfulness they would show him. The one to whom he had forgiven the most would show the greatest thankfulness. This is his explanation about what the woman is doing: her faith has saved her. She has accepted the challenge of the forgiveness of sins in the ministry of Jesus. The forgiveness is for her, even though she is a sinner, one who has made herself as a gentile.

c. The Parable of the Prodigal Son

The parable of the prodigal son in Luke 15:11f. tells about the son who treats his father as if he were dead. The son has become as a gentile, putting himself beyond the scope of God's mercy. Yet when the son turns to his father in penitence, the father receives him, not as a slave—he gives him shoes for his feet. The father receives the son with honor, giving him the best robe and making him the guest of honor at the thanksgiving feast for his return. He puts a ring on his finger, thus retoring him to full authority in his father's house.

Such a story was known to the Jews at the time of Jesus. Rabbi Meyer used to tell the story of a king who had a son who wasted his living in the far country. The king sent for the son, asking him to return. The son said that he was ashamed and dared not return. And the one who had been sent for him asked, "Why should you be? It is your father." In the parable of Rabbi Meyer, the point is that a Jew has the right to regard God as his father, therefore having hope for his forgiveness.

But in his parable of the prodigal son, Jesus carefully makes the son a swineherd, carefully putting him beyond the scope of the forgiveness of God in the eyes of contemporary Jews. Still the father receives the son joyfully and gladly. With this parable, Jesus is apparently defending his own conduct. He is explaining the main purpose of his own ministry—to bring the challenge of the forgiveness of sins to all who will repent. He does not accept the limitations set by his contemporaries to the love and forgiveness of God. The challenge is there even for those Jews who had made themselves as gentiles, if they respond.

Inherent in this message of forgiveness is the gospel for all the world. It is there implicitly. It was to be made explicit in the cross and the gospel of the early church. But here it is implicit in the ministry of Jesus. It is part of the ministry of the one who came claiming to bring the forgiveness of sins to the people of God. It is the ministry of one who refuses to accept the boundaries set by his contemporaries to the love of God. When Jesus is challenged about his forgiveness of sins, he tells the story of the prodigal son. He is describing his own conduct as God's representative by saying in effect "This is what God is like."

C. Summary

By now, we can see a central aspect of the ministry of Jesus—the forgiveness of sins. We have discussed the Jewish conception of sin and forgiveness, a consciousness of sin and its consequences in their lives, their understanding of the means of redemption, and the hope for the messianic forgiveness of sins. In order to understand this particular emphasis of the ministry of Jesus, one has to realize that Jews denied forgiveness of sins to the gentiles and to Jews who had made themselves as gentiles. The Jews strongly believed in this boundary to the love and mercy of God.

Jesus came bringing the forgiveness of sins, claiming that God was acting through him as the Jews expected God to act at the End Time— forgiving sins. But Jesus was also claiming that his contemporaries were wrong. The forgiveness of sins was for all who would respond to his message, for all who would accept it and build their lives on it.

What we need to recognize here is the activity of God in the ministry of Jesus. In the chapter on the kingdom of God, we claimed that God was intervening in the lives of persons in the ministry of Jesus. In this chapter we have seen how Jesus teaches that this intervention is concerned above all with the forgiveness of sins. In the next chapter, we will go on to another aspect—the way this intervention leads to the possibility of a new relationship with God.

The new relationship is intimate. It is summed up by the ability to say to God in prayer "*Abba*, Father." We will take up next the fatherliness of God in the teaching of Jesus. Jesus teaches that because of his ministry, because of God's intervention in history and human experience, and because of the forgiveness of sins, persons can now enter into the true parent-child relationship. Jesus claims that now and only now is this relationship possible.

D. Resource Material

GLOSSARY

ATONEMENT   A theological word meaning "to be once more at one with God." It is used to designate a means whereby sins are absolved. Sin erects a barrier between God and humanity. The means of atonement is the means whereby this barrier is removed, so that God and humankind may be "at one." Another way of expressing atonement is "at-one-ness" with God.

FESTIVAL OF THE DAY OF ATONEMENT   The great festival of the Jewish Temple year. The day in which the sins of the people were laid upon the "scapegoat"—a goat that was driven out into the wilderness. The goat symbolically carried the sins of the people away with him. A significant festival day for the Jews. In the course of the celebration, the High Priest entered the Holy of Holies on behalf of the people.

GENTILE   Although, strictly speaking, the term *gentile* is simply a designation for a non-Jew—one who lived beyond the Law—the term came to have a derogatory emphasis. It designated one who refused to acknowledge God and the Law.

THE GREAT MAN OF GOD   A colloquial expression used to designate the High Priest, the supreme religious personality within Judaism. Immediately before the time of Jesus, the High Priest was both the religious and secular leader of his people. With the coming of the Romans, his secular authority had been taken from him and he was only the religious leader. However, he was highly honored by the Jews. One of the reasons the Jews hated the Romans was that they treated High Priests with disrespect.

THE LAW The requirement God had laid upon the Israelites through Moses. Called the Torah, it was generally regarded as being the contents of the first five books of the Old Testament.

MACCABEAN MARTYRS Jews who suffered death or torture (or both) at the time of the Greek persecution rather than become apostate (deny God). They are called Maccabean Martyrs because Judas Maccabeus led the successful revolt against Syria. Everything connected with this period of time can be called Maccabean. It can be called the Maccabean Revolt, and so on. The Jews who suffered during this period were called the Maccabean Martyrs.

MESSIANIC An adjective from the word *Messiah*. In the Hebrew language, *Messiah* means "the Anointed One." The "Anointed One" was the one whom God would choose and anoint (appoint) to become the means of decisive intervention in history and human experience.

Messianic as an adjective can be used of anything connected with the Messiah. We can speak of a messianic title—a title that designates the Messiah. We can speak of messianic times, meaning the time of the coming of the Messiah. We can speak of the messianic forgiveness of sins, meaning the forgiveness of sins that the Messiah would bring.

MEYER, RABBI One of the men whose names occur in rabbinical literature. He is a rabbi responsible for producing a number of stories and parables. One of the parables taught in his name has striking similarities to the parable of the prodigal son and was probably known by the Jews at the time of Jesus.

REDEMPTION A word that means "delivery from captivity." Because of their sins, the Jews were in captivity to the forces of evil in the world. Redemption was the means whereby they would be delivered from the forces of evil that had made them captive. They looked to the Messiah for the means of redemption or delivery.

SIN The Jews believed that God expected obedience of them, especially obedience to the Law. One who broke the Law sinned—sinned against God (who had laid down the Law) and sinned against other persons (because the actions were often directed against other persons).

In Aramaic, the same word, *hobha*, can be translated "sin" or "debt." To sin is to fail to do what God expected—to keep the Law. One therefore became "indebted" to God. An example of both meanings occurs in the Lord's Prayer, where we read "sin" and forgiveness of those who are "indebted" to us. Those who are "indebted to us" are those who have "sinned against us."

SCRIPTURE REFERENCES

Isaiah 53	Mark 10:1–12	Matthew 13:45–47
Book of Enoch 5:6, 7	Luke 15:3–10	Mark 2:13–17
Galatians 2:15	Luke 15:10f.	Luke 7:36–50
Luke 15:15	Matthew 13:44	Luke 15:15

BIBLIOGRAPHY

Jeremias, Joachim. *The Parables of Jesus.* Rev. ed. New York: Scribner, 1963.
_____. *Rediscovering the Parables.* London: SCM, 1966.

QUESTIONS

1. If a Jew was happy and well, what did he think caused this?
2. If he was not well and unhappy, what did the Jew think was the cause?
3. If there was much sinfulness within a nation, what did the Jews think the result of this would be?
4. How did the Jews explain the fact that a pious man sometimes suffers?
5. How did the Jews explain the fact that many sinners prosper?
6. The Jews were extremely interested in atonement, or redemption of sins. What were some of the ways in which redemption could be gained?
7. What was the Jewish attitude toward the Law?
8. Was the Jew expected to keep the Law perfectly?
9. What if the Jew did keep the Law more perfectly than was expected?
10. Where did the idea derive that suffering and death of righteous individuals should give atonement?
11. Despite all the things the Jews did to gain atonement for sin, there was still sin and persecution. What was their final hope for redemption?

12. How did the Jews define "gentile"?
13. What are the two kinds of sinners as defined by the Jews of Jesus' time?
14. What did Jews think gentiles could expect from the Messiah?
15. In most cases a Jew had hope of atonement, even if he fell by the wayside. How would the person born a Jew lose all hope of salvation, according to Jewish thinking at the time of Jesus?
16. In what case would a Jewish prostitute be a sinner with hope for salvation? In what case would she become as a gentile and be beyond the scope of God's mercy?
17. What does the phrase "tax collectors and other sinners" mean?
18. Was the Jewish Messiah who was to come to be a Messiah for both the Jews and the gentiles?
19. Did Jesus accept boundaries on the mercies of God?
20. In what ways did Jesus claim through his actions to be the Messiah?
21. At the healing of the paralytic, would the Jews have considered the paralytic's sins to have been forgiven if Jesus had not healed him?
22. How is Jesus using the parable of the hidden treasure and the parable of the pearl of great price to explain his own ministry?
23. What if a person should refuse to accept the Messiah?
24. What are three things that Jesus did to cause great disturbances among the Jews?
25. Why did Jesus' call of Levi to follow him cause disturbance among his contemporaries?
26. Why did the fact that Jesus ate at the same table with gentiles cause anger among the Jews?
27. In the story of the incident of the woman who was a sinner (Luke 7:36–50), what do the Pharisees think when they see the woman washing Jesus' feet?
28. Why did the woman wash Jesus' feet instead of saying "thank you"?
29. What is Jesus doing or offering when he tells the story of the prodigal son?
30. What message implicit in Jesus' actions and stories is made explicit later by the teachings of the church?

Chapter 5

THE FATHERLINESS OF GOD

THIS chapter contains a discussion of the concepts of God in Greek thought, in the Old Testament, and in the teaching of Jesus. Special attention is given to the new relationship with God made possible through Jesus' ministry and teaching. An explanation is included concerning the eschatological parent-child relationship evident in the teaching of Jesus.

A widely held and popular concept about the teaching of Jesus is that of the fatherhood of God and the brotherhood of man. This alone is, however, an inadequate understanding of this aspect of his teaching. Jesus emphasizes the activity of God, the forgiveness of sins, and the way these things make possible a new relationship with God—a new relationship in which God is our parent and we are children.

A. God as Progenitor in Greek Thought

The Greek philosopher Plato, in *Timaeus*, expresses the Greek idea of the fatherhood of God. He says that God is "the Maker and Father of this universe." This was the widely held Greek concept—that there is a God who is Maker and Father of the universe.

In the writings of the Greek poet Aratus of Soli (c. 270 B.C.) the line "For we are indeed his offspring," is important to us, because it was quoted by Paul in his speech at Athens as recorded in Acts 17:28. Here we have the same concept that we see in Plato—God is the Maker and Father of this universe and we are offspring. Cleanthes, another Greek poet, (300–220 B.C.) expresses much the same thought in his most famous work, "The Hymn to Zeus." In it, the line "For we are thy offspring" appears exactly as in Aratus of Soli. The understanding here is that people are the offspring of God.

In the Greek concept, God is Father in the sense of Maker and all of us are offspring. God is understood to be the progenitor. In many ancient religious traditions, human beings have expressed this divine-human dimension in familial terms.

B. God as Father in Old Testament Thought

There is a Hebrew parallel to the Greek emphasis on God as Father in the sense of physical generation—the concept of God as creator. In Deuteronomy 32:6-9: "Do you thus requite the Lord, you foolish and senseless people? Is not he your father, who created you, who made you and established you?" This statement could just as easily have been made by a Greek.

1. THE CREATOR

The passage in Deuteronomy is quite similar to Malachi 2:10: "Have we not all one Father? Has not one God created us?" In these two references, the idea of the fatherhood of God is linked with the idea of God as Creator. This concept, common in Greek thinking, is rare in the Old Testament. It constitutes a great difference between Old Testament thought and Greek thought. The major emphasis in the Old Testament is not on God as Creator-Father, but on God as Savior/Father, acting in a fatherly manner toward the children of Israel.

2. ACTING FATHERLY

One theme in the Old Testament deals with God as father, acting in a fatherly manner toward the children of Israel. In Isaiah 63:16: "Thou, O Lord, are our Father, our Redeemer from of old is thy name." God is Father in the sense of a redeemer. A father would act in an emergency to redeem his children.

In Deuteronomy 1:31, we read, "And in the wilderness, where you have seen how the Lord your God bore you, as a man bears his son, in all the way that you went until you came to this place." This is a very vivid metaphor. A father and his son are traveling through the wilderness. The child grows tired and stumbles. The father, naturally enough, picks him up and carries him. This metaphor is applied to the way God guided and helped the people of Israel through the wilderness.

Deuteronomy 8:5 reads: "Know then in your heart that, as a man disciplines his son, the Lord your God disciplines you." Again we have a metaphor on human fatherliness. A father will discipline his child and punish the child when necessary, will seek to teach his children the proper way to go. God likewise acts in this manner toward children, disciplining them when necessary.

In Isaiah 1:2 there is a similar thought expressed: "Hear, O heavens and give ear, O earth; for the Lord has spoken: Sons have I reared and brought up." In this passage, we see that God has acted toward the people as a father acts toward his children—rearing them, bringing them up, educating, disciplining, and caring for them. This is one characteristic of the Old Testament conception—God acting in a fatherly manner.

3. CHILDREN OF GOD

Just as God acts in a fatherly manner toward children, they should respond by acting as children. Deuteronomy 14:1 reads: "You are the sons of the Lord your God; you shall not cut yourselves or make any baldness on your foreheads for the dead." Here it is assumed that the Hebrew who counts God as a Father must respond by acting like a child. A child obeys his father, according to this reference, by avoiding ritual mutilation for the dead.

This same emphasis on response is found in the prophets. For example, in Jeremiah 3:19: "I thought how I would set you among my sons, and give you a pleasant land, a heritage most beauteous of all nations. And I thought you would call me 'My Father,' and would not turn from following me." The fatherly care and attention of God toward children should produce the proper response: love and obedience.

In the prophets, the great indictment of the Hebrews is that they have failed in this responsibility. The cry of the prophets is that Israel has not acted properly in response to the fatherly care and attention of God. Israel has not behaved as the true child of God should have behaved. Referring again to Isaiah 1:2, 3: "Sons have I reared and brought up, but they have rebelled against me. The ox knows its owner and the ass its master's crib; but Israel does not know, my people does not understand." The children of God have not behaved properly as children should behave toward their Father.

Jeremiah 3:20 reads: "Surely, as a faithless wife leaves her husband, so have you been faithless to me, O house of Israel, says the Lord." Here is a different metaphor to express the same thought—the metaphor of marriage and the responsibility of a wife toward her husband. Then we read in verse 21: "A voice on the bare heights is heard, the weeping and pleading of Israel's sons, because they have perverted their way, they have forgotten the Lord their God." Jeremiah indicts Israel for not behaving as children should behave toward their father. He is claiming that much of the catastrophe is afflicting them because they have not responded as children should have responded to God.

Similarly, in Malachi 1:6: "A son honors his father, and a servant his master. If then I am a father, where is my honor? And if I am a master, where is my fear? says the Lord of hosts to you, O Priests, who despise my name." Here the indictment is directed particularly toward the priests. They count God as their Father but they have not behaved as children should behave. This realization that the children of God have not responded as they should leads to a development in the concept of the fatherliness of God. This development is that God is particularly the Father of the God-fearing. As the writings of the Old Testament progress through time, the emphasis that God is Father of all, or even that God is Father of all Israel, is all but lost. And in its place, we have the concept that God is Father particularly of those who behave as children, who fear (stand in awe of) God and obey. An example of this can be found in Psalm 103:13: "As a father pities his children, so the Lord pities those who fear him." A statement like this is moving toward the notion that the parent-child relationship applies only to those who behave as true children.

A similar emphasis is found in Malachi 3:16, 17: "Then those who feared the Lord spoke with one another; the Lord heeded and heard them, and a book of remembrance was written before him of those who fear the Lord and thought on his name. They shall be mine, says the Lord of hosts, my special possession on the day when I act, and I will spare them as a man spares his son who serves him." The concept of a very real personal relationship is presented here. This relationship arises in response to the activity of God as father; it brings privileges and responsibilities.

Jewish theology tended to take on an eschatological note in the first century. The Jews began to think of the moment when God would act decisively for their salvation, for that moment when the kingdom would come. The parent-child relationship with God became a part of this eschatological hope—the day when God would act decisively to visit and redeem the Jews.

4. THE FATHER-CHILD RELATIONSHIP

The father-child relationship as part of the eschatological hope is expressed in Jeremiah 3:22: "Return, O faithless sons, I will heal your faithlessness. Behold, we come to Thee; for Thou art the Lord our God. Truly the hills are a delusion, the orgies on the mountains. Truly in the Lord our God is the salvation of Israel." Jeremiah looked forward to the day when God would establish the new covenant with the Israelites. He looked forward to the day when God would act decisively in their history and their experience. One thing Jeremiah expects in this new day is that the faithlessness of the children would be healed. They would now become faithful children; the true father-child relationship between Israel and God would be restored as part of this hope for the end.

The same thought can be found in the Apocrypha, in The Wisdom of Solomon 2:16: "He [God] will bless the righteous at the End Time. The righteous will exult that God is his Father." Also, in 5:5: "How he [the righteous] will be reckoned among the sons of God. His inheritance will be among the holy ones" (Perrin translation). This refers to the End Time, to the moment when God will act decisively to visit and redeem. Part of this eschatological hope is that the true relationship with God as Father will be restored. Those who are redeemed by God at the End Time and those who become truly righteous through God's activity will exult, because God will be their Father. They will truly be reckoned among the children of God.

We have here the development of what we may call the eschatological parent-child relationship, the new relationship with God arising in response to God's decisive intervention in history and human experience.

C. The Teaching of Jesus about the Fatherliness of God

The eschatological father-child relationship was a characteristic of the Jewish expectation expressed in the Old Testament. As we might expect, this Jewish expectation is also a part of the New Testament. The eschatological parent-child relationship turns up as a presupposition of the New Testament.

1. ESCHATOLOGICAL EXPECTATIONS

We find an example of this eschatological expectation in a discussion between Jesus and the Sadducees about the resurrection in Luke 20:34: "And Jesus said to them 'The sons of this age marry and are given in marriage; but those who are accounted worthy to attain to that age and to the resurrection from the dead neither marry nor are given in marriage, for they cannot die any more, because they are equal to angels and are sons of God!' " Here, Jesus is using the Jewish thought of his period to argue against the Sadducees. This reference to the eschatological relationship with God shows that this was a part of the thought of this age.

Similarly, in the book of Revelation the author uses concepts taken from Jewish apocalyptic thought to express a Christian message. We see this in Revelation 21:7: "He who conquers shall have this heritage, and I will be his God and he shall be my son." This is another instance of the eschatological father-child relationship with God as part of the background to the ministry of Jesus.

Jesus can and does assume this eschatological expectation. What we look for therefore are the new emphases that Jesus himself makes: Jesus implicitly claims to enjoy this new kind of parent-child relationship.

2. JESUS' USE OF *ABBA*

The most striking example of the way Jesus claims to enjoy this eschatological parent-child relationship with God is his use of *abba*. We find this in the prayer in Gethsemane, expressed in Mark 14:36: "And he said, *Abba*, Father, all things are possible to thee; remove this cup from me; yet not what I will, but what thou wilt." This use of *abba* is sufficiently remarkable for Mark to have preserved the actual word used on this occasion. The word *abba* means "father"; what we have here is a quotation of the Aramaic word used by Jesus—*abba*—followed by a translation—"father."

Mark has preserved this word because its use by Jesus in prayer is remarkable. No Jew ever addressed God as *abba*. The Jews addressed God as Father, but they never used this form of the word. They were always careful to say "my Father," "our Father," and "our Father who art in heaven." They would use anything except the simple word "Father." Why? Simply because *abba* is the child's word for "father." It is the first word an Aramaic-speaking child learned, just as we teach our children to say "dada" or the like. In that day children were taught to say *abba*, meaning "daddy." Because *abba* was used by the children in this way, it was thought wrong to use it of God; hence we can explain the careful use of "our Father," "my Father," and similar expressions. Joachim Jeremias discusses this point thoroughly in his book *The Prayers of Jesus* (pp. 11–65).

Jesus breaks with the tradition of his contemporaries, deliberately using the child's word for "father," whereas the Jew would have avoided it. He is stressing the nature of the new relationship that he enjoys with God. He is stressing the fact that he now can address God as *abba*. He is enjoying the eschatological parent-child relationship with God.

This same thing is seen in another Marcan version of the teaching of Jesus. We read in Mark 8:38, "For whoever is ashamed of me and of my words in this adulterous and sinful generation, of him will the Son of man also be ashamed, when He comes in the glory of his Father with the holy angels." Here in this Marcan account, Jesus teaches that the Consummation will come, that the Son of man will come and that the Son of man considers God his Father. Jesus is identified with the Son of man in this passage. Jesus may call God his Father because he enjoys this eschatological parent-child relationship.

Perhaps even clearer is an example in Mark 13:32: "But of that day or that hour no one knows, not even the angels in heaven nor the Son, but only the Father." The evangelist Mark is saying that we have a claim to the new relationship—God is parent; Jesus is child. Jesus apparently enjoys the eschatological parent-child relationship with God.

A further instance is located in Matthew 11:27: "All things have been delivered to me by my Father; and no one knows the Son except the Father, and no one knows the Father except the Son and anyone to whom the Son chooses to reveal him." Although likely not authentic, this saying is remarkably like the kind of thing we read in the gospel of John—the concept of Jesus as the child and God as the parent in a very special way.

If Jesus spoke to God as *abba* in prayer, it is likely because of a consciousness of standing in a new relationship with God. Jesus then teaches that he enjoys this special relationship with God. He also teaches his disciples that they too now enjoy this relationship. Just as he addressed God as *abba* in prayer, he was teaching his disciples to do the same.

3. THE LORD'S PRAYER

The prayer that Jesus taught his disciples is distinctive. The version in Matthew 6:9 begins: "Our Father who art in heaven," which is the common Jewish way to begin a prayer. But in the version expressed in Luke 11:2, it begins simply "Father"—in other words, *abba*. According to Joachim Jeremias, a careful comparison between the Matthean and Lukan versions of the Lord's Prayer shows that the Lukan version likely has the higher claim to authenticity. Matthew's version seems to reflect the influence of the liturgical use of the Lord's Prayer in the church. In this particular instance, the Matthean version shows Matthew's somewhat Jewish prejudices; the notion of addressing God as *abba* has been too much for him. He has gone back to the regular Jewish way of doing things, not the only place in his record of the teaching of Jesus where he modifies that teaching toward traditional Judaism.

Luke is apparently the original here. Luke shows us that Jesus taught his disciples to address God as *abba* in prayer. The relationship that he enjoys with God, the disciples also enjoy. The right he has to address God as *abba*, the disciples also have. By responding to the challenge of the kingly activity of God in the ministry of Jesus and by accepting the forgiveness of sins, the disciples share with Jesus the eschatological parent-child relationship with God.

The apostle Paul saw this relationship very clearly. He makes this point in writing to the Galatians and to the Romans. In Galatians 4:6 we read: "And because you are sons, God has sent the Spirit of His Son into our hearts, crying *Abba*! Father!" Paul too has preserved this remarkable use of the word *abba*. He counts the privilege of addressing God as *abba* the high point of his Christian faith. He shares with Jesus the new relationship with God. Again, in Romans 8:15 we read: "For you did not receive the spirit of slavery to fall back into fear, but you have received the spirit of sonship. When we cry 'Abba! Father!' it is the Spirit himself bearing witness with our spirit that we are children of God." The phrase "children of God" refers to a new way. It identifies people who share in the new relationship. Through Jesus, they enjoy the eschatological parent-child relationship with God.

This is the main drive of the teaching of Jesus concerning the fatherliness of God. He accepts the idea of his Jewish contemporaries that the eschatological father-child relationship would be a feature of the End Time, and that this End Time has now come in his ministry. God is acting as king. The eschatological forgiveness of sins is now here for those who will respond to this challenge. And for those who recognize the kingdom of God as present in Jesus, for those who respond to the challenge of the forgiveness of sins, there is the new relationship with God. God is their parent, they are God's children; they may address God as *abba*.

4. THE ESCHATOLOGICAL PARENT-CHILD RELATIONSHIP

The new relationship with God made possible through the ministry of Jesus is shown in Mark 11:25: "And whenever you stand praying, forgive, if you have anything against anyone; so that your Father also who is in heaven may forgive you your trespasses." In the context of this new relationship with God, one should respond to the challenge of forgiveness by forgiving. It is a new relationship with God that is now possible for those who respond to the challenge of the ministry of Jesus and of his teaching. It is in this relationship that one learns to accept forgiveness and to forgive.

In Luke 11:9–13 are these words: "And I tell you, Ask, and it will be given you; seek, and you will find; knock, and it will be opened to you. For everyone who asks receives, and he who seeks finds, and to him who knocks it will be opened. What father among you, if his son asks for a fish, will instead of a fish give him a serpent; or if he asks for an egg, will give him a scorpion? If you then, who are evil, know how to give good gifts to your children, how much more will the heavenly Father give the Holy Spirit to those who ask him?" It is very probable that this teaching, especially the last part of it, may have been modified somewhat in transmission. References to the "heavenly Father" and the Holy Spirit seem to owe something to the early church. In any event, it assumes the eschatological parent-child relationship. People now share this relationship; they may have confidence as they approach God in their prayer. Because of this relationship they may learn to pray in a new, deeper, and more confident manner.

The most interesting example of the eschatological relationship in the teaching of Jesus is found in Luke 12:22–32: "And he said to his disciples, 'Therefore I tell you, do not be anxious about your life, what you shall eat, nor about your body, what you shall put on. For life is more than food, and the body more than clothing. Consider the ravens: they neither sow nor reap, they have neither storehouse nor barn, and yet God feeds them. Of how much more value are you than the birds? And which of you by being anxious can add a cubit to his span of life?' " Here, of course, we have a general claim that we may learn from nature something of God and God's responsibility toward us. Notice, however, that this is not to be understood as a general teaching about anyone's being able to look to nature and learn something of God. It presupposes sharing the eschatological parent-child relationship. It is only those in the context of faith who can learn these lessons from the world around them.

The text continues: "If then you are not able to do as small a thing as that, why are you anxious about the rest? Consider the lillies, how they grow; they neither toil nor spin; yet I tell you, even Solomon in all his glory was not arrayed like one of these. But if God so clothes the grass which is alive in the field today and tomorrow is thrown into the oven, how much more will he clothe you, O men of little faith. And do not seek what you are to eat and what you are to drink, nor be of anxious mind. For all the nations of the world seek these things; and your Father knows that you need them." Notice the intimate relationship expressed explicitly here. "Your Father knows that you need them." It is because of this new relationship that one can have confidence in God. "Instead, seek his kingdom," that is, look for the evidence of God's activity in your experience, ". . . and these things shall be yours as well."

The person who has come to accept with confidence that God is at work in his/her experience will have confidence with regard to all that God can do for her/him. "Fear not, little flock for it is your Father's good pleasure to give you the Kingdom." You can interpret this "fear not" as meaning that God—the one with whom you share this new relationship—is manifest in your experience. God is concerned that you may learn to build your life around this relationship.

D. Summary

The fatherliness of God is not accidental in the teaching of Jesus. There is clearly a deliberate emphasis on the decisive intervention of God and the new relationship that this makes possible. Jesus has the right to address God as *abba*; he has this new relationship. The disciples may also address God as *abba;* they too may come to share this relationship. And we, of course, come after the original disciples; we also may say *abba.*

We share in this special relationship with God made possible by the ministry of Jesus. Jesus teaches about the God who establishes and maintains a nurturing and caring relationship. We may learn to trust in God, to build our lives on the evidence of God's activity in our experience. We can live joyfully with confidence and hope.

E. Resource Material

GLOSSARY

ABBA   The Aramaic word for "father." Because it was the form taught to children, Jews tended to avoid it in prayer. The teaching of Jesus is significantly different at this point; he used the child's word, *abba,* meaning "dada" and implying a close and familial relationship with God.

ARATUS OF SOLI   A Greek poet who flourished about 270 B.C. Comparatively little of his work is preserved. He is important to the readers of the New Testament since he is quoted by Paul in Acts 17:28.

CLEANTHES   An important Greek poet who lived from about 300 to 220 B.C. His major work is "The Hymn to Zeus."

ESCHATOLOGICAL   *Eschatos* is the Greek word for "end." *Logia* is the Greek word for "sayings." *Eschatology* is the noun meaning "the sayings concerning the End"; *eschatological* is the adjective form. The reference in Jewish eschatology is specifically to the idea of God's decisive intervention in human history and experience to visit and redeem humankind. This visitation from God would bring redemption and insure the forgiveness of sins, the destruction of evil, and the end of death. Three aspects of this expectation are referred to: the eschatological forgiveness of sins, the eschatological parent-child relationship with God, and the new relationship with God.

RITUAL MUTILATION   In the ancient world it was a widespread practice to mutilate or cut oneself as a sign of mourning—a ritual mutilation on behalf of the dead. The practice confronted the Jews as they came into Canaan after the exodus from Egypt. Part of the Jewish Law is concerned with teaching the Jews not to mutilate themselves on behalf of their dead, since this was a pagan, Canaanite practice.

SCRIPTURE REFERENCES

Acts 17:28
Deuteronomy 32:6–9
Malachi 2:10
Isaiah 63:16
Deuteronomy 1:31
Deuteronomy 8:5
Isaiah 1:2
Deuteronomy 14:1
Jeremiah 3:19
Jeremiah 3:20, 21
Malachi 1:6

Psalms 103:13
Malachi 3:16, 17
Jeremiah 3:22
The Wisdom of
    Solomon 2:16
The Wisdom of
    Solomon 5:5
Luke 20:36
Revelation 21:7
Mark 14:36

Mark 8:38
Mark 13:32
Mark 11:27
Matthew 6:9
    (Luke 11:2)
Galatians 4:6
Romans 8:15
Mark 11:25
Luke 11:9–13
Luke 12:22–32

BIBLIOGRAPHY

Ebeling, Gerhard. *On Prayer: The Lord's Prayer in Today's World*. Philadelphia: Fortress, 1978.
Hamerton-Kelly, Robert. *God the Father*. Philadelphia: Fortress, 1979.
Jeremias, Joachim. *The Central Message of the New Testament*. New York: Scribner, 1965 (esp. chap. 1, pp. 9–30).
_____. *The Lord's Prayer*. Philadelphia: Fortress, 1964.
_____. *New Testament Theology: The Proclamation of Jesus*. New York: Scribner, 1971.
_____. *The Prayers of Jesus*. Philadelphia: Fortress, 1978.

QUESTIONS

1. To what is the term *abba* comparable in English?
2. Which Aramaic word would be comparable to *father* in English?
3. What is the Greek concept of God?
4. What Greek poet does Paul quote in Acts 17:28 when he says "For we are indeed His offspring"?
5. Who is another Greek poet who also says "For we are thy offspring"?

6. There are two places in the Old Testament where Hebrew thought about God as Father is similar to Greek thought. In these two places, why is God thought of as Father?
7. Since the idea of God as Father is based on his role as creator in only two places, what does this indicate when compared with Greek and Hebrew thought?
8. Why is God thought of as Father in Hebrew thought?
9. What are several ways in which God is characterized in the Old Testament, particularly in Deuteronomy, as having the characteristics of Father?
10. If God acts as Father, what does this mean about the way we should act?
11. In what way did the Jews think a son should act toward his father?
12. What limitations do the Jews place on God's fatherhood?
13. What is the nature of sonship?
14. What is the eschatological expectation of the Jews concerning the fatherliness of God?
15. Is this same relationship taught by Jesus?
16. Why did the Jews not use *abba* in addressing God?
17. Why did Jesus use the word *abba*?
18. Jesus enjoys the eschatological parent-child relationship with God, which he shows by using the word *abba* to address God. Does Jesus teach the disciples that they also enjoy this new relationship? How?
19. In Mark 11:25, how does Jesus suggest that we should respond to God's forgiveness?

Part III

RESPONSE TO
THE ACTIVITY
OF GOD

Chapter 6

ETHICS AS RESPONSE

THIS chapter contains a discussion of three major topics: the several approaches that have been taken to understand the ethical teaching of Jesus, the context of the ethical teaching of Jesus, and the dynamic of response in the ethical teaching of Jesus.

The thrust of the ethical teaching of Jesus is response to the activity of God. That activity is the kingdom of God as proclaimed by Jesus in his ministry and teaching. This ethical teaching is expressed several places in the teaching of Jesus, but most prominently in the Sermon on the Mount (Matthew 5:1 through 8:27) and the parallel Sermon on the Plain (Luke 6:20–49).

A. The Ethical Teaching of Jesus: Various Interpretations

The expectation of the ethical teaching of Jesus is response. Jesus expects his hearers to understand that their ethical conduct is a response to the love of God. In different scholarly interpretations through the years, many misunderstandings have developed about the ethical teaching of Jesus. Christians have sought to understand and interpret the ethical teaching of Jesus and in the course of time, many different approaches have been used. Usually, these approaches crystallize around the Sermon on the Mount, for the Sermon on the Mount can be conveniently, even if wrongly, used as a representation of the total ethical teaching of Jesus.

Harvey K. MacArthur has written *Understanding the Sermon on the Mount*, which describes twelve approaches to the Sermon on the Mount. Here he points out the different attempts that have been made to understand and interpret the ethical teaching of Jesus (p. 125ff.). Below is his summary of the more common understandings that many people have adopted through the years.

1. ABSOLUTIST VIEW

According to the absolutist view the ethical teaching of Jesus means exactly what it says. The commandments should be interpreted literally, applied universally and absolutely. Of course, some of the commandments contain figures of speech and symbolic language. For example in Matthew 5:29f.: "If your right eye causes you to sin, pluck it out. . . ." But when due allowance is made for the figurative language in the absolutist view, all else is to be taken literally and applied absolutely.

In the history of the Christian interpretation of the ethical teaching of Jesus, the absolutist view has been a popular one. Augustine described the Sermon on the Mount as a perfect standard of the Christian life. He argued that the Sermon on the Mount should be taken literally. Also, Francis of Assisi is regarded as one who took the ethical teaching of Jesus literally. He lived a life of voluntary poverty, trying to carry out the Sermon on the Mount to the letter insofar as his understanding was concerned. The extremist sects at the time of the Protestant Reformation, especially the so-called Anabaptists of the sixteenth century and later, understood the teaching of Jesus literally and attempted to carry it out in their personal and community lives. But perhaps the best known of all the individuals to take an absolutist view of the Sermon on the Mount is the Russian nobleman and novelist Leo Tolstoy. His life, as he tells us himself, was dominated by the understanding that the words of Matthew 5:39, "Do not resist one who is evil," were to be taken literally. He attempted to build his life on this principle.

2. MODIFICATION VIEW

According to the modification view, the teaching of Jesus is to be taken literally, but not absolutely so. At significant points, we may modify it as we apply it. In this understanding, the practice is to introduce what we might call escape clauses into our understanding of the teaching. An example from the text of the New Testament is

Matthew 5:22: "But I say to you that everyone who is angry with his brother shall be liable to judgment; whoever insults his brother shall be liable to the council, and whoever says 'You fool!' shall be liable to the hell of fire." In this text, immediately following "everyone who is angry with his brother," some later manuscripts of the New Testament add the clause "without a cause." In fact, the familiar King James version reads "whosoever is angry with his brother without a cause shall be in danger of the judgment." But the qualifying phrase is not a part of the reading of the original text of the Sermon on the Mount in Matthew's gospel. What has happened is that a later copyist has inserted this as a kind of escape clause. He is taking the teaching of Jesus literally, but modifying it as he applies it.

3. HYPERBOLIC VIEW

Hyperbole is deliberate exaggeration not meant to be taken literally. A sentence such as "He is as strong as a lion" is an example of hyperbole. No one making this statement intends it to be taken literally; it is expressive of a person's great strength. According to this point of view, Jesus himself was using hyperbole in the Sermon on the Mount. His teaching is not to be taken literally, but as expressing a principle; we can therefore tone it down as we apply it.

A good example is found in Luke 14:26: "If any one comes to me and does not hate his own father and mother and wife and children and brothers and sisters, yes, and even his own life, he cannot be my disciple." Another example is Matthew 5:29: "If your right eye causes you to sin, pluck it out. . . ." This view claims that Jesus used hyperbole as a teaching device, that is, that he intended his hearers not to take his teaching literally, but to recognize that he was using this method of emphasizing ethical principles.

4. GENERAL-PRINCIPLES VIEW

The general-principles viewpoint is a popular one. In this understanding, the teaching of Jesus is not concerned so much with specific instruction of commandments; the sayings are not to be taken literally and applied absolutely. Instead, we are to recognize that Jesus is concerned with general moral principles, of which these commandments are illustrations. Therefore, we are to look at the commandment for the principle underlying it, and, having found that principle, to apply it for ourselves.

An example of the general-principles view is the saying about turning the other cheek in Matthew 5:39: "But I say to you, Do not resist one who is evil. But if any one strikes you on the right cheek, turn to him the other also" (the acceptance of a formal insult). Augustine argued that this saying about a backhanded slap gave us a principle that covers all possible forms of injury and one's reaction to it. According to the general-principles view, we are to seek out the principles implicit in these explicit commandments of Jesus. This understanding has been very popular in the church and is obviously valid in many instances.

5. ATTITUDE-NOT-ACTS VIEW

The attitude-not-acts view is also a popular one in the church. In this view we are to understand the teaching of Jesus as dealing with the attitudes we are to have rather than with specific acts we are to do or not to do. It is true that frequently Jesus is concerned with a general attitude rather than a specific act. In the saying about turning the other cheek, for example, it could be argued that this saying is designed to show the attitude that one should take toward personal injury. Having grasped that attitude, we may work out the specific acts for ourselves.

This view obviously has points of validity in interpreting the ethical teaching of Jesus, especially when looking at the so-called antitheses in the Sermon on the Mount. An example is to be found in Matthew 5:21ff.: "You have heard that it was said to the men of old, 'You shall not kill; and whoever kills shall be liable to judgment.' But I say to you that every one who is angry with his brother . . ." Here obviously we have moved from the specific act to the attitude that underlies it. It is clear that Jesus is concerned with what goes on in the hearts of persons, and not merely with their deeds. This aspect of the so-called ethical teaching of Jesus is very popular in Christian thinking and teaching.

6. DOUBLE-STANDARD VIEW

The double-standard viewpoint is widespread in the Roman Catholic church. According to this understanding, we are to distinguish between precepts and counsels. Obedience to the precepts (the fundamental principles) is essential to salvation. Obedience to the counsels (the less essential, but nonetheless important, teaching) is essential for perfection and is a more certain way of insuring salvation. So, in the Roman Catholic church, there actually are two classes of Christians: the perfect class attempts to fulfill both precepts and counsels; the second class attempts to fulfill only the precepts.

Some persons outside the Roman Catholic church are skeptical of this approach to the teaching of Jesus. But even the most skeptical Protestant can have a somewhat similar view. For example, Martin Luther's understanding is very much like the double-standard view.

7. TWO-REALMS VIEW

Martin Luther argues that human activity can be divided into two spheres: the spiritual and the temporal. The Christian, he maintained, participates in both spheres. In the spiritual sphere, the Christian is under obligation to obey all the commands of the Sermon on the Mount. In the temporal or secular sphere, one is to follow a somewhat different standard, apparently one of natural law, or possibly common sense (see MacArthur, pp. 117ff.).

8. INTERIM-ETHICS VIEW

The interim-ethics view is important in any discussion of the ethical teaching of Jesus. It was propounded by Albert Schweitzer, who was following an earlier scholar, Johannes Weiss. Schweitzer maintained that Jesus proclaimed the kingdom of God as imminent—God was about to act and people should prepare themselves for this activity of God. People should repent, and they should show their penitence and prepare themselves for the activity of God by making a superhuman ethical effort. According to this view, such a superhuman effort is demanded by Jesus in his ethical teaching—he sets his standards almost impossibly high because the standards are designed to operate only for a limited period of time—only for the interim between the now of the proclamation and the actual coming of the kingdom.

9. PREPARATION-FOR-THE GOSPEL VIEW

This viewpoint is especially popular in Lutheran circles. This view says in effect that the ethical teaching of Jesus expresses impossible ideals, that no one could in fact keep this teaching perfectly. But no one is intended to keep this teaching perfectly; the teaching is designed to be impossible, designed to prepare persons for the gospel by showing them the impossibility of achieving a real ethical standard on their own. It is designed to drive them to despair so they may be prepared for the good news of the gospel. In this case, the ethics of Jesus would function as law. Luther believed that the law was meant to produce guilt, not righteousness, since no one can keep the law perfectly. Law, then, produces guilt, which prepares one for the gospel.

These nine approaches to an understanding of the ethical teaching of Jesus show that there have been numerous interpretations. With this smattering of possibilities, we naturally ask which one is appropriate to follow for guidance? If we feel that none of the views expresses the matter completely or properly, what alternative do we have?

B. The Context of the Ethical Teaching of Jesus

We must recognize that the ethical teaching of Jesus was not the central focus of his message. Jesus was not simply an ethical teacher, nor was he even primarily an ethical teacher. He came proclaiming the good news that God was active as king in his ministry, that God was intervening in human history and human experience in his ministry—that the kingdom had come. In his book *The Sermon on the Mount*, Joachim Jeremias rejects the various approaches to the Sermon. He maintains that the proclamation of the kingdom of God precedes the ethical teaching. People who came to hear Jesus speak, to whom he directs his ethical teaching, are people who have already heard him proclaim the kingdom as present—God as active. As Mark presents it, Jesus in his ethical teaching presupposes an understanding about the kingdom of God. Professor Jeremias gives five examples of these assumptions.

1. THE LIGHT OF THE WORLD

Jeremias begins with the saying in Matthew 5:14 "You are the light of the world." Jeremias maintains that this presupposes that the disciples had already found in Jesus the light of the world.

2. FORGIVING TRESPASSES

His second example is from Matthew 6:15: "If you do not forgive men their trespasses, neither will your heavenly father forgive your trespasses." Jeremias argues that this saying must be read in the light of the conclusion of the parable of the unmerciful servant in Matthew 18:35: "So also my heavenly father will do to everyone of you, if you do not forgive your brother from your heart." This presupposes the "great debt cancellation" the parable of the unmerciful servant mentions. It is only after our trespasses have been forgiven that we can forgive other people their trespasses. The commandment to forgive presupposes the offer of forgiveness.

3. THE SAYING ON DIVORCE

The third example is in the saying on divorce in Matthew 5:32: "But I say to you that every one who divorces his wife except on the ground of unchastity, makes her an adulteress; and whoever marries a divorced woman commits adultery." This presupposes the hearing of the proclamation that the time of the Law has run out; the time of salvation is beginning. Mark 10:2-12 is parallel to Matthew 5:32 in that it also shows the time of the Law had run out and the time of salvation is beginning. The Marcan version says: "Whoever divorces his wife and marries another, she commits adultery." Again, God's intervention is taking place now; there is really no time to debate about divorce.

4. LOVING ONE'S ENEMIES

The command to love one's enemies is in Matthew 5:44-48: "But I say to you, love your enemies and pray for those who persecute you, so that you may be sons of your Father who is in heaven; for he makes his sun rise on the evil and on the good, and sends rain on the just and on the unjust. For if you love those who love you, what reward have you? Do not even the tax collectors do the same? And if you salute only your brethren, what more are you doing than others? Do not even the gentiles do the same? You, therefore, must be perfect, as your heavenly Father is perfect." The response to the teaching and ministry of Jesus makes possible a new relationship in which one is to be like God. This presupposes the dynamic of the boundless goodness of God, experienced in God's intervention in our history and our experience.

5. TURNING THE OTHER CHEEK

The fifth example Jeremias uses is the saying about turning the other cheek in Matthew 5:38ff.: "But I say to you, Do not resist one who is evil. But if any one strikes you on the right cheek, turn to him the other also." According to Jeremias's interpretation, this passage does not refer to insults in general, but to formal persecution of the followers of Jesus as heretics. The followers of Jesus are being taught how they must respond to the charge of heresy and to persecution as they go on with their Christian ministry. But one cannot go on with the Christian ministry unless one has first responded to the activity of God experientially and responded to the challenge of God in the midst of life. So this commandment, like the others, is preceded by the proclamation.

Jeremias is making a major and important point: the sayings of Jesus concerning ethics are preceded by the proclamation of the gospel. We do not have anything in the teaching of Jesus concerned with ethics that does not follow the proclamation of the kingly activity of God. This, therefore, is the key to understanding the ethical teaching of Jesus. The ethical teaching follows the proclamation of the gospel. Jesus' ethical teaching is designed to illustrate the kind of response that persons must make to the proclamation of God's kingly activity.

C. The Dynamic of the Ethical Teaching of Jesus

It is necessary to keep in mind that the ethical teaching of Jesus is always preceded by the proclamation of the kingdom. In this way we can understand that the dynamic of the ethical teaching of Jesus is response—response to God's activity. The ethical teaching of Jesus is designed to illustrate the kind of response one should make to the activity of God. This assertion can be demonstrated by another close look at the Lord's Prayer.

1. THE LORD'S PRAYER

The central petition in the Lord's Prayer is the petition for forgiveness—"forgive us our sins." This is followed by a second part—"as we ourselves forgive those who have sinned against us." Jewish scholars tend to emphasize that in Judaism there is no condition to the forgiveness of sins. One of the prayers of the Jewish synagogue, certainly known to Jesus, has as one of its petitions "Forgive us, our Father, for we have sinned against Thee. Wipe away our transgressions from before thine eyes. Blessed art thou, O Lord, who dost abundantly forgive." Here, the Jewish scholars say, we have the Jewish understanding of forgiveness—it is unconditional.

But the Christian understanding is slightly different. Jesus adds a condition to forgiveness—"forgive us our sins as we ourselves forgive." If we are to understand the true intent of this second part of the petition, and, of course, it is not simply a condition, we must begin by noting that Matthew and Luke have different tenses to their verb. Matthew has "as we also have forgiven." Luke has "as we ourselves forgive." Matthew has the perfect tense and Luke has the present tense.

Matthew and Luke are translating an Aramaic original here. This is particularly clear because of the play on *sin* and *debt*. Luke has "forgive us our sins as we ourselves forgive everyone who is indebted to us" and Matthew has "forgive us our debts as we also have forgiven our debtors." Here there is a play on the words *sin* and *debt*, because in Aramaic the word *hobha* has both meanings. It is clear that this section of the Lord's Prayer has a translation variant between Matthew and Luke. Matthew has translated the word as "debt" both times (in the noun and in the verb). Luke has translated the noun as "sin," but the verb as "debt."

A hypothetical reconstruction of the Lord's Prayer shows the reason for such a variant. The Aramaic perfect tense indicates an action that takes place here and now. So the emphasis in the original Aramaic would be "as we herewith forgive our debtors." The emphasis would be "forgive us our sins as we *herewith* have forgiven those who have sinned against us." This would be using the Aramaic perfect tense, indicating an action that takes place here and now.

The statement "we ourselves forgive" is not a condition on which God forgives us, since it does not take place before God's forgiveness takes place. The action of this verb is not prior to the action of God in forgiving. Nor is it strictly speaking a consequence of God's forgiving. The Aramaic perfect puts the two together as taking place simultaneously. This leads us to the conclusion that the petition teaches that our willingness to forgive is, as Professor Jeremias once put it, "the outstretched hand whereby we receive God's forgiveness." Or, it could be stated thus: Our willingness to forgive is the response we make to God's forgiveness of us.

This addition to the petition on forgiveness in the Lord's Prayer is one of the places where we can find no parallel in Judaism. There is no one prayer exactly like it, but if we search the prayers of Judaism at the time of Jesus, we can construct one that resembles the Lord's Prayer. There are differences, however. The Lord's Prayer is brief, personal, and direct. The Jewish prayers tend to be rather long, involved, and indirect. But in sentiment, meaning, and intent, there are parallels to the petitions of the Lord's Prayer in the prayers of Judaism of the first century. There are two exceptions—there is no parallel to the address of God as *abba*, nor is there any parallel to this second part of the petition for forgiveness.

Matthew's gospel is designed for Jewish Christians, that is, Christians with a Jewish background. He has modified the address to God; he no longer has the simple *abba*. Matthew 6:9 gives "Our Father who art in heaven," the regular Jewish mode of address to God in prayer, but also uses this second part of the petition for forgiveness. A Jewish Christian would be struck by this addition; it would be a new concept. It is therefore significant that Matthew follows the Lord's Prayer with a saying that occurs elsewhere in the synoptic gospel tradition—from Mark 11:25, 26. This saying is in Matthew 6:14: "For if you forgive men their trespasses, your heavenly father also will forgive you; but if you do not forgive men their trespasses, neither will your Father forgive your trespasses."

The other version of this saying is in Mark 11:25: "And whenever you stand praying, forgive, if you have anything against any one; so that your father also who is in heaven may forgive you your trespasses." This saying makes the same point as the second part of the petition for forgiveness—the essential link between our willingness to forgive and our reception of God's forgiveness. It is for this reason that Matthew puts it immediately after the Lord's Prayer. Having given the prayer to his Jewish Christian readers, he then adds this saying, driving home the point that would be new to them—the point made in the second part of the petition. Our willingness to forgive is the response we make to God's forgiveness.

2. THE SERMON ON THE MOUNT

In addition to the Lord's Prayer, which gives us an understanding of the ethical teaching of Jesus, the so-called antitheses in the Sermon on the Mount likewise reveal a specific attitude. The ethical teaching is illustrated in Matthew 5:43ff.: "You have heard that it was said, 'You shall love your neighbor and hate your enemy.' " These sayings from the Sermon on the Mount are normally taken from the Old Testament. But this particular saying is not to be found there. Leviticus 19:18 is the nearest thing to it in the Old Testament: "You shall not take vengeance or bear any grudge against the sons of your own people, but you shall love your neighbor as yourself: I am the Lord." In this passage there is no mention of "hate your enemy."

However, in the Dead Sea Scrolls, in the Manual of Discipline, we do have exactly this same saying. The Manual of Discipline sets out the principles on which the community is to be founded and by which it is ordered. The first section of the manual deals with fundamental theological principles, one of which is the commandment to love the neighbor who is the son of light, the fellow member of the sect. The other principle is to hate the enemy of that sect. So the Matthew quotation does not come from the Old Testament, but parallels the quote from the Manual of Discipline. Notice how the passage continues: "But I say to you, Love your enemies and pray for those who persecute you." This prayer would certainly not have been offered by a member of the Dead Sea Scroll community! If these people prayed for their enemies or for those who persecuted them, it would only be that God might destroy them, and the sooner the better. "But I say to you, Love your enemies and pray for those who persecute you, so that you may be sons of your Father who is in heaven."

The Dead Sea Scroll people, most likely Essenes, called themselves the Sons of Light. Here we have Jesus playing on the self-designation of the sect. Jesus says "that you may be sons of your Father." The true child responds to the father by exhibiting that same attitude to others that the father has exhibited to him: "for he makes his sun rise on the evil and on the good, and sends rain on the just and on the unjust. For if you love those who love you, what reward have you? Do not even the tax collectors do the same?" (Matthew 5:45, 46). The Dead Sea Scroll people would have hated that statement—they hated tax collectors, since tax collectors were Jews who had made themselves as gentiles.

The passage continues: "And if you salute only your brethren, what more are you doing than others? Do not even the Gentiles do the same?" The Dead Sea Scroll people made a great to-do about salutation—the proper form of greeting. They have instruction in their literature as to the way one member of the sect must greet and respond to another member of the sect. They have very heavy penalties for those who do not behave in accordance with this graduation of greetings. They hated the gentiles; here they are being challenged: "What are you doing more than the gentiles whom you hate do. You, therefore, must be perfect, as your heavenly Father is perfect" (Matthew 5:48). A literal rendering of this passage from the Greek would be "You, therefore, should be progressing toward perfection [maturity, wholeness], as your heavenly Father is [already] perfect." We are not expected to attain the perfection of God, but to be perfect in kind. Just as God is perfect in being, so should we be progressing toward the perfection of our own nature.

In this series of sayings, we can see Jesus not only setting his own teaching over against that of the Dead Sea Scroll people but also exhibiting the same principle—the principle of response. The love of enemies, the praying for those who persecute you—these are not general moral principles implicit in the universe. This is not something you would do because it would make you a better person. This is something God does. This is the kind of attitude God has. We respond to God's activity of forgiving, loving, and helping by exhibiting this same kind of attitude and activity toward others. "You, therefore must be perfect, as your heavenly Father is perfect"—the perfection of response.

3. THE HIDDEN TREASURE AND THE PEARL OF GREAT PRICE

The ethical teaching of Jesus is also illustrated in the twin parables of the Hidden Treasure and the Pearl of Great Price, discussed earlier, in Matthew 13:44–46: "The kingdom of heaven is like treasure hidden in a field, which a man found and covered up; then in his joy he goes and sells all that he has and buys that field." According to the law of that day this was a good act. Palestine was a country that had been conquered many times. People had hidden their treasure in the ground because they were subject to foreign armies and invaders coming through their lands. So often had this happened in this small country that the discovery of hidden treasure was not a rarity.

The Jews had a law that said if you found a treasure in a field and the field belonged to you, you kept the treasure. If you found treasure in a field that did not belong to you, you could buy that field and were legally entitled to do so. There was no sense of deception or anything questionable about it. So, in the parable, the man is behaving as any Jew could behave. Those who heard the parable would probably envy the man who discovered the treasure. "How nice it would be if it could happen to me" they would think. Notice the key phrase here: *"in his joy* he goes and sells" that he may buy the field.

The parable of the treasure hidden in a field makes this point: A person who makes a great discovery full of joy will respond by taking appropriate action to possess what he has discovered. Jesus is saying that you, to whom God is reaching out in kingly activity, whom God is challenging with the forgiveness of sins—you too should be filled with joy. You should respond that you might possess. Response is the way to experience what God is offering.

Similarly, in the parable of the pearl of great price: "The kingdom of heaven is like a merchant in search of fine pearls, who, on finding one pearl of great value, went and sold all that he had and bought it." What is being presented in this parable is the challenge of opportunity. Make the correct response so you may possess what is of greatest value. God is reaching out toward us—we should respond so we can experience what is being offered.

Note that the man "sells all he has," as does the pearl merchant. The point is made that one forsakes all for the surpassing worth of the kingdom of God (cf. Luke 18:22, 28–30; also Luke 9:57–62).

4. JESUS AND SIMON THE PHARISEE

Another illustration of this dynamic of response is the story of Jesus in the house of Simon the Pharisee (Luke 7:36–50). Here is a Perrin translation of the Aramaic underlying the Greek text, beginning with verse 40: "Jesus answered these unspoken words, saying to him, 'Simon, I have something to say to you.' He answered 'what is it, teacher?' 'A certain creditor had two debtors; one owed him 500 denarii and the other 50. When neither of them could pay, he forgave them both. Now, which of these will show him the greater thankfulness?' Simon answered 'the one, I suppose to whom he forgave the more.' Jesus said to him 'you suppose rightly,' Then turning to the woman, he said to Simon 'Do you see this woman? As I entered your house you gave me no water for my feet, but she has wet my feet with her tears and wiped them with her hair. You gave me no kiss of greeting, but from the time I came in, she has not ceased to kiss my feet. You did not anoint my head with oil but she has anointed my feet with this fragrant oil. I may tell you that her sins, which are many, have been forgiven. Therefore she shows much thankfulness. He to whom little has been forgiven shows little thankfulness.' He said to her 'your sins have been forgiven.' Then those who were at table with him began to say among themselves 'who is this who even forgives sins?' He said to the woman 'your faith has saved you. Go in peace!' "

The key to this passage is what the woman was doing in anointing and kissing his feet—showing extreme thankfulness, the conventional way of expressing gratitude. She is responding to the forgiveness of sins in terms of thankfulness, so Jesus commends her for responding appropriately. This is part of what he means when he says "Your faith has saved you." Faith, in this context, means her recognition that Jesus had the authority to forgive sins. Faith also means her willingness to respond. By responding, she is experiencing forgiveness and she is being saved. She may now go in peace to continue in this way.

Here again is a specific principle in the teaching of Jesus—the dynamic of response. Jesus is concerned that people should respond to what is being offered them in his ministry. His ethical teaching is designed to illustrate the kind of response that should be made. We are conscious of the love of God—we should respond by loving. We are challenged by the forgiveness of sins—we should respond by showing forgiveness. We believe that God has treated us as friends and has freely forgiven us—we should respond in a similar way as we deal with even those whom we count as enemies.

D. Summary

In contrast to all the ways in which the ethical teaching of Jesus has been interpreted through the centuries, by building on the foundation laid by Professor Jeremias we now have a far better way of understanding the teaching. We now have a way of entering into the heart of the matter—the recognition that the ethical teaching of Jesus is concerned with response. We are to respond to what Jesus proclaims that God is doing—becoming active as king in our history and our experience. The ethical teaching of Jesus illustrates the kind of response we are to make.

E. Resource Material

GLOSSARY

ANABAPTISTS   A sect that came into prominence at the time of the Reformation. They grouped themselves into communities and lived closely in accordance with doctrines. They formed the nucleus of the free church movement. Their literal interpretation of the scriptures led them to interpret the ethical teaching of Jesus as absolute in meaning and implication. (see Absolutist View)

ANTITHESES IN THE SERMON ON THE MOUNT   In Matthew 5 there is a series of passages from the teaching of Jesus that follows a common pattern. It begins: "You have heard that it was said by men of old . . ." (or a similar statement). Then there follows a quotation from the Old Testament or one that has its parallel in the Dead Sea Scrolls. Next, the teaching of Jesus is set over against the quotation, introduced by: *"But I say to you . . ."* Jesus therefore sets his own teaching in *antithesis* to the teaching he has quoted. Thus the following passages are known as the antitheses in the Sermon on the Mount: Matthew 5:22, 28, 32, 34, 39, 44.

AUGUSTINE   Bishop of Hippo who lived in the fourth century. His writings have influenced Christian thinking throughout the history of the church. He interpreted the Sermon on the Mount to be a standard for Christian life. (See Absolutist View)

COUNSELS   Teaching of Jesus that is taken to be less important for the Christian than the precepts. Obedience to the counsels of Jesus is essential for perfection, a way of assuring oneself of salvation. This view is predominately that of the Roman Catholic church.

FRANCIS OF ASSISI   Founder of the Franciscan Order. A thirteenth-century literalist who renounced worldly goods because of a passage of scripture, Jesus' words to the so-called rich ruler, in Luke 18:22: "And when Jesus heard it, he said to him, 'One thing you still lack. Sell all you have and distribute to the poor, and you will have treasure in heaven, and come, follow me.' " He maintained that the Sermon on the Mount was to be taken literally. (See Absolutist View)

HYPERBOLE   The practice of exaggeration or extravagant statement as a figure of speech. For example, the sentence "Fred is *as strong as a lion*" is hyperbole, expressing a person's strength. One of the interpretations of the ethical teaching of Jesus maintains that Jesus himself uses hyperbole as a teaching device—not to be taken literally, but merely expressing a principle.

INTERIM ETHICS   The interpretation that sees the teaching of Jesus as commands calling for superhuman effort. Interim ethics may be called temporary ethics—temporary in the sense that humanity is waiting for the kingdom of God to come in the future. This view calls for people to have extremely high standards until the kingdom comes. The interim is the time between the life and teaching of Jesus and the kingdom to come (seen as wholly future). Thus interim ethics refers to man's special conduct in preparation for the future Consummation of the kingdom.

LUTHER, MARTIN   The major reformer of the sixteenth century, whose views on the teaching of Jesus were influential in Protestantism until the nineteenth century. He regarded the teaching of Jesus as applying to dual realms or spheres of rule—humankind under the influence of two forces: spiritual and temporal. His understanding in this respect resembles that of Augustine of the fourth century. (See *Natural Law*)

NATURAL LAW   Could be called "common sense." Martin Luther believed in a natural law that a person instinctively knows and can respond to. In Luther's understanding of ethics the Christian has a temporal (secular, earthly) code of conduct which is automatically known. Luther held the view, for example, that the Ten Commandments existed before Moses wrote them on stone, so that the truths in the Commandments, especially those relating to humankind, are intuitive. However, Luther specifically rejected the idea of natural law as expounded by the Scholastics, together with all so-called natural theology. The existence of a real natural law that is universal and applicable to life has been brought into serious question in the twentieth century.

PRECEPTS The fundamental principles of the teaching of Jesus, which must be obeyed in order to gain salvation. This understanding is predominant largely in the Roman Catholic church.

TOLSTOY, LEO A major Russian novelist who wrote with a strong religious, moral, and ethical theme. His writings reflect a strong moralistic interpretation of the scriptures. He took the teaching of Jesus literally and wrote of the sayings of Jesus as though they were commandments. (See Absolutist View)

SCRIPTURE REFERENCES

Matthew 5:29f.	Matthew 6:15	Mark 11:25, 26
Matthew 5:22	Matthew 18:35	Matthew 6:14
Luke 14:26	Matthew 5:32f.	Matthew 5:43f.
Matthew 5:29f.	Mark 10:2–12	Leviticus 19:18
Matthew 5:39	Matthew 5:44f.	Matthew 13:44–46
Matthew 5:21f.	Matthew 5:38f.	Luke 7:36–50
Matthew 5:14	Matthew 6:9–13	
	(Luke 11:2–4)	

BIBLIOGRAPHY

Crossan, John Dominic. *Finding Is the First Act*. Philadelphia: Fortress, 1979.
Davies, W. D. *The Setting of the Sermon on the Mount*. Cambridge: Cambridge University Press, 1964.
Jeremias, Joachim. *The Sermon on the Mount*. Philadelphia: Fortress, 1963.
MacArthur, Harvey K. *Understanding the Sermon on the Mount*. New York: Harper & Brothers, 1960.
Perrin, Norman. *Rediscovering the Teaching of Jesus*. New York: Harper & Row, 1967 (esp. chap. 3, pp. 151–53).
Sanders, Jack T. *Ethics in the New Testament*. Philadelphia: Fortress, 1975.

QUESTIONS

1. Around what part of the teaching of Jesus are most approaches to his ethical teaching based?
2. Who are three people and one religious group who hold the absolutist view of interpreting the Bible?
3. What is the "escape clause" found in Matthew 5:22 concerning being angry with one's brother?

4. What is the absolutist view of interpreting the ethical teaching of Jesus?
5. What is the modification view of the ethical teaching of Jesus?
6. What is the hyperbolic view of the ethical teaching of Jesus?
7. What is the general-principles view of the ethical teaching of Jesus?
8. What is the attitude-not-acts view of interpreting the ethical teaching of Jesus?
9. What is the double-standard view of interpreting the ethical teachings of Jesus?
10. According to the Roman Catholic church, what are the two classes of Christians?
11. What is the view held by Martin Luther, which is very similar to the "double-standard" view held by the Catholic church?
12. What is the two-realms view?
13. Are there distinctions to be made in the ethical teaching of Jesus that would substantiate the double-standard view and the two-realms view?
14. What is the interim-ethics view of the teaching of Jesus?
15. Who advanced the interim-ethics view?
16. Upon what man's ideas was the view of Albert Schweitzer based?
17. What is the preparation-for-the Gospel view?
18. What are nine different views of the ethical teaching of Jesus?
19. By what is the ethical teaching of Jesus preceded?
20. What do we mean by the proclamation of the kingdom of God?
21. What does Jesus presuppose when he gives his ethical teachings?
22. What does Jesus presuppose when he tells his disciples that they are the "light of the world" in Matthew 5:14?
23. What does Jesus presuppose in Matthew 18:35 when he says, "So also my heavenly father will do to every one of you, if you do not forgive your brother from your heart"?
24. What does Jesus presuppose in his saying on divorce in Matthew 5:32?
25. What does Jesus' command to love one's enemies presuppose in Matthew 5:44ff.?
26. Does the suggestion by Jesus to "turn the other cheek" (according to Jeremias) refer to a response to general persecution in Matthew 5:38?
27. What does this command presuppose?
28. What is the key to understanding the ethical teaching of Jesus?
29. What is the ethical teaching of Jesus designed to do?
30. How does the Lord's Prayer differ from other Jewish prayers in terms of the petition for forgiveness?

31. Why did Luke use the term *sins* in "forgive us our sins," and why did Matthew use the word *debts* in "forgive us our debts" in the Lord's Prayer?

32. Which interpretation of the Lord's Prayer is correct: Luke, who says, "forgive us our sins, for we ourselves forgive everyone who has sinned against us," or Matthew, who says, "as we have forgiven our debtors"?

33. Is the forgiving of our debtors a condition of God's forgiveness?

34. What is the meaning of "forgiving others as God forgives us"?

35. Does the addition to the petition of forgiveness in the Lord's Prayer have a parallel in Judaic prayers?

36. What are adjectives describing the Lord's Prayer and Kaddish prayer showing how they contrast?

37. In the Sermon on the Mount, Matthew 5:43, 44, Jesus says, "You have heard that it was said, 'You shall love your neighbor and hate your enemy.' But I say to you ..." This saying is not in the Old Testament. Where is it to be found?

38. To whom does the antithesis in the Sermon on the Mount, which directs you to love your neighbor, seem to be directed?

39. What is the man like who finds the treasure in the field and sells everything he has to possess this field?

40. Why does Jesus commend the woman who visits him to offer thanks in the house of Simon the Pharisee in Luke 7:36–50?

41. What does Jesus mean when he says to the woman, "your faith has saved you"?

Chapter 7

ETHICS AND
THE WILL OF GOD

THIS chapter is a presentation of the view that the will of God is the central concern of the ethical teaching of Jesus. Three major discussions are included: Jesus as a rabbi, Jesus as an interpreter of the will of God, and the new understanding of the will of God.

A. Definition of a Rabbi

In first century Palestine, a rabbi was both a theologian and a civil judge—a religious teacher and one who settled civil disputes. The rationale behind this practice was that the Law of God—the Mosaic Law—was the Law of the community, and the Law of the community was regarded as the Law of God. Therefore the one who was expert in this Law, the rabbi, had an essential role in the community, giving advice and help both in religious or theological matters and in civil matters. The Mosaic Law was a medium of revelation showing the will of God, a means of gaining God's favor.

1. JESUS AS A RABBI, OR EXPERT IN THE LAW OF GOD

Jesus was regarded as a rabbi, an expert in the Law of God. Often called "rabbi" in the gospel tradition, he would be known as Rabbi Jesus (Yeshua) of Nazareth. In the gospels we have many occasions where his opinion is asked on theological and religious matters. For example, in Mark 12:13ff.: "They sent to him some of the Pharisees and some of the Herodians, to entrap him in his talk. And they came and said to him 'Teacher [rabbi], we know that you are true and care for no man; you do not regard the position of men, but truly teach the way of God. Is it lawful to pay taxes to Caesar or not?' "

This was a question that very much concerned the Jews at the time of Jesus. Because they hated the Roman occupying authorities, whether it was in accordance with the law of God to pay taxes to this godless occupying power was a question that concerned them greatly. The question is a trick question designed to trap Jesus. If Jesus answered "It is lawful," his opponents could turn to the Jews and say "This man teaches us to pay taxes to the godless Romans." If Jesus said, "It is not lawful," then his opponents could turn to the civil authorities, the Romans, and say "This man teaches sedition." The fact that such a question was asked of Jesus indicates his public stature and recognition as a rabbi.

Another example of Jesus' status as a rabbi appears when the Sadducees come to him with a question about the resurrection (Mark 12:18–27; Matthew 22:23–33). The Sadducees believed that there was no resurrection, so they were asking Jesus a trick question. Their question dealt with a man who had seven brothers; each one of the brothers took the same woman as his wife in succession. They asked Jesus whose wife would she be at the resurrection? (This passage is an example of the levirate law, Deuteronomy 25:5–10.) Because this question is a theological matter, the fact that Jesus' opinion is asked shows his public standing as a theologian, as a rabbi.

In Mark 12:28–34, the question is asked of Jesus about which commandment is the first of all. This matter was much discussed in the rabbinical schools, and the occasion indicates that he had standing as a rabbi.

Further, Jesus is asked to adjudicate matters of civil dispute. For example, the question addressed to him in Luke 12:13ff.: "One of the multitude said to him 'Teacher [rabbi] bid my brother divide the inheritance with me.' " Here Jesus is asked to adjudicate a civil dispute with regard to a will, a matter in the Jewish community that called for a rabbi.

The gospel tradition clearly testifies to the fact that Jesus was regarded as a rabbi. His opinion was asked on theological and religious matters and he was asked to adjudicate civil disputes. Thus, as a rabbi, Jesus interpreted the will of God.

B. Jesus as an Interpreter of the Will of God

1. THE SCRIPTURES

All rabbis interpreted the scriptures because they believed the scriptures had been given to the Jews through Moses as a revelation of what God required. In the first century, sacred scriptures were what we now call the Old Testament. Rabbis interpreted and applied the teaching of scriptures so that people might know the will of God in specific situations. By knowing the will of God, people could then do the will of God. All rabbis, therefore, were concerned with interpreting and applying the scriptures in this light. Jesus interprets the scriptures, applies them and, shows how, in his view, they reveal the will of God. He talks about the ways the will of God is known and what the will of God is in specific situations. This much he has in common with his contemporaries, first-century rabbis such as Hillel and Shammai. But the way Jesus interprets the scriptures—the way in which he claims the will of God is known—is new and radically different from that of his contemporaries.

2. HOW JESUS DIFFERS FROM HIS CONTEMPORARIES

There are at least three ways in which Jesus is different from his fellow rabbis. First, Jesus rejects tradition—in his teaching the time for tradition is past. Second, Jesus has no concern for ritual cleanliness—in his teaching the new relationship with God makes it unnecessary. Third, Jesus can even reject the specific Law of Moses—in his teaching there is a new law for the new situation.

a. Tradition

An example of how Jesus shows contempt for tradition is expressed in Mark 2:18–22: "Now John's disciples and the Pharisees were fasting; and people came and said to him, 'Why do John's disciples and the disciples of the Pharisees fast, but your disciples do not fast?' And Jesus said to them 'Can the wedding guests fast while the bridegroom is with them? As long as they have the bridegroom with them, they cannot fast.' " And then he continues with another saying: "No one sews a piece of unshrunk cloth on an old garment; if he does, the patch tears away from it, the new from the old, and a worse tear is made." This is a reference to the fact that the new cloth would not be preshrunk and would surely cause more harm than good.

He continues: "And no one puts new wine into old wineskins; if he does, the wine will burst the skins, and the wine is lost, and so are the skins; but new wine is for fresh skins." New wine is unfermented wine; it would be put into new wineskins. As it fermented, the suppleness of the new skin would be able to take the pressure of expansion. Once this process of fermentation had taken place, the skins would become hard and stiff. They would never be able to take the pressure of a second lot of wine for fermenting.

Jesus is rejecting the practice of fasting here because in his view the time for this particular aspect of the Law has passed. Traditionally, the Jews fasted two days a week. It was required of them. But there were certain times when this requirement could be lifted. For example, when one was invited to a wedding the invitation superseded the requirement for fasting, if the wedding day was a day of fasting. So Jesus is saying in effect: "In my ministry we have the wedding feast of God. We have the Messiah and his community. We have the joy of the new relationship with God. For us the time for fasting is passed. This particular aspect of the tradition does not apply to us. We need a new way to express our relationship with God. The old way will not do."

This point is more clearly expressed in Mark 2:23–28: "One sabbath he was going through the grainfields; and as they made their way the disciples began to pluck ears of grain. And the Pharisees said to him, 'Look, why are they doing what is not lawful on the sabbath?' And he said to them, 'Have you never read what David did, when he was in need and was hungry, he and those who were with him: how he entered the house of God, when Abiathar was high priest, and ate the bread of the Presence, which it is not lawful for any but the priests to eat, and also gave it to those who were with him?' And he said to them, 'The sabbath was made for man, not man for the sabbath.'" Plucking the ears of grain and rubbing them was considered work. This was harvesting and threshing, even if it was just one ear of corn and even if the rubbing was done with the palm of the hand, as it was in this instance—it was still work.

Literally hundreds of regulations were used to determine what was work on the sabbath and what was not. The regulations were designed to help a person know the will of God. For example, a doctor could attend a man who had had an accident, such as a broken leg.

He could do whatever was sufficient to keep the man alive on the sabbath, but he could not start the process of healing—healing was work and work was forbidden on the sabbath.

Jesus rejects the idea that their "harvesting" of the grain and eating was work, and he rejects the implied criticism that his disciples were breaking the law. He points to an incident in the Old Testament where David similarly broke the Law of God—in this instance the law about eating the show bread. The show bread was twelve loaves of bread put on a table outside the Holy of Holies to symbolize that the people of God (the twelve tribes) were perpetually in the presence of God. Only the priests could eat the show bread. David and his companions, who were not priests, did eat the show bread on one occasion. In the Jewish tradition this was justified by the fact that David and his companions were on a special mission for God. This special mission superseded the requirement about eating and not eating the show bread.

Jesus is therefore implying in Mark 2:23–28 and Mark 2:18–22 that he and his disciples are on a special mission—a mission that supersedes the requirement of work on a sabbath. So far he is doing what any other rabbi of his time would have done. A first-century rabbi would have gladly discussed whether a certain mission for God carried with it the right to abrogate the tradition of the Law in some respects. But Jesus goes beyond this. He makes a flat statement that no other rabbi would ever have made: "The sabbath was made for man, not man for the sabbath." In this moment, Jesus claims that the requirements of God must be reexamined. The requirements of God must be seen in the light of the needs of persons. This characterizes the new relationship with God that his ministry makes possible.

In these instances it can be seen that Jesus rejects the tradition by means of which the Law was interpreted and applied to everyday life. He will set it aside to meet the requirements of his own ministry. He will also set it aside to meet the requirements of persons in the new relationship with God.

b. Ritual Cleanliness

Jesus has no concern for ritual cleanliness. We can see this attitude expressed in Mark 7:14–23: "And he called the people to him again, and said to them 'Hear me, all of you, and understand: there is nothing outside a man which by going into him can defile him; but the things which come out of a man are what defile him.' " Then the discussion continues, as Jesus elaborates on the parable for his disciples.

This saying marks a definite break with the rabbinical teaching of the period. The rabbis were concerned with the distinction between what we would call the sacred and the secular—the things of God and the things of everyday life. They were concerned that a person might have the means of meeting God, of working for God, of having a living relationship with God. In order to achieve this, the rabbis were concerned that the things of everyday life might be made ritually pure and clean so they would not defile a person, hindering the relationship with God. In itself, this is a fine ideal and a great step forward from the previous position in which the things of God were totally separate from the things of the world. Here we have a means whereby the things of the world can be made a means to a relationship with God, if they are kept ritually clean and pure.

But Jesus tosses this concept aside. It is not just the things of the world that can hinder a person in a relationship to God. Only a person's attitude is important—the way a person uses the things of this world, the way things are approached. It is not just what a person eats or drinks or the ritual cleanliness or uncleanliness or the tools used—it is also the way a person eats and drinks, the way tools are used. It is the kind of life a person lives, not just the means that one uses to live, that determines the relationship with God.

This emphasis of Jesus was a bold new stroke. It redefines the distinction between the sacred and the secular. Jesus stresses the heart (the affections, or will) in contrast to the dietary laws (v. 21–23). Defilement comes from an impure heart, not from ceremonial uncleanliness. The new relationship with God arises out of response to the will of God and results in a different attitude about life, the world, and the things of the world. It is this attitude with which God is concerned.

c. The Law of Moses

Jesus rejects the Law of Moses. We can see an example of this in Mark 10:1–9. Jesus is discussing the question about divorce, and Pharisees come up and ask, "Is it lawful for a man to divorce his wife?" Like all rabbinical schools of the period, Jesus refers to the commandment of Moses in Deuteronomy 24:1 and asks, "What did Moses command you?" In other words, what is commanded in the Law of God? The reply to Jesus is that "Moses allowed a man to write a certificate of divorce, and to put her away." Deuteronomy 24:1 says: "When a man takes a wife and marries her, if then she finds no favor in his eyes because he has found some indecency in her, he writes her a bill of divorce and puts it in her hand and sends her out of his house. . . ."

The rabbis of the first century interpreted this passage in different ways, as we discussed earlier in another context. The school of Shammai said a man shall not put away his wife unless he has found in her "something shameful," interpreting the "indecency" in that verse. The "indecency" refers to adultery or fornication. Rabbi Hillel said a divorce was possible even if the wife lets his food burn, because then he has found something "unseemly" in her. This is a wider interpretation of "indecency"—anything that causes offense to the husband. Rabbi Akiba interpreted the Deuteronomic passage to mean that if the husband found a woman more beautiful than his wife, divorce was allowed under the law of Moses. Rabbi Akiba was interpreting the phrase "if she find no favor in his eyes," which was quite a liberal conclusion.

Notice what Jesus does in this passage from Mark 10. Jesus does not offer a new interpretation of Deuteronomy 24:1, as his questioners rightly expected him to do. He does not comment on Rabbis Shammai, Hillel, or Akiba, nor does he offer a fourth interpretation of this verse. He brushes the verse aside, almost contemptuously: "But Jesus said to them, 'For your hardness of heart he wrote you this commandment' " (v. 5). The Law of Moses is being rejected here because it does not apply except under certain circumstances—the circumstances of the "hardness of heart," the situation of the fallen state of humankind. Jesus is saying that these circumstances do not apply to him and to his disciples because they are responding to the kingly activity of God. They are living the life of the new age.

It was a feature of the Jewish expectation of the new age that in some respects it would be like the paradise age. The new age would be like the age in the garden of Eden before the fall. In Mark 10, Jesus turns to the paradise will of God before the fall of man in the Old Testament. He quotes: "But from the beginning of creation, 'God made them male and female. For this reason a man shall leave his father and mother and be joined to his wife, and the two shall become one.' So they are no longer two, but one" (v. 6–8). These references to Genesis 1:27 and 2:24 are references to the paradise will of God.

In this passage from Mark, Jesus claims that the new relationship with God that he and his disciples enjoy demands a new understanding of the will of God. But insofar as the Law of Moses applies to the "hardness-of-heart" situation of humankind, it is no longer applicable to the new community of God's people. This was a bold assertion and something that no other rabbi would have said.

So we see through these examples that although Jesus did interpret the scriptures and declare the will of God as did the other rabbis of his day, his way of doing it was quite different. The situation for him and his disciples was new and quite different. This new relationship with God demands a new understanding of the will of God.

C. A New Understanding of the Will of God

In his teaching, Jesus demands obedience to the will of God. This obedience arises as a response to what God has done. It comes from the new relationship with God made possible by the ministry and teaching of Jesus. The obedience Jesus demands is more radical than that demanded by the teaching of his contemporaries.

1. RADICAL OBEDIENCE

Radical obedience to the will of God in Jesus' teaching is always directed at specific situations.

a. Murder

Notice what happens in the saying about murder in Matthew 5:21–26: "You have heard that it was said to the men of old 'You shall not kill; and whoever kills shall be liable to judgment.' But I say to you that every one who is angry with his brother shall be liable to judgment; whoever insults his brother shall be liable to the council, and whoever says, 'You fool!' shall be liable to the hell of fire." Here we have a saying that radicalizes the Law against which it is set. The Law of Moses said, "You shall not kill; and whoever kills shall be liable to judgment." The demand of Jesus is more radical. He says that not only shall you not kill, but you shall not even be angry with your brother.

The radical nature of this commandment is emphasized by the fact that it is directed to specific situations. We have not only the general concern with anger, but the specific concern with insulting: "For whoever insults his brother . . ." And still more, "and whoever says, 'You fool!' "—this does not sound as though it belongs in this saying, because we are not concerned with a general insult to somebody. The word translated here is probably a play on the Hebrew word for a fool—*moreh*. This word carries with it the connotation of someone who denies God and rejects the will of God.

Here we have the radical movement from the external act of killing to the internal attitude of being angry. The attitude is made specific with two examples; insulting your brother and being prepared to regard him as one who denies God—in other words, passing judgment on his religious and moral life.

This movement from the external act to the attitude is not unknown in rabbinical Judaism. There is a saying attributed to a rabbi who was almost a contemporary of Jesus that goes as follows: "He who hates his neighbor, lo, he belongs to the shedders of blood." In other words, he who hates his neighbor is classed with the murderers. A rabbi could argue that to hate one's brother was the moral equivalent of murder. What is new in the teaching of Jesus here is not only the preparedness to move from external acts to attitude, but the deliberate way in which this is contrasted with the old Law. A rabbi contemporary with Jesus would have added his own saying as an element of interpretation. But Jesus contrasts his interpretation with the old Law: "You have heard that it was said . . . but I say to you . . ." So we have a contrast—the new contrasted with the old. The deliberate nature of this contrast is what is really important.

The deliberate contrast with the old puts the emphasis on the fact that we are moving from external act to internal attitude. And this is in accordance with the general ethical teaching of Jesus—his concern for response. It also matches his own concern with a person's attitude. We have to understand this radical insistence on obedience in a specific situation in terms of responding to God. It is responding out of the new relationship with God that makes such a radical obedience possible.

b. Adultery

The movement from external act to attitude shows up in the saying on adultery in Matthew 5:27–30: "You have heard that it was said, 'You shall not commit adultery.' But I say to you that every one who looks at a woman lustfully has already committed adultery with her in her heart. If your right eye causes you to sin, pluck it out and throw it away; it is better that you lose one of your members than that your whole body be thrown into hell. And if your right hand causes you to sin, cut it off and throw it away; it is better that you lose one of your members than that your whole body go into hell."

We can see here the insistence on a radical and specific obedience. As in the saying about murder, we are moving from an external act to the attitude. We are concerned not only with the act of adultery— after all, a person may refrain from adultery physically, yet be adulterous in attitude. We are to be concerned with the attitude that produces adultery. The obedience that Jesus demands is the radical obedience that goes inward to the attitude itself and does not restrict itself to the external act alone.

In this particular saying the radical nature of this obedience is emphasized pictorially by the saying about plucking out the eye and cutting off the hand. Again, such a radical obedience is possible only out of the new relationship with God—the new relationship with God that is implied as the background to all the ethical teaching of Jesus. In this particular instance Jesus is not saying anything absolutely new. The rabbis have a saying: "He who looks at a woman with desire is as one who has criminal intercourse with her." The rabbis also would interpret adultery in terms of one's attitude. But they would have never contrasted their interpretation with the old Law. They would have simply added their interpretation to the Law. Once again, as in the saying on murder, Jesus contrasts his teaching with the old Law. For him the attitude has become all-important because, as we have seen already, it is in terms of attitude that the response to God has to be made.

c. Lex Talionis

Jesus radicalizes the Law concerning the saying an eye for an eye and a tooth for a tooth in Matthew 5:38–42: "You have heard that it was said, 'And eye for an eye and a tooth for a tooth.' But I say to you, Do not resist one who is evil. But if any one strikes you on the right cheek, turn to him the other also; and if any one would sue you and take your coat, let him have your cloak as well; and if any one forces you to go one mile, go with him two miles." Notice here the same radical obedience as in the other two passages on murder and adultery.

The *lex talionis*—the law of an eye for an eye and a tooth for a tooth—was in its origin a great step forward. It ended the whole business of vendetta. It ended the way the family of a wronged person would take it on itself to right the wrong. They would avenge themselves as a family on the one who had done the wrong and also on that person's family. This situation was common in the ancient world, in Teutonic culture—the Anglo-Saxon era of Beowulf. It is also traditional today in Corsica and in the hill country of America. The *lex talionis* limited retaliation and was therefore a step forward.

But Jesus radicalizes this in three ways. First, "Do not resist one who is evil." That means not to exercise vengeance on another person. The Christian resists evil with good, returns love for hate, returns prayer for insult, and the like. This is the Christian resistance—not the exercising of vengeance on the evil person, not even when that vengeance is limited to the eye for the eye or the tooth for the tooth.

Second, Jesus refers to the lawsuit: "If any one would sue you and take your coat, let him have your cloak as well." Again, this is a radical example of Christian generosity—the returning of love for hate.

Third, Jesus makes a reference to the system in the Roman Empire whereby the Roman authorities have the right to impress civilians into their service. A Roman authority, a legionnaire, or a centurion could impress into service a civilian of the country in which he was serving. In this instance, the reference probably is to impressing into service someone to carry the baggage. You will remember that Simon of Cyrene was impressed into service to carry the cross of Jesus at the crucifixion.

Anyone impressed into service by the authorities is not to resist, and certainly not to grumble and moan, but to be prepared to do with joy and gladness more than is expected. This particular kind of teaching is not new in the ancient world. The Stoic philosopher Epictetus says if there is a requisition and a soldier seizes your animal, let it go; do not resist or complain, otherwise you will first be beaten and you will lose the animal anyway. Epictetus, the moral philosopher, is simply facing a fact of life. But notice the difference between Epictetus and the teaching of Jesus—an important difference. The Christian is to go two miles, not on the practical grounds that he has to go anyway and that he might as well go unresisting and not get beaten for his pains. The Christian is to go two miles on the idealistic grounds that one should exercise love in this specific situation.

Jesus demands a more radical obedience than his contemporaries. He contrasts this radical obedience with the more external obedience demanded by the Jewish Law. He radicalizes the command because obedience arises out of the new relationship with God. In all the instances mentioned there is an insistence on the radical nature of the obedience. There is an implication that the point of reference in any situation is the new relationship with God, of which this kind of obedience is an expression. This kind of obedience is response. These specific commandments are accompanied by specific illustrations: the insult, judging your brother's religious life, the pictorial plucking out of the eye and cutting off of the hand, the illustrations of insult, the lawsuit, and impressment into service.

We have to be careful to avoid legalizing the teaching of Jesus. He has moved from external act to attitude. He is concerned with the attitude that expresses a response to what God has done in the context of the new relationship with God. But we must never take the same attitude toward these commandments that the Jews took to those commandments with which these are set in deliberate contrast. It is not a question of our plucking out eyes and cutting off hands. It is not a question that we must never, under any circumstances, file a lawsuit or resist someone who is trying to take something away from us. No, the question is always whether what we are doing expresses the kind of attitude of which these sayings are illustrations.

2. IMITATION OF GOD

Exactly what is expected of a person according to the ethical teaching of Jesus? Jesus requires a true imitation of God.

a. The New Relationship

In the Sermon on the Mount, we read in Matthew 5:43f.: "You have heard that it was said, 'You shall love your neighbor and hate your enemy.' But I say to you, Love your enemies and pray for those who persecute you." The first part of this saying has a parallel in the Manual of Discipline, one of the writings of the Dead Sea Scroll community. The Qumran community was organized on the principle of loving your neighbor and the fellow member of the community but hating your enemy. Jesus contrasts his teaching with this understanding: "love your enemies and pray for those who persecute you." Notice why he says this: "So that you may be sons of your Father who is in heaven" (v. 45). And he continues: "You, therefore, must be perfect, as your heavenly Father is perfect" (v. 48).

The parallel to this saying is in Luke 6:36: "Be merciful, even as your Father is merciful." Here we have the heart of the matter so far as the new understanding of the will of God is concerned. The will of God in the teaching of Jesus is that people should imitate God, with whom they have entered into this new relationship. They have known God's love—they should love one another. They know God's forgiveness—they should forgive one another. They know something of God's perfection—they should strive to respond by being merciful.

The teaching of Jesus reminds us of the kind of radical obedience expected in specific situations. It is to remind us of the way we should be expressing this new relationship as we live. In another age, different from the first century, we are to find new ways of expressing it.

b. The Nature of Love

The parable of the good Samaritan (Luke 10:29ff.) is preceded by a discussion concerning the nature of love. In Luke 10:25–28 we read: "And behold, a lawyer stood up to put him to the test, saying, 'Teacher [rabbi], what shall I do to inherit eternal life?' He said to him, 'What is written in the law? How do you read?' And he answered, 'You shall love the Lord your God with all your heart, and with all your soul, and with all your strength, and with all your mind; and your neighbor as yourself.' And he said to him, 'You have answered right; do this, and you will live.' " According to Luke, here is one instance in which Jesus does not set his own teaching in contrast with the Jewish Law. He does not make the Jewish Law more radical because in this instance the Jewish Law itself is radical. Here is a commandment that applies in the new situation just as well as it did in the old.

Our concern here must be with the meaning of these commandments. What does it mean to love God and to love your neighbor as yourself? It does not mean that the love of God must be regarded as identical with the love of one's neighbor—the two are not the same thing. If we try to understand this as indicating that the love of God is the love of one's neighbor and that the love of one's neighbor is the love of God, we will end up by regarding the love of God as a kind of symbol. If we regard the two as identical—love of God and love of one's neighbor—the tendency will be for the love of God to be swallowed up in the love of one's neighbor, and that would never do. Nor can we argue that the love of neighbor is a means whereby we love God, because that would lead to our making our neighbor less than a real person. The person would simply become a symbol by means of which we love God; that must not happen.

What we have to recognize is that God challenges us in the specific relationship with our neighbor. The love of God and the love of our neighbor become a unity if we respond to the challenge of our neighbor's situation as being the challenge of God to us. To love God and to love our neighbor means to recognize in the neighbor and the neighbor's situation the challenge of God. This is well illustrated by the parable of the good Samaritan (Luke 10:30–37). In this parable, we have the priest and the Levite turning away from the man who has been beaten and left for dead on the Jericho road. They were legally right to do this. If the man were dead, they would be defiling themselves by ceremonially handling him. They would thus be hindered from keeping their responsibilities and fulfilling them as priest and Levite. Here they are asking "What is our responsibility to

God?" The answer is: to serve God as a priest or Levite. They also ask "What is our responsibility to this neighbor of ours?" The answer is "none" in this situation because it would interfere with their service of God.

What does the Samaritan do that is different? The Samaritan recognizes in the situation of the neighbor the challenge of God. It is not a question of "what is God's will" and "who is my neighbor?" It is a question of: "to whom am I neighbor?" "Where does the neighbor's situation challenge me?" "Where is God challenging me through my neighbor's situation?" This is the point of the parable. "Which of these three, do you think, proved neighbor to the man who fell among the robbers?" (v. 36). The Samaritan recognized that the man who fell among thieves was his neighbor and that God was challenging him in his neighbor's situation.

D. Summary

The challenge of Jesus to us is to see our specific personal circumstances as situations in which and through which God is challenging us to be God-like. If our relationship with God is vital and real and if we are alert to God's challenge in our situation, it will not be difficult to discern God's will. Thus, the confrontation with a neighbor in need is a challenge to do God's will, as participants in the new relationship we enjoy as the children of God.

E. Resource Material

GLOSSARY

EPICTETUS A Stoic philosopher. Born a slave, he was allowed to study philosophy and was eventually freed. He lived from about A.D. 50 to about A.D. 130. His teaching is in the Stoic tradition. He left no written works behind him, but some of his pupils published his lecture notes. The school he founded was very influential in the second and third centuries of our era.

HERODIANS Jews who supported Herod the Great and his sons. Herod was installed as ruler of Palestine by the Romans. Only a half-Jew himself (he was an Idumean), he was hated by the Jews for two reasons—because he was not wholly a Jew and because the

Romans had installed him into power. He did, however, develop some followers among the Jewish people called Herodians. The only time the Herodians got together with the more religious Jews (Sadducees and Pharisees) was in condemning Jesus.

LEVIRATE LAW   A provision in Hebrew Law whereby, if a man died without leaving an heir, his brother was obliged to take the widow as his wife and sire an heir for the deceased man. This was deemed to prevent his line from dying out. *Levir* is Latin for "brother-in-law." See Deuteronomy 25:5–10.

LEX TALIONIS   The Latin name for the law governing retaliation. The law stated that retaliation for a personal injury cannot exceed the injury done: an eye for an eye, a tooth for a tooth, and so on. (Not two eyes for one eye, and so on.) In the Old Testament the law is found in Exodus 21:22–25, Leviticus 24:19f., and Deuteronomy 19:21. In the New Testament, a reference can be found in Matthew 5:38–42.

MOREH   The Hebrew word for "fool." A fool is one who denies God and rejects the will of God.

RABBI   Among the Jews of the first century, a rabbi was a theologian and a civil judge—a religious teacher and one who settled civil disputes. The reason behind this was that the Law of God was the Law of the community, and the Law of the community was regarded as the Law of God. The rabbi was expert in the Law and was consulted for advice and help in both "theological" and "civil" matters. Jesus was a rabbi—an expert in the Law of God. The term *rabbi* is often translated as "teacher" or "master." In the first century the term had not taken on the formal meaning of "one who is ordained."

SADDUCEES   One of the main parties in Judaism at the time of Jesus. The Sadducees are the Temple party, i.e., the families who controlled the Temple. From the Sadducees came the High Priests and the major figures within the priesthood. Theologically, the Sadducees were conservative. They accepted only the first five books of our Old Testament as authoritative, rejecting the Prophets and the later writings. This led them to reject the idea of resurrection, since there is no teaching on this subject in the first five books of the Bible.

SHOW BREAD   Sometimes called the "bread of the presence." Also spelled "shewbread." Twelve loaves of bread baked under conditions of special ritual cleanliness were installed on a special table just outside the Holy of Holies. The installation of the show bread took place weekly and was a special service within the Temple. The bread symbolized the presence of the twelve tribes of Israel in the holy place. Therefore, the bread symbolized the fact that the Jews were continually in the presence of God.

SCRIPTURE REFERENCES

Mark 12:13f.	Mark 7:14–23	Matthew 5:27–30
Mark 12:18f.	Mark 10:1–9	Matthew 5:38–42
Mark 12:28f.	Deuteronomy 24:1	Matthew 5:43f.
Luke 12:13f.	Genesis 1:27	Luke 6:36
Mark 2:18–22	Genesis 2:24	Luke 10:25–28
Mark 2:23–28	Matthew 5:21–26	Luke 10:36

BIBLIOGRAPHY

Bornkamm, Günther. *Jesus of Nazareth*. 3rd ed. New York: Harper & Brothers, 1960 (esp. pp. 96–143).
Bultmann, Rudolph. *Jesus and the Word*. New York: Scribner, 1958 (esp. pp. 57–132).
Lewis, C. S. *The Four Loves*. New York: Harcourt Brace Jovanovich, 1960.
Macquarrie, John. *The Humility of God*. Philadelphia: Westminster, 1978 (esp. chap. 3).

QUESTIONS

1. Why were rabbis experts in civil as well as religious matters?
2. What is the purpose of the question to Jesus in Mark 12:13 when he is asked whether Jews should pay taxes to the godless occupying power of Rome?
3. What does the fact that Jesus is asked a question whether Jews should pay taxes to the Romans indicate about Jesus?
4. Where are three places in the gospels where Jesus is asked to make an interpretation of a simple question, showing that he has stature as a rabbi?
5. Rabbis of Jesus' time had as one of their major tasks to interpret the will of God as they understood it from the scriptures and to teach it. Did Jesus do this?

6. Did Jesus interpret the scriptures in the same way that other rabbis interpreted it concerning the will of God?

7. In what three ways does Jesus differ most radically from his contemporaries, the other rabbis?

8. What are two things Jesus specifically indicates as a rejection of tradition?

9. What are three ways Jesus shows his contempt for tradition?

10. What is Jesus' response when he is accused of not keeping the practice of fasting?

11. What did Jesus mean by his interpretation of the wedding feast?

12. What was Jesus' response when he was accused of breaking the regulation that says to keep the sabbath day holy and do no work?

13. What does Jesus imply by this?

14. What other statement does Jesus make that goes further than this?

15. What is Jesus' response in Mark 7:14–23 when he is accused of uncleanliness?

16. What does Jesus mean by his response?

17. What is Jesus' reaction when he is asked to interpret Moses' teaching about divorce in Mark 10:1–9?

18. What does Jesus say about divorce?

19. Is the obedience Jesus demands more or less radical than that demanded by his contemporaries?

20. At what is the obedience to the will of God always directed in the teaching of Jesus?

21. The Law of Moses says, "Thou shalt not kill." How does Jesus amend and extend this law?

22. The Law of Moses is directed at the specific act. What does Jesus also add to this overt behavior?

23. There are examples in rabbinical literature that are similar to Jesus' saying on murder, in which he implies that not only the act but also the attitude is important. In what way is Jesus' teaching different from rabbinical Judaism?

24. The Mosaic Law about adultery says, "Thou shalt not commit adultery." How does Jesus extend and amend this law?

25. There are similar teachings of this viewpoint in rabbinical literature, so Jesus has not come up with a completely new idea. Just how does Jesus' teaching differ from those of rabbinical literature?

26. The law of lex talionis or "an eye for an eye ..." was common during Jesus' time. How did he view this law?

27. There were similar teachings to this in rabbinical literature in which it is said "if a man asks for your animal, give it to him, for he might beat you." This is very practical; in what way is Jesus' saying different from this?

28. Jesus says that if someone asks you to go one mile, you go two miles. What does Jesus imply in this teaching?

29. What must one guard against in interpreting the ethical teaching of Jesus?

30. What does Jesus mean when he says such things as "love your enemies, so that you may be sons of your Father who is in heaven" and also, "you must be perfect as your Father in heaven is perfect"?

31. Do we love God and our fellow man in the same way?

32. What did Jesus say about loving God and your neighbor?

Chapter 8

DISCIPLESHIP

THIS chapter presents a discussion of the various meanings of discipleship. Included in the discussion are three major topics: discipleship in Judaism at the time of Jesus, the disciples of Jesus, and Jesus' teaching about discipleship.

A. Discipleship in First-Century Judaism

1. RABBINICAL SCHOOLS

In Judaism at the time of Jesus, rabbis attracted schools of pupils. For example, there is the school of Shammai, which simply means Rabbi Shammai and his pupils. There was also the school of Hillel. These two are the best-known groups among all the rabbis and their pupils at this time, but of course there were many others.

A rabbi who became well known for his teaching attracted pupils who came to him and studied with him. Such a pupil was called a *talmid*, the Hebrew word for "pupil." The students spent their time studying sacred writings—what later became the Old Testament—and other literature. They attended lectures where the rabbi would speak on the interpretation of the Old Testament, the so-called oral tradition. There would be discussion of difficult cases so that the pupil became trained in the exegesis and interpretation of the Law.

When the pupil had finished his training with the master teacher, he in turn became a rabbi. But not all rabbis became sufficiently well known to attract pupils and to found schools. The majority of them worked as theological teachers, judges, and settlers of civil disputes. Although there is no evidence that Jesus had formal training, he was recognized as a rabbi by his friends and opponents. The fact that Jesus attracted a group of followers would arouse no comment. In this respect, Jesus simply would have been thought of as Rabbi Jesus of Nazareth, surrounded by his pupils.

The work of a rabbi is well illustrated in the New Testament. There is a story of the synagogue worship at Capernaum in Luke 4:16f., where Jesus goes to the synagogue on the sabbath, as was his custom, and stands up to read. As a recognized rabbi, he has apparently been asked to address the congregation at regular synagogue worship. This happened to Jesus and it also happened to Paul on his journeys. For example, in Acts 13:14-16, "And on the sabbath day they went into the synagogue and sat down. After the reading of the law and the prophets, the rulers of the synagogue went to them, saying, 'Brethren, if you have any word of exhortation for the people, say it.' So Paul stood up . . ." and delivered his sermon.

Other examples of the activities of rabbis, discussed in the previous chapter, are found in John 9:2, Luke 12:13, and Mark 10:1-9.

So the work of the rabbi is rather clear. He collects pupils; he trains them, and the pupils in turn become rabbis. If they become well known, they in turn collect pupils and train them. If the rabbi does not become well known, he does his work singly, settling religious, civil, and theological questions, teaching and preaching.

2. JOHN THE BAPTIST

The disciples of John the Baptist are mentioned several times in the New Testament. For example in Mark 2:18: "Now John's disciples and the Pharisees were fasting; and people came and said to him, 'Why do John's disciples and the disciples of the Pharisees fast, but your disciples do not fast?' " In this verse we can see the situation very clearly. The Pharisees (rabbis) have their disciples, John has his disciples, and Jesus has disciples.

The disciples of John the Baptist are recognized, just as were the disciples of the rabbis and the disciples of Jesus. The disciples of John the Baptist have a rather different function from that of the regular disciples of the rabbis. John not only teaches, he also proclaims the imminent coming of the kingdom of God and conducts a ministry of preparation for that coming. He challenges people to repent in view of the imminence of the kingdom. They were to prepare themselves for the kingdom by being baptized and therefore purified from the world and its evil. They also were to prepare by living a special kind of life and, like other disciples, following high ethical teaching. This was the moral aspect of their preparation, just as the baptism was the ceremonial aspect.

The disciples of John the Baptist likely shared in his work—the preaching of the imminence of the kingdom, the work of baptism, challenge, and instruction. Indeed, we can be sure that this is the case, because a movement survived after the death of John the Baptist. One reference to this is in Acts 19:1–4: "While Apollos was at Corinth, Paul passed through the upper country and came to Ephesus. There he found some disciples [of John the Baptist]. And he said to them, 'Did you receive the Holy Spirit when you believed?' And they said, 'No, we have never even heard that there is a Holy Spirit.' And he said, 'Into what then were you baptized?' They said, 'Into John's baptism.' And Paul said, 'John baptized with the baptism of repentance, telling the people to believe in the one who was to come after him, that is, Jesus.' "

We do not know a great deal about the John the Baptist movement, but we do know that there was such a movement. John's disciples went out preaching the coming of the kingdom and preparing persons for that coming by baptism.

John the Baptist and his disciples are persons preparing themselves for the future coming of the kingdom. This is the difference between Jesus and John the Baptist: John the Baptist prepares people for a kingdom to come in the future, but Jesus declares the kingdom to be present in his own ministry. Because John the Baptist is a religious teacher, the people learn from him. But in the other respects his disciples are different. John's disciples do not go out to teach the normal interpretation of the Law. Instead, they share their master's emphasis on the future coming of the kingdom; their work is a work of preparation for that coming.

In the light of what we have said about the disciples of first-century rabbis and of John the Baptist, we now turn to Jesus and his disciples to identify some characteristics of discipleship.

B. Jesus and His Disciples

We have already seen that Jesus and his disciples have some similarities to the Pharisees and John the Baptist and his disciples. But there are certain distinctive characteristics about Jesus and his disciples that should be examined.

1. THE CALL

Jesus challenges individuals to discipleship. An example is located in Mark 1:16–20: "And passing along by the Sea of Galilee, he saw Simon and Andrew the brother of Simon casting a net into the sea; for they were fishermen. And Jesus said to them, 'Follow me and I will make you become fishers of men.' And immediately they left their nets and followed him." Here is Jesus seeking men and personally challenging them to discipleship. This is different from the other rabbis because their pupils (disciples) came to the rabbi. But Jesus challenges persons whom he has found to follow him. We do not know how John the Baptist got his disciples.

The fact that Jesus chooses, or calls, his disciples is seen again in the call of Levi in Mark 2:14: "And as he passed on [by the sea], he saw Levi the son of Alphaeus sitting at the tax office, and he said to him, 'Follow me.' And he rose and followed him." Again, there is the same note of personal challenge. Jesus personally calls people to discipleship.

2. APPRENTICES

There is an interesting saying about discipleship in Matthew 10:37, 38 (with parallels in Luke 14:26 and Thomas, Log. 55): "He who loves father or mother more than me is not worthy of me; and he who loves son or daughter more than me is not worthy of me; and he who does not take his cross and follow me is not worthy of me." The Lukan version of this passage in 14:26, 27 reads: "If any one comes to me and does not hate his own father and mother and wife and children and brothers and sisters, yes, and even his own life, he cannot be my disciple. Whoever does not bear his own cross and come after me, cannot be my disciple." A similar saying has also turned up in the gospel of Thomas, Log. 55: "Jesus said, 'Whoever does not hate his father and mother will not be able to be a disciple to me, and whoever does not hate his brethren and his sisters and does not take up his cross in my way will not be worthy of me." Notice in these sayings the difference between Matthew and Luke. Matthew has "is not worthy of me"; Luke says, "cannot be my disciple"; Thomas has both.

In his book, *The Teaching of Jesus*, T. W. Manson investigated this point thoroughly (pp. 237–40). Manson shows that if one translates the Greek back into Aramaic using the word *talmid* for "disciple," this difference is inexplicable. But if you translate the Greek back into Aramaic, using not the word *talmid* for "pupil," but another word, *shewilya*, the difference between "is not worthy of me" and "cannot be my disciple" is one very small letter, *jot*, which is a small dot. Now this difference is that in one manuscript you have "is not worthy of me" and in the other one you have the translation "cannot be my disciple." A person reading this saying in Aramaic could readily read either translation. This is the only possible explanation for this difference in translation. It is unlikely that Jesus would have said the same thing twice with two different endings. It is more likely that they are the same saying. In one translation tradition, Matthew has rendered it "is not worthy of me"; another, the Lukan tradition, has rendered it "cannot be my disciple." Still another tradition, Thomas, knows both forms of the sayings.

If Jesus did call his disciples not *talmid* but *shewilya*, what does this mean? The word *shewilya* means "apprentice"—not so much a pupil, like an academic student, but an apprentice in the sense of a practical student. A carpenter has apprentices, and so does a builder and other tradespersons. Manson's arguments are convincing; Jesus apparently makes a distinction between his disciples and the disciples of the rabbis. The disciples of Jesus are not called to theoretical work such as learning, reproducing teaching, and interpreting—they are called to become proficient in doing a task. An apprentice imitates his master until he has learned a task and then goes out and does it on his own. This is what the disciples of Jesus do. They come to be with Jesus, to learn the task of ministry from him, then go out and do it. This brings us to the key text with regard to Jesus and his disciples.

The appointing of Jesus' disciples is described in Mark 3:13–19 (and its parallels in Luke 6:12–16 and Matthew 10:1–4): "And he went up into the hills, and called to him those whom he desired; and they came to him. And he appointed twelve, to be with him, and to be sent out to preach and have authority to cast out demons." The disciples are appointed to be with him as apprentices; they are to be sent out to preach—that is, to proclaim the presence of the kingdom of God— and they are to have the authority that Jesus has to manifest this kingdom in exorcisms, casting out demons.

There is another dimension to the calling of the disciples, that of the eschatological characteristics of the teaching of Jesus. We read in Mark 1:17: "And Jesus said to them, 'Follow me and I will make you become fishers of men.'" This is a reference to the End Time, cast in the traditional wording about fishers. The End Time was the day when God would act decisively as king. The traditional reference to fishermen comes from Jeremiah 16:16: "Behold, I am sending for many fishers, says the Lord, and they shall catch them; and afterwards I will send for many hunters, and they shall hunt them from every mountain and every hill, and out of the clefts of the rocks." It was believed that the coming of the kingly activity of God would involve fishermen and hunters as instruments through whom God would manifest the kingdom. The kingly activity would be carried out through the disciples, just as God was carrying it out through the ministry and teaching of Jesus. Again, the disciples of Jesus are called to share his task, to do what he is doing in places where he cannot personally go.

So the disciples of Jesus are challenged by Jesus and then trained by him to a specific task. He trains his disciples so they may go out to proclaim what he is proclaiming, to do what he is doing, to teach what he is teaching. They have definitive tasks to perform: to proclaim the presence of the kingdom of God, to manifest that kingly activity of God in exorcisms, and to teach men and women about the kingdom of God.

C. The Teaching of Jesus about Discipleship

Up to this point we have discussed Jesus and his disciples in general terms. Now it is appropriate to look closely at the teaching of Jesus on discipleship.

1. IMMEDIACY

The impression we get from Mark 1:16 and Mark 2:14—the stories of the call of the disciples—is one of immediacy. "And as he passed on, he saw Levi the son of Alphaeus sitting at the tax office, and he said to him, 'Follow me.' And he rose and followed him." Jesus says, "follow me," and the disciples leave all and follow him. Notice that in the case of the call of Levi, Jesus breaks with the tradition of Judaism in that Levi, as a tax collector, would be regarded as a gentile. A Jew who had made himself as a gentile certainly would have had no place in a group of disciples of a rabbi, perhaps not even of John the Baptist. In calling Levi, Jesus is making the same point as in the parable of the prodigal son—the forgiveness of God knows no bounds. The challenge of the kingly activity of God is for all persons. To have a former tax collector as one of the disciples makes this point very well indeed.

Then there is the teaching of Jesus in Luke 9:59–62: "To another he said, 'Follow me.' But he said, 'Lord, let me first go and bury my father.' But he said to him, 'Leave the dead to bury their own dead; but as for you, go and proclaim the kingdom of God.' Another said, 'I will follow you, Lord; but let me first say farewell to those at my home.' Jesus said to him, 'No one who puts his hand to the plow and looks back is fit for the kingdom of God.' " There must be no delay in responding to the call to discipleship, not even the honored task of caring for father and mother by burying them, not even the humanitarian act of going to say farewell. Not even these things must be allowed to stand in the way. God is challenging and the call must be obeyed and must be obeyed immediately.

In this respect, the teaching of Jesus is more drastic than that of the Old Testament. Notice what happens in the call of Elisha in 1 Kings 19:19–21: "So he [Elijah] departed from there, and foud Elisha the son of Shaphat, who was plowing . . . Elijah passed by him and cast his mantle upon him [symbolically calling him to discipleship]. And he left the oxen, and ran after Elijah, and said 'Let me kiss my father and my mother, and then I will follow you. And he said to him, 'Go back again; for what have I done to you?' " The "what have I done to you?" means for Elisha to go and tell his parents farewell, then come and follow Elijah. The teaching of Jesus is obviously a deliberate contrast to this because the call of Elisha would be well known to Judaism at the time. Jesus simply allows no delay in the call of his disciples.

We get a very vivid sense of urgency in the mission of the disciples as Jesus sees it. God is acting as king, decisively intervening in personal experience. Nothing must come between those who are challenged by this—specifically those who are challenged by Jesus to become a real part of this intervention by becoming his disciples. Nothing is to come between them and this challenge. Notice the urgency of the challenge and the authority that Jesus claims. Jesus is claiming a supreme authority—greater than that of Elijah because he is saying in effect that although Elijah could grant a disciple time to say farewell, he cannot do this. In the new eschatological age, Jesus is claiming that the new era is present—that the time for discipleship is now.

2. CAUTION

The fact that the call to discipleship allows no delay does not mean that the call is to be answered hastily and without thought of consequences. People are to think seriously about what they are doing and what may be required of them. This thoughtfulness is well expressed in the twin parables of the tower builder and the king going to war in Luke 14:28–33: "For which of you, desiring to build a tower, does not first sit down and count the cost, whether he has enough to complete it? Otherwise, when he has laid a foundation, and is not able to finish, all who see it begin to mock him, saying, 'This man began to build, and was not able to finish.' Or what king, going to encounter another king in war, will not sit down first and take counsel whether he is able with ten thousand to meet him who comes against him with twenty thousand? And if not, while the other is yet a great way off, he sends an embassy and asks terms of peace. So therefore, whoever of you does not renounce all that he has cannot be my disciple." Discipleship is demanding and urgent, but it must be considered carefully and well. One who builds a tower counts the cost first. A king going to war considers his chances. Thus, the disciple must not rush in heedlessly.

The parable of the murderer in the gospel of Thomas also deals with the conditions for discipleship. It is in Thomas, Log. 98: "Jesus said, 'The kingdom of the father is like a man who wishes to kill a powerful man. He drew the sword in his house, he stuck it into the wall in order to know whether his hand would carry through. Then he slew the powerful man.'" Here again is the idea of deliberate action, of measuring chances. Discipleship is not something to be entered without caution and trepidation. Far from it. But it is also something not to be entered into heedlessly. Jesus challenges a person to discipleship, but one must first be prepared to pay the price. The real tragedy, of course, would be for those who answered the call but who were not prepared.

3. CONFLICT

The challenge of Jesus to discipleship and his teaching about discipleship is that his call is a call to conflict. Discipleship involves one in conflict. There are many sayings that demonstrate this point, but we can restrict ourselves to a few. We read in Matthew 10:34–56: "Do not think that I have come to bring peace on earth; I have not come to bring peace, but a sword. For I have come to set a man against his father, and a daughter against her mother, and a daughter-in-law against her mother-in-law; and a man's foes will be those of his own household." There are sayings of parallel meaning in Luke 12:51-53: "Do you think that I have come to give peace on earth? No, I tell you, but rather division; for henceforth in one house there will be five divided, three against two and two against three; they will be divided, father against son and son against father, mother against daughter and daughter against her mother, mother-in-law against her daughter-in-law, and daughter-in-law against her mother-in-law." It is likely that the present form of these sayings owes something to the experience of the early church. Members of the early Christian church likely found their allegiance dividing them from their own families. But the part of the saying about "not bringing peace, but a sword" has high claim to authenticity.

A similar saying is found in Thomas, Log. 16: "Jesus said 'Men possibly think that I have come to throw peace upon the world. And they do not know that I have come to throw division upon the earth; fire, sword, war. For there shall be five in a house; three shall be against two and two against three, the father against the son, the son against the father, and they will stand as solitaries.' " This saying undoubtedly owes something to the interpretation in the Gnostic Christian church from which this gospel comes. But you will notice that it is the same general saying. We may be fairly sure that Jesus did teach that he had come to bring "not peace, but a sword." To put it in contemporary terminology, Christian discipleship is not a kind of cosmic insurance policy that guarantees one against all possible evils. Far from it. Christian discipleship means involvement in conflict.

A point where this call to conflict becomes clear is in the Lord's Prayer, especially in the petition, "lead us not into temptation" (Matthew 6:13, Luke 11:4). This is a very difficult petition to understand; a detailed discussion is available in Perrin's *The Kingdom of God in the Teaching of Jesus* (pp. 196-98). There are two problems in this passage: first, in the meaning of "lead us not" and second, in the words "into temptation." Two ancient Jewish prayers to help us in interpretation are the Eighteen Benedictions and an evening prayer. Both of these must certainly go back to the first century.

The sixth and seventh of the Eighteen Benedictions are as follows: "Forgive us, our Father, for we have sinned against thee; wipe away our transgressions from before thine eyes. . . . Look thou upon our afflictions, and strive in our strivings; Redeem us for thy name's sake. . . ." The evening prayer is as follows: "Do not let me come into the hand of sin, nor into the hand of temptation, nor into the hand of shame."

In the prayers from the Eighteen Benedictions, it is easy to see that prayers of the contemporaries of Jesus moved from a prayer for forgiveness to a prayer for help from God in their everyday experience. We also assume that Jesus' prayer moves likewise from forgiveness to the concept of God striving in our strivings. The evening prayer helps by shedding light on the phrase "lead us not into temptation" in the Lord's Prayer. The phrase "lead us not" indicates a Semitic causative tense; that is, a tense that expresses a relationship based upon cause. We have to add a helping verb to make it read "cause us not to come . . ."

So we can deduce that Jesus actually said, "cause me not to come into the power of temptation." This phrase has been translated into Greek, which does not have the causative tense, so that it reads "lead me not." The Lord's Prayer is a prayer by Jesus that teaches us to ask for the continuous help of God in our own personal experience. It was also a prayer for the help of God in the personal experience of the disciples—"May he so strive in our strivings that we may not come into the hand of [under the power of] temptation."

The word *temptation* in the New Testament has to be understood more widely than what we understand it to mean in the English language. The Greek word here is *peirasmos*. The word usually translated as "temptation" actually means "temptation," "trial," "tribulation," "distress" and refers to anything that can bring doubt or difficulty, cause trouble or distress. What Jesus is saying in effect in teaching his disciples this prayer is that as his disciples they may expect trial and tribulation, difficulty and distress. But he is teaching them that in this experience they may turn to God and pray that God may so "strive in their strivings" that they might become victorious in their struggle.

This struggle can be seen in the garden of Gethsemane as Jesus struggles with doubt and difficulty; Mark 14:32–42 (Luke 22:40–46; Matthew 26:36–46): "And they went to a place which was called Gethsemane; and he said to his disciples, 'Sit here, while I pray' . . . and he said, 'Abba, Father . . . remove this cup from me; yet not what I will, but what thou wilt.' " And his disciples fall asleep. He comes to them and is distressed by this: "Could you not watch one hour?

Watch and pray that you may not enter into temptation. . . ." Of course we cannot know how far this story is accurate in detail, but it does illustrate vividly the meaning of the word *temptation, peirasmos*. Jesus is suffering doubt, is knowing extreme difficulty—this is temptation. The Lord's Prayer therefore assumes that the disciples will have similar experiences. They will know persecution and difficulty. They will know personal doubt and even despair. They will wrestle with an attempt to understand the will of God and the purpose of God. In this agony, they are sharing the agony of Gethsemane. In this situation they can pray and find God. God is the one who so "strives in their strivings" that they overcome, just as Jesus overcame in the garden of Gethsemane.

Therefore Jesus teaches that the call to discipleship is the call to conflict. And he helps his disciples in teaching them this prayer to turn to God in their hour of need, just as he himself does in the garden.

4. THE TWELVE

The fact that there were twelve disciples is significant. This choice of twelve was obviously not an accident. It was not that Jesus could find only twelve, rather than eleven or thirteen or fifteen. The number twelve is highly symbolic. In Judaism at the time of Jesus, the number twelve symbolized the twelve tribes of Israel and, therefore, symbolized the people of God. A good illustration of this symbolism appears in the so-called bread of the Presence. Remember the account of the dispute between Jesus and the Pharisees about working on the sabbath in Mark 2:25f.: "Have you never read what David did, when he was in need and was hungry, he and those who were with him: how he entered the house of God, when Abiathar was high priest, and ate the bread of the Presence, which it is not lawful for any but the priests to eat, and also gave it to those who were with him?"

The bread of the Presence was twelve loaves of bread baked under conditions of special purity, then placed on a table just outside the Holy of Holies in the Temple. At the time of Jesus the ceremony for placing these twelve loaves—the bread of the Presence—was the main feature of the weekly worship of the Temple. It was done each week just before the sabbath. The bread was left there for a week and changed as a part of the weekly service. As long as those twelve loaves were there, the people of God were symbolically in the presence of God. The number twelve did that; it symbolized the twelve tribes.

Jesus, then, in choosing the twelve disciples, is saying in effect that his disciples are the people of God—the new people of God. He is saying that in his ministry God is active as King—the kingdom of God is present, intervening decisively in human history and human experience. One result of this intervention is the formation of a new people of God: those who respond to the challenge of the hour become the new Israel. All of this is communicated by the choosing of twelve disciples rather than some other number.

D. Summary

In thinking about discipleship, we end on the note of the kingly activity of God and its consequences. There are consequences for the individual who responds and becomes a member of the new people of God. There are consequences for the disciples and what they symbolize. The disciples of Jesus are the messianic community—the new and true people of God.

E. Resource Material

GLOSSARY

DISCIPLE In the case of the rabbis of Jesus' day, disciples were pupils (*talmid*) and were followers of a particular rabbi. The pupils chose a rabbi under whom they studied. In contrast with this pattern, Jesus selected his disciples from among his followers. Jesus called his disciples *shewilya*, meaning "apprentice."

EIGHTEEN BENEDICTIONS Short prayers in use at the time of Jesus. The prayers of the first century shed light on the meaning of discipleship as shown in the Lord's Prayer.

EVENING PRAYER A prayer in use at the time of Jesus that uses the word *temptation* (*peirasmos*). The understanding of *peirasmos* in the evening prayer illuminates the meaning of *temptation* in the Lord's Prayer. From the Lord's Prayer comes one aspect of the teaching of Jesus concerning the meaning of discipleship.

EXEGESIS Explanation; critical analysis of a word or passage of scripture. The rabbis of Jesus' day were skilled in exegesis of the Old Testament. They interpreted passages for the Jewish people and especially for their own pupils.

JOT (or *yodh*) The smallest letter of the Hebrew (and Aramaic) alphabet. It is a small dot. The *jot* becomes important in interpreting what Jesus means by his use of the word *disciple*. As the texts of the gospels were written down (from Aramaic, which Jesus used, to the Greek, which the early church used), different writers produced different narratives. Thus different accounts of the same event occur in different form in the gospels. This produces a problem for the New Testament scholar; he has to decide which of the accounts is most likely the authentic saying of Jesus.

ORAL TRADITION One of the functions of a rabbi at the time of Jesus was to interpret sacred writings. The rabbis' interpretation of the law of Moses was authoritative (although there was frequently much disagreement among rabbis). The interpretations they made are known as oral tradition.

PEIRASMOS A Greek word in the Lord's Prayer that has been translated as "temptation." The meaning in Greek includes: "temptation," "trial," "tribulations," "difficulty," and "distress"—or anything that brings doubt or difficulty or causes trouble.

SEMITIC CAUSATIVE TENSE A tense requiring the addition of a helping verb to complete the meaning of the main verb; this step is necessary in translating a Semitic language into English. An example is "lead us not" which actually would be "cause us not" in the original. This linguistic situation has a meaning for the understanding of discipleship as found in the Lord's Prayer.

SHEWILYA Apprentice. Jesus used this term to designate the *disciples* he chose to be his followers. *Shewilya* means a "practical apprentice" (as opposed to a *talmid*—an "academic apprentice").

TALMID The Hebrew word for "student." The students of the scriptures studied under a rabbi. Rabbis in Judaism gathered pupils into a "school" and created a "following" or group of students who were influenced by the particular emphases of their rabbi.

SCRIPTURE REFERENCES

Luke 4:16f.
Acts 13:15, 16
John 9:2
Luke 12:13
Mark 2:18
Acts 19:1
Mark 1:16f.
Mark 2:14
Matthew 10:37f.
(Luke 14:26)

Thomas, Log. 55
Mark 3:13–19
(Matthew 10:1–4,
Luke 6:12–16)
Mark 1:17
(Jeremiah 16:16)
Luke 9:59–62
1 Kings 19:19–21
Luke 14:28–33
Thomas, Log. 98

Matthew 10:34
Luke 12:51–53
Thomas, Log. 16
Matthew 6:13
(Luke 11:4)
Matthew 26:36–46
(Mark 14:32–42
Luke 22:40–46)
Mark 2:25f.

BIBLIOGRAPHY

Jeremias, Joachim, *The Parables of Jesus*. London: SCM, 1958.
_____. *The Prayers of Jesus*. Philadelphia: Fortress, 1978.
Manson, T. W. *The Teaching of Jesus: Studies of Its Form and Content*. 2d ed.
Cambridge: Cambridge University Press, 1959, (see especially pp. 237–40).
Perrin, Norman. *The Kingdom of God in the Teaching of Jesus*. Philadelphia:
Westminster Press, 1963 (see esp. pp. 196–98).
_____. *Rediscovering the Teaching of Jesus*. New York: Harper & Row, 1967
(esp. chap. 3).

QUESTIONS

1. What did most rabbis at the time of Jesus teach their pupils?
2. What were the pupils (disciples) of most rabbis called at the time of Jesus?
3. What were some of the functions of the rabbi?
4. Since most of the rabbis in Jesus' time attracted a following of students and followers, is it unusual that Jesus also attracted a following?
5. Name a person in the New Testament besides Jesus who attracted disciples.
6. In what ways did John's disciples differ from the disciples of other rabbis of his time?
7. What was the difference in the baptism of John and the baptism of Jesus?
8. What is the difference between John's work and Jesus' work?
9. The disciples of most rabbis at the time of Jesus wished to learn

from the rabbi, and on their own initiative requested discipleship. In what way did the disciples of Jesus differ from this?

10. Most rabbis of Jesus' time called their disciples *talmid*. What did Jesus call his disciples?
11. What does the term Jesus used for disciples imply?
12. What tasks are Jesus' disciples called on to perform?
13. What are some of the characteristics of Jesus' call to discipleship?
14. How should "lead us not . . ." in the Lord's Prayer be translated?
15. How should the word *temptation* in the Lord's Prayer be translated?
16. The choosing of twelve disciples by Jesus does not seem to be an accident. Where does the number twelve come from?

Chapter 9

JESUS AND THE FUTURE

THIS chapter is a presentation of the teaching of Jesus concerning the future. Two major themes are developed: first, the understanding of the kingdom of God as expressing the future and its relationship to the present; second, teaching concerning the Consummation, an understanding of the future.

A. The Kingdom of God: Present and Future

One element in the teaching of Jesus is the characteristics of the future to be expected by his disciples. One major source of how Jesus understood the future is his teaching on the kingdom of God.

1. THE LIBERALS

The scholars of the past generation believed that when Jesus taught about the kingdom of God he was concerned with the "spiritual" order of things, that his message was a message of a reformation—moral and even political reform. The message, they believed, was concerned with the transformation of society and human relationships. They argued that the kingdom of God is the transformed society and transformed relationships—the world, or the human community, reformed according to the guidance of the spirit of God. This reformation, they held, begins in the ministry of Jesus himself and will continue until it is complete.

The difficulty with this interpretation is that it represents a basic

139

misunderstanding of the phrase "kingdom of God." "Kingdom of God" does not refer to a society or community, but to the activity of God. A notable feature of books that present this understanding is that they do a great deal of talking in general terms about the kingdom of God, but very little exegesis of the teaching of Jesus itself. The scholar who really brought an end to this viewpoint was Albert Schweitzer.

2. ALBERT SCHWEITZER

In his famous book *The Quest of the Historical Jesus*, Albert Schweitzer points out that "kingdom of God" has reference to the activity of God breaking into the world, breaking into history. He maintains that Jesus expected God to irrupt into history at some point in the immediate future. For Schweitzer, the teaching of Jesus is concerned with this irruption of God into history and the references are always to the immediate future. In Schweitzer's view, Jesus was a kind of deluded fanatic; he expected God to break into history in the immediate future, but was mistaken in his expectation.

Schweitzer's views are important in that he exploded the misunderstanding of the kingdom of God. Today we recognize that he was right insofar as he understood "kingdom of God" to refer to God's activity intervening into human history. But he was wrong in believing that in the teaching of Jesus there is only an emphasis on the immediate future.

3. C. H. DODD

The next important stage in this discussion was the work of C. H. Dodd. Dodd's major work in this field is his book *The Parables of the Kingdom*, which had a strong scholarly impact. Dodd says that "kingdom of God" does refer to God's activity. But far from being wholly future in the teaching of Jesus, this activity was regarded as wholly present. According to Dodd's understanding, Jesus taught that the kingdom of God—God active in human history—was present in his ministry; now was the hour of salvation, now sins were being forgiven, God was active now in a way that he had never been active before. With this view of "realized eschatology," Dodd says there is nothing further to be expected. He argues that any emphasis in the teaching of Jesus referring to the future is a misunderstanding, or at best an accommodation of language. In Dodd's interpretation, so far as Jesus was concerned, the kingdom was present and this present activity of God was all that was to be expected or looked for.

4. JESUS' TEACHING

The discussion has continued beyond Dodd's view of wholly present activity. Gradually, it became evident that neither Schweitzer's wholly future emphasis nor Dodd's wholly present emphasis did in fact do justice to the teaching of Jesus. Today we understand Jesus' teaching about the kingdom of God to refer both to the present and the future. There is ample evidence of kingdom as present and evidence for kingdom as future in the teaching of Jesus. And the kingdom of God does indeed refer to God's intervention into human history and human experience. In the teaching of Jesus, this intervention is certainly present—the forgiveness of sins, the casting out of demons, and the like. The kingdom of God also has a future dimension in the teaching of Jesus—Jesus' teaching is concerned with future time.

If we recognize that the kingdom of God is both present and future in the teaching of Jesus, the question naturally arises, "What is the relationship between these two concepts?"

B. The Relationship between Present and Future

To restate the situation, we have the kingdom understood as present in the teaching of Jesus. God's decisive, eschatological activity is intervening in a new and drastically different way in personal experience. The claim of Jesus is that in his ministry, God is forgiving sins. Thus there is a possibility for a new relationship with God such as never had been known before.

The present time of the kingdom must be understood to be in tension with future time. The End Time of the future conditions and challenges the present moment. The present and future, therefore, coexist.

1. THE PRESENT

a. The Parables

The presence of the kingdom is part of the message of the parables of Jesus. In the following parables it is implied that God's decisive activity is now present, and persons are challenged to respond to it: the hidden treasure and the costly pearl (Matthew 13:44–46), the tower builder and the king going to war (Luke 14:28–33), the fig tree (Mark 13:28), and the lamp under the bushel (Mark 4:21–25, Luke 8:16–18). In these parables, there is no doubt that there is emphasis on God's present activity in the ministry of Jesus.

b. Eschatological Imagery

Jesus was considered to be an eschatological figure in the first century—his ministry was understood by the evangelists as referring to the End Time. For example, in reply to the question about fasting, there are three eschatological images in talking about his work (Mark 2:18–22, Luke 5:33–39, Matthew 9:14–17). The pictures are the wedding feast, the new patches and old garments, and the new wine and the old wineskins. All of these images imply a claim that the messianic times had begun in his work. His disciples do not fast, because the old order in which fasting had its part had passed away. The evangelists depict Jesus using distinctively eschatological figures to describe himself.

In several passages, the evangelists link Jesus with the theme of the shepherd: Matthew 9:36 (Mark 6:34); Matthew 10:6; Matthew 25:32; Mark 14:27 (Matthew 26:31); Luke 15:3–7; Luke 12:32. In each of these passages Jesus is referred to in some way as the shepherd. In the Judaism of the first century, the shepherd was an eschatological figure symbolizing the Messiah. When the Messiah came, he would shepherd the sheep of God.

Jesus is also spoken of as the husbandman who sends out his servants to reap the harvest (Matthew 9:37ff.; Luke 10:1ff.). In the Judaism of the first century, the harvest was a figure of the End Time, a metaphorical way of pointing to what God would do when he intervened decisively in history and human experience.

c. Prophecies

Also applied to Jesus and to his ministry are the Old Testament prophecies traditionally referring to the joys of the messianic age. Luke 4:16–21 claims the fulfillment of Isaiah 61:1ff. in the ministry of Jesus. Matthew 11:2–6 claims the fulfillment in the work of Jesus of

Isaiah 35:5ff. and Isaiah 61:1. Both of these prophecies were understood in the first century to be prophecies referring to the End Time.

d. Messianic Times

According to Matthew, Jesus speaks of himself and his ministry in terms that imply that the messianic times have begun. Two examples are the saying about the blessedness of the disciples in Matthew 13:16ff. (Luke 10:23ff.) and the saying about something greater than Solomon or Jonah in Matthew 12:41ff. (Luke 11:32ff.). The references to the exorcisms of Jesus carry this same claim, as do the instances of the forgiveness of sins. Perhaps even more important is the implied claim that his teaching supersedes the law of Moses. All of these aspects of the teaching of Jesus seem to indicate that in his ministry the new day has dawned. But the emphasis on the present activity of God is not the only dimension.

2. THE FUTURE

The evangelists depict Jesus teaching that God is decisively, eschatologically active in his ministry and in the experience of those who respond to the challenge of his message. But this is not all. The gospel writers imply that there is still something further to be expected. They claim that he looks toward the moment when God will act to consummate what has begun in his ministry and in the experience of his disciples.

a. "With Power"

The evangelist says in Mark 9:1: "Truly, I say to you, there are some standing here who will not taste death before they see the kingdom of God come with power." Parallel sayings are located in Matthew 16:28 and Luke 9:27. It is likely that this saying is not original with Jesus. It is a difficult saying, one that is reinterpreted by both Matthew and Luke and is itself likely a Marcan redaction.

It is obvious that this Marcan saying refers to the future. It contrasts the present coming of the kingdom in the ministry of Jesus and in the experience of his disciples with a future moment when that kingdom will come with power. To say that the kingdom will come "with power" poses a problem of meaning. Our task now is to understand the key phrase from the Aramaic, which has been translated into "with power."

The writings of Paul are helpful in interpreting this phrase. Paul is often helpful to us because he spoke Aramaic and wrote in Greek. When he uses a phrase we can sometimes tell what that phrase might have meant in Aramaic. In Romans 1:4, he used the phrase "with power." He speaks about the designated son of God "in power" according to the "spirit of holiness by his resurrection from the dead, Jesus Christ our Lord." Jesus is therefore designated the Son of God in power by his resurrection from the dead. What difference has the resurrection made? It has not made Jesus "Son of God" in the sense that he was not Son of God before. That would be nonsense to Paul (See Philippians 2:5–11). What the resurrection has done is to make self-evident that which was only implicit before. By the resurrection of the dead, Jesus is declared to be Son of God unmistakably and without further discussion. This is the difference that the phrase "in power" makes.

C. The Consummation

In the teaching concerning the future, there are a series of pictures of what will be involved in the Consummation. Jesus leaves unanswered the questions as to how, when, and where the Consummation will take place. His emphasis is on the certainty that the Consummation will take place.

1. REVERSAL OF PRESENT CONDITIONS

According to two of the evangelists, Jesus teaches that the future state will reverse the conditions of the present. The beatitudes reveal this emphasis in Luke 6:20–26 (Matthew 5:3–12): "Blessed are you poor, for yours is the kingdom of God. Blessed are you that hunger now, for you shall be satisfied. Blessed are you that weep now, for you shall laugh. Blessed are you when men hate you, and when they exclude you and revile you, and cast out your name as evil, on account of the Son of man! Rejoice in that day, and leap for joy, for behold, your reward is great in heaven; for so their fathers did to the prophets." These beatitudes present the idea of a future state of things in which the conditions of this world will be reversed. It is not simply a question of reversal, but rather a recognition that the future state of things will involve the establishment of the values of God. These values may well turn out to be the reverse of the values of this world. It is not necessarily the case that the poor literally will be rich and vice versa; rather, it is a case in which the values of God will be established that may involve this kind of change.

Another illustration of the reversal of present conditions is located in Matthew 19:30 (Luke 13:30, Mark 10:13): "But many that are first will be last, and the last first." This saying is more evidence that at the Consummation a reversal of present conditions may take place. The future is being described in contrast with the present, with the strong implication that God will be involved in the ultimate and final decisions.

Another reversal is illustrated in Matthew 10:26 (Mark 4:22, Luke 12:2): ". . . nothing is covered that will not be revealed, or hidden that will not be made known." This saying reflects the understanding that the values of God will be established. Things now hidden will be revealed, things now valued will turn out to be valueless, people regarded as first will turn out to be last, and so on. In all of this teaching the emphasis is the same: the values of God will be all in all. Whatever else the Consummation may or may not involve, it involves of necessity the complete and final establishment of those things that are valuable in the sight of God.

2. THE NEW TEMPLE

There is no saying left to us from the teaching of Jesus about the new Temple—the Temple not made with hands. We know about the saying because of the accusation at his trial in Mark 14:57: "And some stood up and bore false witness against him, saying 'We heard him say, "I will destroy this temple that is made with hands, and in three days I will build another, not made with hands." ' " At the crucifixion there is the same emphasis. In Mark 15:29: "And those who passed by derided him, wagging their heads and saying 'Aha! You who would destroy the temple and built it in three days, save yourself, and come down from the cross!' "

The idea of a new Temple not made with hands is a common feature of Jewish thought at this period of time. It is imagery about the future blessed state. The Temple is the place where God and humankind come closest together, the place where people enter most nearly into a perfect relationship with God. The temple symbolizes this relationship; it was believed that in the future this relationship would be perfected. What the Temple symbolized would become a fact of experience. The teaching of Jesus looks toward a future in which persons enjoy perfectly what the Temple symbolizes—a pure relationship with God.

3. THE MESSIANIC BANQUET

Another illustration about the future consummation and imagery about the messianic banquet is found in Matthew 8:11: "I tell you, many will come from east and west and sit at table with Abraham, Isaac, and Jacob in the kingdom of heaven." The parallel saying is located in Luke 13:28: "There you will weep and gnash your teeth, when you see Abraham and Isaac and Jacob and all the prophets in the kingdom of God and you yourselves thrust out. And men will come from east and west, and from north and south, and sit at table in the kingdom of God."

This concept begins in the Old Testament in Isaiah 25:6–8: "On this mountain the Lord of hosts will make for all peoples a feast of fat things, a feast of wine . . ." This idea of a future feast had become popular in Judaism. It is also found in an apocalyptic work from about this time, the Book of Enoch 62:14: "And the Lord of Spirits will abide over them and with that Son of man shall they eat and lie down and rise up forever and ever." The idea of a future feast is, of course, heavily symbolic. Neither the Jews nor Jesus literally visualized a great feast. Eating and drinking symbolize participation in the benefits of God, sharing God's supreme gifts.

So the feast of the End Time, the Messianic Banquet, is a way of saying that people will enjoy the closest possible kind of fellowship with one another. In the East, table fellowship is a very sacred thing. The saints of all the ages symbolize the eternal blessings of God. The people of God will feast in the kingdom.

4. PARABLES ABOUT THE FUTURE

The so-called parables of growth can be interpreted as parables about the future: the parable of the sower (Mark 4:3–9; Matthew 12:3–9; Luke 8:4–8), the parable of the mustard seed (Mark 4:30–32), the parable of the leaven (Matthew 13:33), and the parable of the seed growing secretly (Mark 4:26–29). These are well-known parables, and their message is quite graphic. In the parable of the sower, the sower sows his seed; only a portion survives, but that portion produces fruit in great quantities. The mustard seed is the smallest of all seeds, but grows into a great bush. A small piece of leaven is put into a large lump of dough and overnight leavens the whole lump. The seed growing secretly refers to the farmer's casting on the ground seed that grows day and night without his doing anything else to it.

At first glance, these parables appear to be parables of growth. It would appear as though Jesus is saying that what is begun in his ministry will go on growing gradually but inevitably. Scholars of the past generation used to interpret these parables this way, saying in effect that the parables describe the growth of the kingdom of God—the gradual transformation of society, the gradual reform of human relationships, the inevitable working out of the will of God in the world.

But Joachim Jeremias, in his book *The Parables of Jesus* (pp. 89–92), has shown that in the first century a Jew would not think of growth when confronted with pictures like this. The idea of gradual growth in agricultural processes is a comparatively modern idea. In the ancient world the process of agriculture was understood as a miracle. The people compared the handful of seed with the tremendous yield of the harvest. A small bit of leaven was able to change a large lump of dough. They saw the tiny mustard seed contrasted with the large bush. But they did not speculate about the process that caused this to take place—they simply saw the miraculous contrast between the beginning and the ending.

So in these parables there is no emphasis on growth as such. There is emphasis on the contrast between the beginning and the end and the fact that God produces this difference. The beginning will lead to the end, just as seed leads to harvest, the leaven to leavened dough, and the mustard seed to the great bush.

5. DISCIPLESHIP

There is a strong emphasis in the teaching of Jesus about the climax to discipleship, about what his disciples could expect. Professor T. W. Manson, in *The Sayings of Jesus* (pp. 114–48), shows that there is a strong element in the teaching of Jesus about what his disciples are to expect. Luke 12:35–46 says, "Let your loins be girded and your lamps burning, and be like men who are waiting for their master to come home from the marriage feast, so that they may open to him at once when he comes and knocks. Blessed are those servants whom the master finds awake when he comes; truly, I say to you, he will gird himself and have them sit at table, and he will come and serve them. . . . But know this, that if the householder had known at what hour the thief was coming, he would have been awake and would not have left his house to be broken into. You also must be ready. . . ." Here there is an emphasis on the fact that the disciples are to watch and wait for something further in their experience. They are to orient themselves to the future as well as to the present.

This emphasis is also present in Luke 13:22–30: "He went on his way through towns and villages, teaching, and journeying toward Jerusalem. And someone said to him, 'Lord, will those who are saved be few?' And he said to them, 'Strive to enter by the narrow door; for many, I tell you, will seek to enter and will not be able. When once the householder has risen up and shut the door, you will begin to stand outside and to knock at the door, saying, "Lord, open to us." He will answer you, "I do not know where you come from." Then you will begin to say, "We ate and drank in your presence and you taught in our streets." But he will say, "I tell you, I do not know where you come from; depart from me, all you workers of iniquity." There you will weep and gnash your teeth, when you see Abraham and Isaac and Jacob and all the prophets in the kingdom of God and you yourselves thrust out.' " Here we have the same teaching with an emphasis on preparation for the inevitable future.

Another point concerning the coming of the end and the necessity of being prepared for it is made in Luke 17:22–37: "And he said to the disciples, 'The days are coming when you will desire to see one of the days of the Son of man, and you will not see it. And they will say to you, "Lo, there!" or "Lo, here!" Do not go, do not follow them. For as the lightning flashes and lights up the sky from one side to the other, so will the Son of man be in his day. . . .' " Here the end time is depicted as the coming of the Son of man. This is a very real emphasis in the teaching of Jesus. What does it mean?

In Judaism of this time, the Son of man is the one who comes from God as the judge. He comes to hold judgment on the earth. The Son of man is therefore a symbol for the judgment of God. In Judaism, judgment means two things—to establish the good and to destroy or punish the evil. The coming of the Son of man is a reference to the coming of the judgment of God, the coming of that moment when good will be established truly and forever and evil destroyed completely and for all time.

When Matthew interprets Mark 9:1, he understands it in the light of the Second Coming (Matthew 16:28): "Truly, I say to you, there are some standing here who will not taste death before they see the Son of man coming in his kingdom." Most likely Jesus taught that judgment would be a part of the End Time; this moment when God would act for the last time would be a moment of judgment. Later on, the church could think only of the coming of the Son of man. For them, Jesus was the coming Son of man, so they thought of his returning. But this is not necessarily what Jesus likely meant—he apparently meant a judgment in which he would be vindicated.

6. THE FINAL JUDGMENT

The final judgment refers to the Son of man coming in his glory. In Mark 8:38 (Matthew 16:27, Luke 9:26), we read: "For whoever is ashamed of me and of my words in this adulterous and sinful generation, of him will the Son of man also be ashamed when he comes in the glory of his Father with the holy angels." This saying is a Marcan contribution to the Jesus tradition. It teaches that the Son of man is coming in his glory with the angels. This is teaching concerning judgment. The last act will be, among other things, judgment. Notice what else is taught here. The judgment will turn one's reaction to the challenge of Jesus: "Whoever is ashamed of me and my words, of him will the Son of man also be ashamed."

The same emphasis is found in Matthew 10:33: "But whoever denies me before men, I will also deny before my Father who is in heaven." This form of the saying carries the same teaching, although not in reference to the coming of the Son of man; it is a reference to standing before God in heaven—which is the same thing! To stand before God in heaven is a symbolic way of saying "to be judged by God." The coming of the Son of man is a symbolic way of saying "the coming of the judgment of God."

D. Summary

The claim of the evangelists is that there will be a final act in the drama of humankind—the act of judgment. The criterion by which persons will be judged is their response to the challenge of Jesus. This criterion has great implications for Jesus' apparent understanding of himself and the significance of his person and ministry.

Jesus seems to be teaching that there will be a further act of God, a climax to that which has begun in his ministry and in the experience of his disciples. This climax will establish the values of God. It will establish men and women in a perfect relationship with God—the symbolism of the new Temple. The Consummation will involve judgment, a judgment that will turn on the response that one has made to the challenge of Jesus and his ministry. We do not know when, where, or how, but we do know that it will be.

E. Resource Material

GLOSSARY

CONSUMMATION   The climax to that which was begun in the ministry of Jesus. The Consummation is the final establishment of the values of God.

ESCHATOLOGICAL IMAGERY   Jesus refers to himself and his work in terms that were understood in the Judaism of the first century to mean the End Time. The image of the shepherd is an example of Jesus' way of pointing to the End.

FEAST OF THE END TIME   See definition of *Messianic Banquet*. The two terms are interchangeable.

MESSIANIC BANQUET (Feast of the End Time)   An idea found in first-century Judaism that carried over from Old Testament times (Isaiah 25:6–8) to the time of Jesus. The future holds the promise of a banquet—a symbolic way of saying that people will enjoy the closest possible kind of relationship with one another. The Messianic Banquet is another way of saying that people will participate in the eternal blessings of God.

SHEPHERD   Throughout the teaching of Jesus in the gospel accounts there is the theme of the shepherd. Jesus is referred to as the shepherd. In the Judaism of the first century, the shepherd is an eschatological figure—a figure used for the Messiah. When the Messiah came he would shepherd the sheep of God. The figure is used to point to the activity of the Messiah.

TEMPLE   In the Judaism of the first century, the Temple of Jerusalem is the place where people and God come closest together, the place where people enter most nearly into a perfect relationship with God. The Temple symbolizes this relationship. The New Temple "not made with hands" is one in which the relationship between God and humankind would be perfected. That which the first-century Temple symbolized would become a fact of experience in the New Temple. The Temple was destroyed in A.D. 70.

SCRIPTURE REFERENCES

Matthew 13:44–46
Luke 14:28–33
Mark 13:28
Mark 4:21–25
 (Luke 8:16–18)
Mark 2:18–22
 (Luke 5:33–39,
 Matthew 9:14–17)
Matthew 9:36
 (Mark 6:34)
Matthew 10:6
Matthew 25:32
Mark 14:27
 (Matthew 26:31)
Luke 15:3–7
Luke 12:32
Matthew 9:37ff.
Luke 10:1f.
Luke 4:16–21
 (Isaiah 61:1f.)

Matthew 11:2–6
 (Isaiah 5:35f.)
Matthew 13:16f.
 (Luke 10:23f.)
Matthew 12:41f.
 (Luke 11:32f.)
Mark 9:1
 (Matthew 16:28,
 (Luke 9:27)
Romans 1:4
Luke 6:20–26
 (Matthew 5:3f.)
Matthew 19:30
 (Mark 10:31,
 (Luke 13:30)
Matthew 10:26
 (Luke 12:2,
 Mark 4:22)
Mark 14:58

Mark 15:29
Matthew 8:11
 (Luke 13:28)
Isaiah 25:6–8
Enoch 62:14
Mark 4:3–9
Mark 4:30–32
Matthew 13:33
Mark 4:26–29
Luke 12:35–46
Luke 13:22–30
Luke 17:22–37
Mark 8:38
 (Matthew 16:27,
 Luke 9:26,
 Matthew 10:33)
Matthew 16:27
 (Luke 9:26,
 Matthew 10:33)

BIBLIOGRAPHY

Dodd, C. H. *The Parables of the Kingdom*. Rev. ed. New York: Scribner, 1961.
Jeremias, Joachim. *The Parables of Jesus*. London: SCM, 1958 (pp. 89–92).
_____. *The Problem of the Historical Jesus*. Philadelphia: Fortress, 1964.
Perrin, Norman. *The Kingdom of God in the Teaching of Jesus*. Philadelphia: Westminster, 1963.
_____. *Rediscovering the Teaching of Jesus*. New York: Harper & Row, 1967 (chap. 4).
_____. *The Resurrection According to Matthew, Mark and Luke*. Philadelphia: Fortress, 1977.
Schweitzer, Albert. *The Quest of the Historical Jesus*. New York: Macmillan, 1968.
Tödt, H. E. *The Son of Man in the Synoptic Tradition*. Philadelphia: Westminster, 1965.

QUESTIONS

1. Did the scholars of the past generation believe that the kingdom of God as Jesus taught it refers to the present and future?
2. What was the understanding of the teaching of Jesus about the kingdom of God by scholars of the past generation?
3. Do the liberals represent an accurate understanding of the phrase "kingdom of God"?
4. To what does the term "kingdom of God" refer, as taught by Jesus?
5. How did Albert Schweitzer understand the phrase "kingdom of God" in the teaching of Jesus?
6. What is the importance of Schweitzer's view?
7. How does C. H. Dodd understand the phrase "kingdom of God" in the teaching of Jesus?
8. What interpretation of the phrase "kingdom of God" do most scholars present today?
9. What did the image of the shepherd mean in Judaism of the first century?
10. Does the teaching of Jesus support the idea that the eschatological relationship is present in the here and now?
11. What are some of the indications in the teaching of Jesus that show he is referring to the kingdom of God as present in his ministry?
12. Does the belief of the eschatological activity of God as future have support in the teaching of Jesus?
13. Interpret the phrase "the coming of the Son of man."
14. Several parables (the sower, the mustard seed, the leaven, the seed growing secretly), called the parables of growth, need to be reinterpreted. The liberals interpreted these parables to mean that the influence of Jesus would gradually transform society. Jews at the time of Jesus would not have understood this idea of growth. Why?
15. Describe Jesus' teaching about the consummation.

Part IV

THE NEW RELATIONSHIP

Chapter 10

JESUS' UNDERSTANDING
OF HIMSELF

THIS chapter presents the view that Jesus never made any direct reference to himself as the Messiah, the anointed one of God. A case is made for Jesus' understanding of himself as implied from his teaching on other subjects. Included is a discussion of the authority of Jesus' words and deeds and how this authority is meaningful for an understanding of the ministry and teaching of Jesus.

A. The Messianic Consciousness of Jesus

Until recently most books on the teaching of Jesus included chapters on the messianic consciousness of Jesus. It was assumed that Jesus explicitly claimed to be the Messiah, that he reinterpreted his messiahship in terms of the suffering servant of Isaiah 53, and that his favorite self-designation was Son of man. It was argued that he chose this particular title because although it was a messianic title, its actual meaning was rather vague; Jesus could therefore fill it with his own particular understanding of himself and his ministry.

All this has changed. Scholars no longer make any of these statements. For example, Günther Bornkamm expresses one view of current New Testament scholarship in *Jesus of Nazareth* in chapter 8 on the "Messianic Question" (pp. 169–78 and appendix 3, pp. 226–31). His view is that Jesus did not claim explicitly to be the Messiah, that we do not know how he understood his own death, and that there are questions about the use of the term *Son of man*.

1. THE UNIQUE NATURE OF THE GOSPELS

The gospels are definitely not sources for understanding the thought processes of Jesus himself. If we talk about the messianic consciousness of Jesus, we are talking about how he himself thought—what he believed about himself. The only material we have about Jesus in this regard is the material in the gospels. But the material in the gospels simply is not concerned with this kind of question. Nowhere in the gospels is there any kind of material that would be included in a modern autobiography or biography, no account of any kind of experience that Jesus may or may not have had. The only thing that could come close to this would be the experience of the temptation. But the temptation narratives in the gospels are not accounts of any experience that Jesus actually had; they are merely a pictorial way of expressing an understanding of Jesus' messiahship. Almost certainly those narratives owe nothing to the historical Jesus himself.

Our sources do not tell us anything about the consciousness Jesus had or did not have. They do not tell us anything about the way Jesus thought of himself. So we cannot speak of the "messianic consciousness" of Jesus if by this we mean something about his thought processes.

2. EARLY CHURCH PROCLAMATIONS

The gospels are proclamations of the faith of the first century believers. The early church believed that Jesus was the Messiah, that his death fulfilled Isaiah 53, and some believed that he was the Son of man who would come again. The gospels express this belief by reading it back on to the lips of Jesus. What they actually do is to superimpose the early church's understanding on the life of Jesus. As proclamations of the faith of the early church, the gospels are almost sermonic in their construction and intent. Therefore the material in them in which Jesus claims to be the Messiah or accepts such a designation is an expression of the faith of the church. The statements do not tell us what Jesus himself actually said or did not say.

3. THE BURDEN OF PROOF

Since the gospels are primarily proclamations of the early church—that is, they were written by committed members of the church and in response to problems that the church was facing—the material in them is heavily affected; in some instances is actually reproduced by the faith and understanding of the early church. Any material we find in the gospels therefore must be accepted as representing this faith and understanding of the early church unless we can prove the opposite, namely, that it represents the actual teaching of Jesus. That is, we presume that the gospel statements do come from the early church rather than from the historical Jesus unless we can definitely prove otherwise.

Concerning the sayings in which Jesus claims to be the Son of God, we must conclude that these sayings represent the understanding, the theology, and the vocabulary of the early church. An example of this treatment is in Matthew 11:27, where the reading has Jesus claiming to be the Son of God: "All things have been delivered to me by my Father; and no one knows the Son except the Father, and no one knows the Father except the Son and any one to whom the Son chooses to reveal him." Another example is the servant of God saying in Mark 10:45: "For the Son of man also came not to be served but to serve, and to give his life as a ransom for many." Still another example is the claim in Matthew 16:17: "And Jesus answered him, 'Blessed are you, Simon Bar-Jona! For flesh and blood has not revealed this to you, but my Father who is in heaven.' " A final example is the Son-of-man claim in Mark 9:31: ". . . for he was teaching his disciples, saying to them, 'The Son of man will be delivered into the hands of men, and they will kill him; and when he is killed, after three days he will rise.' "

No proof is possible as to whether these sayings represent the actual teaching of the historical Jesus. The burden of proof is on any person who claims a saying to represent the teaching of Jesus. Sayings like those cited above must remain outside serious consideration when we are concerned with the teaching of Jesus himself.

The truth is, we cannot know anything directly about the messianic consciousness of Jesus because we simply do not have the source material for such an understanding. We cannot use any direct teaching about his messiahship from the gospels, for there is no way to prove that these writings represent anything other than the understanding of the early church. But we do not give up in the quest for some understanding of how Jesus understood himself and his ministry. What we have to do is to turn to the teaching of Jesus itself. That is, instead of starting with the statements attributed to Jesus, we can start with the teachings of Jesus and work backward to those statements. We look for what is implied about Jesus' understanding of himself in authentic teaching on other subjects.

B. Jesus' Self-Understanding Derived From Other Teaching

Jesus' understanding of himself as implied in his teaching on other subjects involves concentrating attention on the implications of the teaching. In the teaching of Jesus that we regard as authentic, we look for what is implied about his understanding of himself and his ministry.

We have discussed several topics in earlier chapters in which we can look for Jesus' understanding of himself. The first topic is the major subject in the teaching of Jesus, the kingdom of God.

1. KINGDOM OF GOD

We have already seen how hope for the coming of the kingdom of God was the supreme hope of ancient Judaism and that the desire for God's decisive intervention into human history and experience was strong. In fact, in the first century the Jews prayed every day in the Kaddish prayer for the kingdom to come. We know also, that Jesus taught that the kingdom had come in his ministry, that is, that the kingdom of God was present in the experience of the individual confronted by the kingly activity of God in him and in his ministry. It is certain that this teaching definitely comes from the historical Jesus.

Accepting these emphases as given, we can observe what is implied. If the kingdom of God is present in the experience of the individual confronted by the kingly activity of God in the ministry of Jesus, Jesus is himself claiming to mediate this kingly activity to humankind. The Jews had always expected that the kingly activity of God—God's decisive intervention in human history and human experience—would come through a mediator, through the Messiah, an archangel, angel, and so on. Thus, in teaching that the kingdom is present in his ministry, Jesus is implying that he is the Messiah. He is not claiming it explicitly, but he is most emphatically claiming it implicitly.

2. FORGIVENESS OF SINS

The message of Jesus to his contemporaries was his claim to confront them with the eschatological and messianic forgiveness of sins. He also ventured to make a radical challenge of their understanding of the limitation they felt God had set to this forgiveness. Jesus refused to accept the exclusion of the gentiles and of the Jews who had made themselves as gentiles. What is more, he brought these sinners into the community of the forgiven.

The parable of the prodigal son in Luke 15:11–32 shows Jesus daring to act as if he stood in the very place of God. This parable implies a tremendous amount with regard to Jesus' understanding of himself. He does not defend his action by pointing to the scriptures; he does not defend himself by pointing to some of the arguments from the traditional theology of Judaism; he does not venture any kind of an apologetic. Through the parable, Jesus is apparently proclaiming the forgiveness of sins. On his own personal authority he dares to correct the misunderstanding of his contemporaries about the limitations they had set on God's forgiveness.

3. FATHERLINESS OF GOD

Jesus addressed God as *abba* and taught his disciples to do the same, implying a claim that he himself enjoyed the eschatological father-son relationship of the End Time. Furthermore, in teaching his disciples to do this, he implies the claim to have the authority to include others in this same relationship. Like the other claims, this is not a direct claim. But there is a tremendous implication; the only figure in Jewish expectation who would have this kind of authority was the Messiah.

4. REINTERPRETATION OF THE JEWISH LAW

Jesus had a contempt for oral tradition, because the time for such tradition had passed. Also, Jesus had no concern for ritual cleanliness; the new relationship with God made possible by his ministry caused such a concern to be unnecessary. He even rejected the specific Law of Moses in the teaching about marriage because the new relationship with God necessitates a new understanding of the will of God (Mark 10:6, Matthew 19:4).

These actions transcend those of a rabbi. They imply that a new era has dawned in the relationship between humankind and God, an era that supersedes the era beginning with Moses. The implication by Matthew is that Jesus himself supersedes Moses, that he is the Messiah, and that his teaching is the messianic law. The radical reinterpretation of the Jewish Law is an implicit claim to messiahship.

5. THE CONSUMMATION

The teaching of Jesus looks toward a Consummation of that which had begun in his ministry. One particular aspect of Jesus' teaching concerning that Consummation is the judgment. Jesus certainly taught that the future Consummation would include the element of judgment. In the Son-of-man saying in Mark 8:38, Jesus is not identified with the Son of man. But this saying turns on the nature of one's response to the challenge of the ministry of Jesus. Mark 8:38 says: "For whoever is ashamed of me and of my words in this adulterous and sinful generation, of him will the Son of man also be ashamed when he comes in the glory of his Father with the holy angels." According to Mark, this means that one's reaction to the ministry of Jesus seals one, so to speak, for the final judgment. Reaction to his ministry determines one's standing at the final judgment.

The conclusion to be drawn is that Jesus did not directly claim to be the Messiah. But he implicitly claims the following: to mediate the kingdom of God to humankind; to proclaim the eschatological forgiveness of sins; to enjoy and to be able to bring others to share the eschatological parent-child relationship with God; to have the authority to supersede the law of Moses where he deems it necessary; that one's response to the challenge of his person and his ministry seals one for judgment at the Consummation.

Jesus may not have claimed directly to be the Messiah. But he certainly implies claims so strong that the response of the early church, "Thou art the Christ [Messiah]," was then and is now an appropriate response to the resurrection event. This response may have been read back into the tradition, but it is completely in accord with what Jesus implies about the significance of his person and his ministry.

C. The Authority of Jesus' Words and Deeds

A point that still needs to be discussed is the directness and immediacy of the manner with which Jesus teaches people and deals with them. Günther Bornkamm elaborates on this point in *Jesus of Nazareth* (pp. 57–63). His insight is a valuable supplement to the following discussion.

1. EXTERNAL AUTHORITY

First, it is interesting to note that Jesus refused to authenticate his ministry by having some external authority for what he was doing. There are three categories of representatives of God known to first-century Judaism and each one had his own kind of authority. The three representatives were the prophet, the apocalyptic seer, and the rabbi.

a. The Prophet

The Jews were very conscious of the prophets in their history and they looked for the return of prophetic activity at the End Time. Characteristic of the prophet is the claim of a direct experience of God, which gives prophetic authority. In the Old Testament there are several prophets who were authenticated in this way. For example, Amos 1:1, 2: "The words of Amos, who was among the shepherds of Tekoa, which he saw concerning Israel in the days of Uzziah king of Judah and in the days of Jeroboam the son of Joash, king of Israel, two years before the earthquake." Also, in Isaiah 6:1: "In the year that king Uzziah died I saw the Lord sitting upon a throne, high and lifted up; and his train filled the temple." And in Jeremiah 1:1, 2: "The words of Jeremiah, the son of Hilkiah, of the priests who were in Anathoth in the land of Benjamin, to whom the word of the Lord came in the days of Josiah the son of Amon, king of Judah, in the thirteenth year of his reign." Notice that in all three of these examples the following things are present: the date, the time, sometimes the place, and the manner of the direct experience of God. The authority of this direct experience of God gives the prophet the right to say, "The Lord says" or "Thus says the Lord" or "The word of the Lord to Israel is," and so on.

The prophet comes with a message and the message is in some sense its own authority. But in the classic Old Testament prophets, there is an additional authority—the authenticating personal experience of God.

b. The Apocalyptic Seer

The apocalyptic seer is the writer of apocalyptic literature. Like the prophet, he also authenticates his message. He describes the vision that gave him the message. It is a vision which God personally granted him and in which he found the truth that he is to proclaim. All apocalyptic writers have this kind of authenticating experience.

The author of the book of Revelation refers to his authenticating experience in Revelation 1:9ff.: "I, John, your brother, who share with you in Jesus the tribulation and the kingdom and the patient endurance, was on the island called Patmos on account of the word of God and the testimony of Jesus. I was in the Spirit on the Lord's day, and I heard behind me a loud voice like a trumpet. . . ." This experience is characteristic of most Jewish apocalyptic seers; it was this experience that gave them their authority.

c. The Rabbi

The rabbi also has a message—teaching about God and the Law, although he does not claim the authority of a direct experience with God, like the prophets, nor of a vision, like the apocalytpic seer. He claims authority derived from the chain of tradition in which he stands. This posture can best be explained by an example from rabbinical literature, verses 1–4 of the first chapter of the Aboth (The Fathers), a section of the Mishnah: "Moses received the Law from Sinai and committed it to Joshua, and Joshua to the elders, and the elders to the prophets. And the prophets committed it to the men of the great synagogue. They said three things: be deliberate in judgment, raise up many disciples, and make a fence around the Law. Simeon the Just was of the remnants of the great synagogue. He used to say 'By three things is the world sustained: by the Law, by the temple service, and by deeds of loving kindness.' Antigonas of Socho received the Law from Simeon the Just. He used to say 'Be not like slaves that minister to the master for the sake of receiving a bounty, but be like slaves that minister to the master not for the sake of receiving a bounty, and let the fear of heaven be upon you.' Jose ben Joezer of Zeredah, and Jose ben Johanan of Jerusalem received the Law from them. Jose ben Joezer of Zeredah said 'Let thy house be a meeting house for the sages, and sit amid the dust of their feet and drink in their words with thirst. . . .' "

Each one of these men—Simeon the Just, Antigonas of Socho, Jose ben Joezer, and Jose ben Johanan—claims authority. Each stands at a certain place in a direct chain of tradition that began with Moses and came down to the time each taught. A rabbi (teacher) of Jesus' day stood up and taught, deriving his authority from such a statement. He would set his place in the chain of tradition, stating who his teacher was and who his teacher's teacher had been, and so on. This would establish his place in the tradition. Such was the authentication of the rabbi.

d. Jesus' Authentication

In constrast with the prophet, the apocalyptic seer, and other rabbis, Jesus apparently refused to authenticate his message by any kind of appeal to a call of God, to a vision, or to a chain of tradition. This is the overall impression we get from the gospels. This impression is trustworthy, because the gospel writers themselves actually attempt to fill in this gap. For example, at the baptism of Jesus in Mark 1:11 we read: "And a voice came from heaven, 'Thou art my beloved Son; with thee I am well pleased.' " Here the gospel writer is authenticating the ministry of Jesus by having a voice come from heaven to speak of his authority.

A similar situation is observed in the account of the transfiguration in Mark 9:7: "And a cloud overshadowed them, and a voice came out of the cloud 'This is my beloved Son; listen to him.' " The gospel writer is authenticating Jesus and his message.

The Jews believed that the Messiah would bring an authentication with him. They believed that there would be some means of evaluation to determine whether or not he was the Messiah. In A.D. 132 Simon bar Kochbah claimed to be the Messiah and was tested by the rabbis to see whether or not his claim was valid. We do not know how they tested him, only that they did. Some people apparently believed he was the Messiah, because they supported him, leading to the revolt against Rome, which collapsed in A.D. 135.

There is a conspicuous absence of any authority expressed by Jesus except for the authority of the teaching itself.

2. DIRECTNESS

The directness with which Jesus teaches is quite remarkable. The impression that the teaching of Jesus made is evident in Mark 1:22: "And they were astonished at his teaching, for he taught them as one who had authority, and not as the scribes." The scribes taught on the derived authority of the chain of tradition. Jesus teaches directly. He proclaims the kingdom of God, challenges people to repentance, proclaims the will of God, and announces the forgiveness of sins. He does all of this directly; he does not say, "in the name of Moses" or "in the name of rabbi so-and-so"—he just says, "Your sins are forgiven you."

The impression as reported in Mark 1:22 is reliable. It is much too widespread and uniform in the gospel tradition to have been the result of something read back on to the lips of Jesus. The disciples and the early church did believe in Jesus and did regard him as having an immediate authority. But as we have already seen, the early church felt that there ought to be some kind of authenticating experience. We have already seen authentication by the voice of God in the baptism and transfiguration narratives. So we may claim with some degree of reliability that this directness is a true characteristic of the teaching of Jesus, not something read back in the tradition.

3. JESUS' DEALINGS WITH PEOPLE

Jesus showed authority in his dealings with people. One example is the healing of the paralytic in Capernaum, described in Mark 2:12: "And he rose, and immediately took up the pallet and went out before them all; so that they were all amazed and glorified God, saying 'We never saw anything like this.' " This Marcan report is like everything else manifest in every aspect of the tradition, whether it is the call of the disciples, the healing of the sick, the casting out of demons, forgiving sinners, or rebuking the sons of Zebedee (Mark 10:35ff.). Whatever aspect of Jesus' dealings with people, it is always the same story—the directness of his dealing with them, the immediacy of his challenge, and the authority that he exercises. This approach is far too widespread and consistent in the tradition to be something read back on to the lips of Jesus by the early church.

This manner is clearly an exhibition of the authority that Jesus himself claimed in practice by refusing to authenticate his ministry by referring to a call, a vision, or a chain of tradition. By teaching in such a manner as to exhibit a direct authority, by dealing with people showing direct authority, Jesus is implying a very high claim. It is a claim that can be answered by saying, "Thou art the Christ, the Son of the living God."

D. Authority: Direct and Indirect

On the question of authority we must deal with a general impression rather than centering on an exegesis of any single saying or group of sayings. A careful study of the teaching of Jesus leads one to believe that Jesus did in fact have a very high claim to authority, but this claim was revealed indirectly, rather than directly.

1. JESUS' CLAIM TO AUTHORITY

That Jesus manifested an indirect claim to authority rather than a direct claim cannot be proved. It is doubtful that Jesus ever said anything like, "I am the Messiah," or anything similar. It appears that he acted as if he were the Messiah and let people draw their own conclusions.

If he had come claiming specifically to be the Messiah, he would have been tested. The rabbis would have set out to test him as they set out to test Simon bar Kochbah. Then there would have been the objective question, "Is Jesus the Messiah or is he not?" Questions would have been put to Jesus and tests would have been set for him. But he who questioned and he who tested would be standing over against Jesus, looking at him objectively, trying to determine something about him in the realm of objectivity. What would have been gained by this procedure?

By not claiming authority directly, but by acting and teaching with this authority, Jesus creates the situation wherein a person must first wrestle with his teaching, must first take serious notice of what Jesus is doing. Then one is face to face with the question "What do I think of this man?" Already, you see, there is an element of personal involvement before the question arises. And when the question does arise, it does not arise in an objective manner from the outside; but it arises from within, from the context of one's experience. This change of perspective appears to be the reason for the indirectness in the claims of Jesus.

It seems that above all Jesus wanted persons to become involved with him, involved with the challenge that God was acting as king in his ministry, involved with the challenge that now sins were being forgiven, involved with the challenge that God was acting as king in the personal experience of the one confronted—in other words, involved in the challenge that my sins are forgiven. Only after this is recognized should one ask oneself whether or not Jesus is the Messiah.

A claim by Jesus to be the Messiah, objectively and therefore intellectually proven or disproven would not mean a great deal. Personal involvement in the ministry of the Messiah and personal involvement with the challenge the Messiah brought—that is a very different matter.

E. Summary

Our understanding of the nature of the gospel tradition and our manner of interpreting and understanding the teaching of Jesus has hopefully brought us significantly closer to what Jesus himself likely intended. He apparently intended an element of involvement out of which questions arise, rather than giving a direct claim to which one can say, "yes" or "no" or "so what." Jesus' words and deeds, his healing and ministry, were signs of his authority and power. Each individual is to decide whether to respond by saying, "Thou art the Christ, the Son of the living God."

F. Resource Material

GLOSSARY

ORAL TRADITION   The term is mentioned to illustrate Jesus' understanding of himself and his mission. A knowledge of Jesus' self-understanding comes from his teaching on other subjects, including his radical reinterpretation of the Jewish Law. In this connection, Jesus had a contempt for oral tradition—apparently the time for oral tradition had passed because of his ministry and teaching.

PROPHETIC AUTHORITY   Hebrew prophets had their authority because they claimed a direct experience with God. The experience gave them "prophetic" authority so that they could speak on behalf of God (see Amos 1:1,2). The Jews of the first century looked for a return of prophecy at the End Time. Jesus, however, did not claim to take his authority in the customary prophetic tradition.

SIMON BAR KOCHBAH   In A.D. 132, Simon bar Kochbah came claiming to be the Messiah. He was tested by the rabbis to see whether his claim was valid. They supported his claim, leading to the revolt against Rome (which collapsed in A.D. 135).

SON OF MAN   In first-century Judaism, the Son of man is the one who comes from God as the judge. He comes to hold judgment upon the earth. The Son-of-man designation is not necessarily a synonymous designation for Jesus.

SCRIPTURE REFERENCES

Isaiah 53	Mark 10:6	Aboth 1:1–4
Matthew 11:27	(Matthew 19:4)	Mark 1:11
Mark 10:45	Mark 8:38	Mark 9:7
Matthew 16:17	Amos 1:1,2	Mark 1:22
Mark 9:31	Isaiah 6:1	Mark 2:12
Luke 15:11–32	Jeremiah 1:1	Mark 10:35f.
	Revelation 1:9f.	

BIBLIOGRAPHY

Anderson, Charles C. *The Historical Jesus: A Continuing Quest.* Grand Rapids: Eerdmans, 1972.

Bornkamm, Günther. *Jesus of Nazareth.* 3rd ed. New York: Harper & Brothers, 1960 (see chap. 8, pp. 169–78 and appendix 3, pp. 226–31; pp. 57–63).

Danby, Herbert, ed. and trans. *The Mishnah.* London: Oxford University Press, 1958.

Jeremias, Joachim. *The Problem of the Historical Jesus.* Philadelphia: Fortress, 1964.

Kähler, Martin. *The So-Called Historical Jesus and the Historic Biblical Christ.* Philadelphia: Fortress, 1964.

Keck, Leander E. *A Future for the Historical Jesus.* Nashville: Abingdon, 1972.

Küng, Hans. *On Being a Christian.* New York: Doubleday, 1978.

Lapide, Pinchas. *Israelis, Jews and Jesus.* New York: Doubleday, 1979.

Pannenberg, Wolfhart. *Jesus: God and Man.* Philadelphia: Westminster, 1979.

Perrin, Norman. *The New Testament: An Introduction.* New York: Harcourt Brace Jovanovich, 1974 (esp. chapter 12, pp. 277ff.).

The Sayings of the Fathers. New York: Schocken, 1962 (Hebrew and English).

Schillebeeckx, Edward. *Jesus: An Experiment in Christology.* New York: Seabury, 1979.

Tödt, H. E. *The Son of Man in the Synoptic Tradition.* Philadelphia: Westminster, 1965.

Wrede, William. *The Messianic Secret.* London: J. Clarke, 1971.

QUESTIONS

1. What are three main characteristics of Jesus' understanding of himself and his mission?
2. Are the synoptic gospels the source of understanding the thought processes of Jesus himself?
3. There are accounts in the gospels in which Jesus claims to be the Son of man. Explain these accounts.
4. What is the primary nature of the gospels aside from reporting the teaching of Jesus?
5. What is the possibility of knowing directly anything about the messianic consciousness of Jesus?
6. How can we learn about the messianic consciousness of Jesus?
7. The Jews at the time of Jesus expected the Messiah to come to mediate between humanity and God. Jesus claimed that the kingdom of God was present in his teaching. What is the implication of this claim?
8. What claim is implied in Jesus' proclamation of the forgiveness of sins?
9. Jesus addressed God as *abba* in a way that indicated a close relationship with God. What is the implication of this claim?
10. What is the implication of Jesus' reinterpretation of the Jewish Law of the tradition of Moses?
11. What in Jesus' teaching about the Consummation (such as Mark 8:38) implies that he is the Messiah?
12. What conclusion can be drawn about the messianic consciousness of Jesus?
13. Summarize evidence from Jesus' actions and teaching that implied that he was the Messiah.
14. What was the authenticating authority claimed by the prophets in early Judaism?
15. What was the authenticating authority of the apocalyptic seer?
16. Did the rabbi claim authority by direct experience of God or by a vision, as the seer claimed?
17. What was the authenticating authority of the rabbi?
18. Jesus was a rabbi. Did he attempt to authenticate his message, as did other rabbis of his time, by referring to his tradition? Did he use, as the prophets did, a statement of direct experience with God? Did he refer to a vision of God, as the apocalyptic seer did?
19. Did the gospel writers attempt to authenticate the teaching of Jesus in a way not employed by Jesus himself?

20. Jesus gave no authentication of his teaching; was this consistent with the Jewish expectation about the Messiah?
21. What seems to be the only authentication of the teaching of Jesus?
22. Explain the baptism and transfiguration narratives in the New Testament.
23. What characteristic of Jesus' dealings with people implied his authority?
24. Jesus never makes his claim to authority explicit. In what way does he show his claim to authority?
25. Why does Jesus not claim directly to be the Messiah?

Chapter 11

THE FIRST CENTURY
AND THE TWENTIETH

THIS chapter contains a discussion of the relationship between the
historical Jesus and the Christ of the *kerygma*. (*Kerygma* is a Greek
word that means "message" or "proclamation.") It investigates the
relevance of a study of the historical Jesus and how this study relates
to the Christian faith. The chapter includes the implications of a study
of the teaching of Jesus to the Christian believer in the twentieth
century.

Thus far we have treated the teaching of Jesus from a historical and
theoretical perspective, which is in keeping with the nature of the
documents that present Jesus to us. Now, in keeping with the intent
of the gospel records of the teaching of Jesus, we move to a response
to the activity of God. This naturally takes us into a more subjective
and personal realm, as opposed to a detached and scholarly study.
But it is our impression that the Jesus of history and the Christ of faith
cannot be effectively separated, and the teaching/preaching nature of
the gospels allows for an individualized response, not dictated by
strict conventions of scholarship.

A. The Concern of the Christian Faith

Our purpose in looking at the teaching of Jesus historically has
been to arrive at an understanding of what Jesus taught in the first
century. We have also dealt with the question of what the teaching
of Jesus meant to those who heard him then. Now we go beyond this
and ask the question, "What does the teaching of Jesus mean to us
in the twentieth century?"

1. THE CHRISTIAN BELIEVER

With whom is the Christian believer concerned? The quick and apparently obvious answer, "the historical Jesus," is an incorrent answer. The early church was interested in the historical Jesus and what he had said and done. But the early church was even more concerned with the risen Lord of its own experience. Further, the early church modified what Jesus actually said in light of an understanding reached in later days; this understanding came out of a later experience of the risen Lord, what he was saying and doing.

In the early church, faith was concerned with the Lord present to the Christian congregations in their worship. The Lord was also present to the Christian believers in their devotions. Christian faith was concerned, as was Paul on the Damascus road, with the risen-Lord experience. The Lord appeared to Paul from then on and guided him in every aspect of his thought and life and work. This model was true for the early church as a whole. Their first and primary concern was with the risen Lord of their Christian experience. It was the risen Lord who spoke to them. It is the words of this risen Lord that are recorded in the gospels.

2. THE RISEN LORD

The details of what happened at the resurrection are of relatively minor importance; that the resurrection took place is of supreme importance. Thus artifacts such as the Shroud of Turin are interesting from a scientific or historical standpoint, but such things materially add nothing to the faith perspective. In other words, understanding the resurrection as an act of God does not require scientific proof.

What was true for the early church must also be true for us today. True Christian faith today is faith in the risen Lord of our Christian experience. We individually come to faith because of what we are told about Jesus by the church. We come to faith through the gospels, in lessons by church schoolteachers, and in sermons preached by ministers and evangelists. The crucial moment of Christian faith for any one of us is the moment we become conscious of his presence—the crucified and risen Lord, challenging us to discipleship, challenging us to live a life in his name.

3. THE CHRIST

Our concern is always with the Lord present with us in our experience, with the Lord proclaimed to us by the church. In technical language, this is the Christ of the *kerygma*. *Kerygma* is the Greek word for "preaching" or "proclamation," and we speak of the Christ of the *kerygma* to mean Christ proclaimed by the church as the crucified, risen, and redeeming Lord. It also means the Christ of Christian experience—the Christ who confronts us in the Eucharist or Lord's Supper, the Christ who confronted Paul on the Damascus road, and the Christ who has challenged the great figures in the church since the first century.

4. JESUS

Contrasted with the Christ of the *kerygma* is the historical Jesus, the Jesus we come to know through historical research. This is the Jesus we have been talking about throughout the book. This is the Jesus whose teaching we have been seeking to reconstruct by the methods of historical science.

Christian faith, however, is always faith in the risen and redeeming Lord, who confronts us in the immediacy of our personal Christian experience, who is proclaimed to us by the church—the Christ of the *kerygma*. From a faith perspective, the words of the historical Jesus must be confirmed in a personal experience of the Christ of the *kerygma*.

5. THE SECOND COMING

The relationship between the historical Jesus and the Christ of the *kerygma* can be illustrated by the second coming. The second coming is the church's reinterpretation of Jesus' teaching about the Consummation and activity in the kingdom of God. In the light of our previous discussion, it is difficult to believe literally that Jesus will come on a cloud, on some hilltop in Turkey, Palestine, or Colorado, or wherever. In the history of the church, some people have gone out and waited a thousand times for this Christ to return, and their bones still molder on the hillsides where they have waited. They have waited in vain.

Professor T. W. Manson of Manchester University believed that he was able through historical research to reconstruct the teaching of Jesus. In his conclusions about the teaching, Manson maintained that Jesus was wrong about the Consummation. He believed that the Consummation would come, not necessarily in the form of the return of Jesus, but in some form in a few months or a few years from the date of his study. Manson did not accept Jesus' own teaching because it brought forth no confirmation in his own personal experience of the risen and redeeming Lord.

Jesus did in fact teach the certainty of the Consummation, but he did not teach how, when, or where. This statement can be believed, but not because of historical research that has reconstructed it. One can find meaning in this if one finds confirmation of it in the immediacy of one's experience of the risen and redeeming Lord, the Christ of the *kerygma*. This is always the way. The Christian faith is concerned with the risen and redeeming Lord, the Christ of the *kerygma*, the Jesus of personal experience. It is his word we believe and accept. Personal faith is not directly concerned with the historical Jesus, nor is it directly concerned with the words of that historical Jesus except insofar as they find confirmation in the Christ of our personal experience.

B. The Historical Jesus and the Christ of Faith

The question that next comes to mind is, "What is the relationship between the risen and redeeming Lord of our experience (the Christ of the church's *kerygma*) and the historical Jesus?" We have spoken of these two figures as if they were separate. Yet the early church clearly identified the two.

1. THE EARLY CHURCH

For the early church, the risen Lord of their experience was the historical Jesus. They could and did read back on to the lips of the Jesus of the gospel record what they understood the risen Lord to be saying to them. The risen Lord who spoke in their experience was the historical Jesus who had spoken in Galilee and Judea. The early believers identified the historical Jesus and the Christ of the *kerygma* as one and the same.

2. THE HISTORICAL JESUS

There are certain differences between the historical Jesus and the Christ of the *kerygma*. The historical Jesus proclaimed the kingdom of God. He came with a message about the kingdom of God. He is the proclaimer. But the risen Lord is proclaimed in the gospel message as the eschatological event. His ministry, death, and resurrection is proclaimed by the church as the decisive salvation activity of God. The proclaimer thus has become the proclaimed.

3. THE CROSS AND RESURRECTION

The Christ of the church's *kerygma* is the crucified and risen Lord. The historical Jesus is the Jesus of Galilee and Judea before the crucifixion and the resurrection. Indeed, by reading the works of the scholars from the past generation who said they believed in the historical Jesus, one will see that they are almost embarrassed by the cross and resurrection; for to believe in the historical Jesus merely as reformer, spiritual guide, and moral teacher makes the cross and resurrection seem irregular. This difficulty underlines the very real difference between the two figures. One figure, the historical Jesus, is a pre-cross-and-resurrection figure; the other, the Christ of the *kerygma*, is inevitably a post-cross-and-resurrection figure.

4. THE CONTINUITY

The difference between the two figures must not hide from us the very real continuity that exists between them. If there had been no historical Jesus, there obviously could have been no Christ of the church's *kerygma*. The church did not make up a figure to proclaim as the crucified and risen Lord. And the early believers did not choose just any figure to proclaim, such as Barabbas or some martyr from the period. No, the church proclaimed as crucified and risen the Jesus of Nazareth, who had taught and been known by many present in those early days of the first proclamation. Therefore, there is obviously a very real continuity between these two figures. However much we may stress the difference, in order to get them clear in our minds, we must at the same time stress the continuity that exists between them. The historical Jesus becomes the crucified and risen Lord of present day proclamation.

5. BEYOND CHRONOLOGICAL CONTINUITY

Does the continuity between the two figures imply anything more than simply a chronological relationship? This discussion has been carried out most ably by James M. Robinson in *The New Quest of the Historical Jesus.*

The discussion revolves around the relationship between the historical Jesus and the Christ of the church's *kerygma.* The question asked is, "What is the significance of the historical Jesus to Christian faith?" The historical Jesus is not the primary concern of Christian faith; the true concern of the Christian faith is the Christ of the *kerygma.*

To speak of Jesus is to refer to a historical figure. To speak of Christ is to make a theological statement. As an actual, historical, and preresurrection person, the name Jesus refers to Rabbi Yeshua bar Joseph of Nazareth, who preached and taught in the first century. The term *Christ* is a postresurrection designation which accepts the historical Jesus as being identical to the Christ of the faith. Jesus as rabbi means the Jesus of history. Jesus Christ means the risen Lord and the Messiah—a declaration of faith. Although the designation of Jesus and Christ may be referring to the same figure, to the nonbeliever Jesus is Jesus and not the Christ, or anointed one, or the risen Lord of the believer's experience.

The Jesus of history becomes the Christ of the *kerygma* to the believer. There is a very real parallel between the ministry and teaching of the historical Jesus and the ministry and message of the risen and redeeming Lord. The early believers proclaimed Christ as the eschatological event, especially his cross and resurrection. The historical Jesus proclaimed the kingdom of God.

When the historical Jesus proclaimed the kingdom of God, he was talking about God's decisive, eschatological activity. When the church proclaims the cross and resurrection today, it proclaims this message as God's decisive, eschatological activity. There is a difference of reference, but a very real parallel in concern. Theologically speaking, the two proclamations mean the same thing—God is decisively, eschatologically active. Indeed, the proclamation of the cross and resurrection becomes the means whereby persons in the twentieth century are confronted by God's decisive, eschatological activity, just as the ministry of Jesus itself was the means whereby the people of the first century were confronted by that activity. That parallel is clear and marked.

6. THE ACTIVITY OF GOD

The teaching of Jesus was designed to elicit a response to the activity of God. The ethical teaching, for example, is concerned with the kind of response persons would make to this activity of God. This is what Christianity means by faith. Faith in the crucified and risen Lord is the response we make to the God who is active in our personal experience.

7. JESUS' CLAIMS

In the chapter on "Jesus' Understanding of Himself" we discussed the claims that Jesus makes for himself by implication. Although Jesus seems not to have said, "I am the Messiah," he nonetheless acted as if he were. The parallel between the claims Jesus implied concerning himself and his ministry and the claims early believers made concerning him and his ministry is a real parallel.

C. How the Early Church Used the Teaching of Jesus

1. INTERPRETATION, MODIFICATION, AND ADDITION

We have seen that the early church interpreted, modified, and added to the Jesus tradition. It took sayings and reinterpreted them; it took sayings and added to them other sayings spoken by a prophet, and so on. Nonetheless, the tradition of the teaching of Jesus is constantly the starting point for the work of present day Christians. The very fact that the church modified, interpreted, and added to the tradition of the teaching of Jesus testifies to the conviction of the church that this tradition itself was significant. One does not constantly add to, modify, and interpret something that is not of real concern. The tradition of the teaching of Jesus was a very real concern to the Christian church. It was the starting point for its own work.

2. DISCOVERING JESUS' TEACHING

By modern historical study, we have arrived at the point where we can know something about what the historical Jesus actually taught. The teaching of the historical Jesus as reconstructed through modern research must become the starting point for new endeavors in understanding and application. This teaching will constantly open up new possibilities for faith.

The early church interpreted, modified, and added to the teaching of Jesus, and we have its tradition in the gospels. Using our knowledge of the teaching of Jesus, we can open up new possibilities for an understanding and application of his teaching for contemporary faith. This is the significance of the knowledge of the historical Jesus and his teaching—to open up new possibilities for faith, in addition to those possibilities always present to the reader of the New Testament who takes at face value what the scriptures say.

D. The Teaching of Jesus and Contemporary Faith

1. KINGDOM OF GOD

The kingdom of God is an apocalyptic concept in the teaching of Jesus. It refers to God's kingly activity, to God's irruption into personal history and experience to visit and redeem humanity. This is what the Jews expected and this is what Jesus proclaimed as present in his ministry. The early church does not proclaim the kingdom of God. In fact, the early church rarely used the concept of the kingdom of God in its teaching. When it does use this phrase, it does so with a meaning different from what it has in apocalyptic literature and in the teaching of Jesus. When Christians talk about the decisive activity of God in human history and human experience, they are talking about Jesus, especially about his cross and resurrection.

Although the church is using different terms, it is referring to the same thing Jesus talked about. Jesus' proclamation of the kingdom of God and the Christian proclamation of Christ as the eschatological event are two ways of talking about the same thing. We are no longer talking about the experience of Peter in first-century Galilee or of any other person who first heard the proclamation of Jesus. We are talking about people in the twentieth century as well as about men and women of the first century. God speaks through the risen and crucified Lord, through Christ identified as the eschatological event. This is the possibility we must hold open for faith. As the cross of Jesus confronts us, God moves toward us acting as king, irrupting into our history and our experience.

2. FORGIVENESS OF SINS

It is clear that the message of the historical Jesus to his contemporaries in Galilee is also the message of the risen and redeeming Lord to us today. However different the circumstances, however different the clothes, language, culture, and the times, the relationship with God is the same. The technician of the twentieth century in the West is every bit as much a sinner as the peasant of the first century in the East. In particular, persons in the twentieth century have exactly the same needs for forgiveness and reconciliation.

The forgiveness of sins, central to the teaching of Jesus, is perhaps more directly meaningful than any other aspect of his teaching. The parable of the prodigal son, which speaks of sin and forgiveness, will always be a favorite story with people because it speaks to the universal human situation. It is concerned with the permanency of the human relationship with God. The proclaimer still proclaims. Christ and his cross, God and God's love are ways of experiencing the forgiveness of sins. The teaching of Jesus helps us to appreciate God's concern for humanity.

3. FATHERLINESS OF GOD

In discussing the fatherliness of God, we are focusing upon the constant human relationship with God. God is a nurturing and caring God. This is a prime tenet of our faith and always has been. From the day when Paul first wrote of the "spirit whereby we cry *abba*" (Galatians 4:6; Romans 8:15), the fatherliness of God has been one of the great concepts of the Christian faith.

The fatherliness of God is not a platitude but a dynamic expression of the intimacy of the relationship with God now possible for humankind because of Jesus. This is every bit as true for the man or woman in the twentieth century as it was for any person in the first century. A deeper understanding of exactly what Jesus meant by the fatherliness of God can serve only to strengthen and deepen our faith.

4. RESPONSE

The ethical teaching of Jesus must be understood as indicating the kind of response the believer can make in order to experience God. In the case of the forgiveness of sins, we enter ever more deeply into the experience of the forgiveness of sins as we ourselves forgive. In the case of the love of God, we enter ever more deeply into the experience of the love of God as we ourselves learn to love.

For all the difference in clothes, language, culture, and time, we are the same as the persons of the first century. We are equally confronted by the forgiveness of sins, equally confronted by the love of God, equally in need of guidance as to how we can best respond to God's forgiveness, to God's love.

The teaching of Jesus about response can become directly important to contemporary faith. The teaching of Jesus is concerned with examples of the way persons may respond. The striking feature about the teaching of the historical Jesus as the evangelists present it is that it consists almost solely of examples. They do not have Jesus giving specifics as to what should be done in any and every situation; they have him giving examples of what can and should be done in a specific situation.

The examples Jesus gives and the parables he teaches are always designed to illustrate the kind of response that will lead to a new thinking in new situations—to a seeking for new ways of doing things. Love is the constant among all the changing examples. The means of expressing that love are not limited, for example, to doing exactly what the good Samaritan did. The means of expression is found by seeking to have the same spirit the Samaritan revealed when we confront situations in our everyday lives.

5. THE WILL OF GOD

We have a responsibility to be like God. We are to exercise in our lives the qualities we find in God. By seeking to do this, we do God's will for us in the immediacy of our own personal situations in our own personal lives. The challenge to be like God is a challenge to seek the will of God in personal experience and specific situations.

6. DISCIPLESHIP

In the teaching of Jesus about discipleship, our main interest is with the twelve and the teaching of Jesus to them. One thing is clear: we are not members of that inner group of first-century disciples. Circumstances in the ministry of Jesus are also different from our present situation. We no longer have a small group of persons following one leader; we have the organized church with millions of members. We also have two thousand years of Christian history behind us and the multitudinous organization of the church. From this perspective, the immediate relevance of what Jesus taught is not obvious.

Discipleship in the first century meant leaving everything to follow Jesus. Today discipleship may involve practicing the Christian faith in everyday life. The disciples were commissioned to extend and continue the ministry of Jesus. The same message is committed to the disciples—the proclamation of the kingdom; the same authority—to forgive sins; the same power—to cast out demons.

However different our suburban and inner-city life may be from that group of Galilean fishermen, in discipleship we have the same function. We are Jesus' lips in twentieth-century places where he cannot speak, his hands in situations where he cannot personally be present. If there is any function in discipleship, it is this. The more we know about the teaching of Jesus to the twelve disciples, the better we can understand our own personal responsibilities as members of his own body, the church, and the more we can respond to God's will.

E. Summary

Knowledge of the teaching of Jesus must be confirmed by the risen Lord of personal experience before it becomes truly meaningful. The confirmation by the risen Lord of our experience is necessary to transform knowledge of the teaching of the historical Jesus from something interesting to something vitally important. Knowledge of the teaching of the historical Jesus offers new opportunities in what he may have to say to the twentieth century believer.

F. Resource Material

GLOSSARY

CHRIST OF THE KERYGMA *Kerygma* is the Greek word for "preaching" or "proclamation." Technically, "Christ of the *kerygma*" means the Christ proclaimed by the church as the crucified, risen, and redeeming Lord. It also means the Christ of Christian experience; the Christ who confronts believers in the Lord's Supper; the Christ who confronted Paul on the Damascus road.

CONSUMMATION Understanding the Consummation as related to the second coming points to a difference between the historical Jesus and the Christ of the *kerygma*. There is a difference in what the Consummation means to Jesus himself, to the early church, and to the twentieth-century believer. (See *Second Coming*)

HISTORICAL JESUS The Jesus we come to know through historical research. The Jesus whose teaching has been reconstructed by methods of historical science. (Compare *Christ of the kerygma*). The words of the historical Jesus must be confirmed in personal experience by the Christ of the *kerygma*.

NAZARENE The usual designation for the word *Christian* in Hebrew. Contemporary Jewish scholars usually refer to Christians as Nazarenes. Their usual designation for Jesus is Yeshua or Yesha, a very common given name for a male. The name *Jesus* in English is translated Joshua.

SECOND COMING The early church's reinterpretation of Jesus' teaching about the Consummation. It does not refer to a literal return of Jesus.

SCRIPTURE REFERENCES

Luke 15:11–32   Galatians 4:6   Romans 8:15

BIBLIOGRAPHY

Aulen, Gustaf. *Jesus in Contemporary Historical Research*. Philadelphia: Fortress, 1976.

Baird, William. *The Quest of the Christ of Faith*. Waco: Word Books, 1977.

Connick, C. Milo. *Jesus: The Man, The Mission and the Message*. 2d ed. Englewood Cliffs, N.J.: Prentice-Hall, 1974.

Gogarten, Friedrich. *The Reality of Faith*. Philadelphia: Westminster Press, 1959.

Jeremias, Joachim. *The Problem of the Historical Jesus*. Philadelphia: Fortress, 1964.

Kummel, W. G. *Promise and Fulfillment*. London: SCM, 1957.

Küng, Hans. *Signposts for the Future*. New York: Doubleday, 1978.

Macquarrie, John. *The Humility of God*. Philadelphia: Westminster, 1978.

Marxsen, Willi. *The Resurrection of Jesus of Nazareth*. Philadelphia: Fortress, 1970.

Moltmann, Jürgen. *The Passion for Life: A Messianic Lifestyle*. Philadelphia: Fortress, 1978.

Perrin, Norman. *Jesus and the Language of the Kingdom*. Philadelphia: Fortress, 1976 (esp. chap. 4).

_____. *A Modern Pilgrimage in New Testament Christology*. Philadelphia: Fortress, 1974.

_____. *The Promise of Bultmann*. Philadelphia: Fortress, 1979.

_____. *Rediscovering the Teaching of Jesus*. New York: Harper & Row, 1967 (chap. 5).

_____. *The Resurrection according to Matthew, Mark and Luke*. Philadelphia: Fortress, 1977.

Robinson, James M. *The New Quest of the Historical Jesus*. London: SCM, 1959.

Royce, Josiah. *The Problem of Christianity*. Chicago: University of Chicago Press, 1968.

QUESTIONS

1. Whom should we be concerned with as the focus of our Christian faith—the historical Jesus, the Christ of the *kerygma*, or the risen Lord?
2. Do we have faith in the historical Jesus?
3. What about Jesus' expectation concerning the Consummation, which he expected to take place within a few months or a few years?
4. How did the early church think of the Christ of the *kerygma* and the historical Jesus?
5. What is the difference in our experience between the Christ of the *kerygma* and the historical Jesus?

6. The historical Jesus proclaimed the kingdom of God and the early church proclaims Christ as the eschatological event. What about the compatibility of these two proclamations?
7. What are some of the things the early church did to the teaching of Jesus?
8. What is the implication of knowledge discovered in the twentieth century regarding the teaching of the historical Jesus?
9. Jesus did not give a specific teaching for every possible situation; what did he do?
10. Jesus proclaims the kingdom of God and the early church seldom used the term "kingdom of God." Instead, it proclaimed Jesus. How would you reconcile these two emphases?
11. What does Jesus offer as a central aspect of his teaching?
12. What does the fatherliness of God mean to a twentieth-century person?
13. Discipleship in the time of Jesus meant leaving all and following him. What does discipleship mean today?

Chapter 12

REVIEW, SUMMARY, AND CONCLUSION

THIS chapter is a brief review of the contents of the previous chapters. It includes a short presentation of the major points presented throughout the book and a general summary of the teaching of Jesus as it relates to the Christian faith.

A. Review of Topics

Now that we have covered the teaching of Jesus, it may be helpful to review the things we have discussed, recalling the points that have been made and attempting to get an overview of the teaching of Jesus as we have depicted it. In order to do so, we will first review the chapters in sequence and summarize the contents of each. Then, we can speak in broad terms of the main emphases of the teaching of Jesus as our study has revealed it.

1. SOURCES AND METHODOLOGY

The sources for our knowledge of the teaching of Jesus are the synoptic gospels of Matthew, Mark, and Luke and some of the non-canonical sayings, those found outside the canonical gospel tradition, especially in the Coptic gospel of Thomas. The material in the fourth gospel, the gospel of John, has been much too drastically reinterpreted to be used directly in a reconstruction of the teaching of the historical Jesus.

But even in the case of the material in the synoptic gospels we have a similar problem. The teaching of Jesus presented in the synoptic gospels is teaching that has been modified and interpreted from the insights, understanding, situation, and faith of a later time. Strictly speaking, the synoptic gospels do not present the teaching of Jesus as he spoke it. They present it as it was understood and interpreted at a later date. This claim is defended by referring to and discussing certain passages in the synoptic gospels. Sometimes by bringing in the tradition from the noncanonical sayings, we have access to additional versions of the sayings or parables; therefore, we can compare these versions with one another—the various traditions in Mark, Luke, Matthew, or Thomas. This process gives us material with which we can work in order to reconstruct the teaching of Jesus.

The methodology we use in reconstructing the teaching of Jesus from this synoptic and noncanonical gospel material includes five points. First, we compare the various forms of a saying or parable by using the method of literary analysis or form criticism, attempting to find the earliest form of the saying or parable.

Second, we seek to understand the kind of changes and modifications introduced in the tradition of the teaching as it was transmitted in the early church. We seek for example, to learn what kind of emphasis Matthew brings to the teaching. We therefore know to take these particular emphases into account as we study the material.

Third, we work by retranslation into Aramaic. This leads us to the earliest tradition because, for the most part, the tradition was transmitted in Greek. Once we arrive at an Aramaic form of the saying, we have likely moved closer to the historical Jesus.

Fourth, and perhaps one of the more important steps, we accept this criterion: What could not have come from Judaism and what does not represent the particular interest of the early church may well be authentic material. This criterion of dissimilarity has called our attention to major aspects of the teaching of the historical Jesus.

Fifth, we concentrate our attention at places where we can be reasonably sure that we do have access to the actual teaching of the historical Jesus. In the case of the parables, the work of Professor Joachim Jeremias has shown that it is possible to reconstruct the original form of these parables. In the case of the Lord's Prayer, he has shown that it is possible to reconstruct the original form of this prayer. In the kingdom-of-God teaching, it is possible to show that Jesus spoke of the kingdom of God in a way different from that of the early church.

By concentrating our attention upon such principles, we may construct a picture of the teaching of Jesus as a whole. We then use this as the basis for further work.

2. FIRST-CENTURY JUDAISM

The purpose of understanding first-century Judaism is this: If we are to reconstruct certain elements in the teaching of Jesus, it is important to learn to understand the setting of the teaching. To reconstruct this context, we need to know something about Jews and Judaism at the time of Jesus. For example, Jesus constantly used certain words and phrases, giving them the same meaning they had to his contemporaries. One example is "kingdom of God." Jesus uses this term in ways comparable to those used by his contemporaries. If we are to understand his teaching, therefore, we need to know how he and his contemporaries understood and used this phrase.

The sources for our knowledge of Jews and Judaism at the time of Jesus are the Old Testament, the Apocrypha and Pseudepigrapha, apocalyptic literature, the Dead Sea Scrolls, the writings of Flavius Josephus, and rabbinical literature. We gave an example of how this knowledge helps us to interpret and understand the teaching of Jesus in the discussion of the parable of the prodigal son.

Having discussed the introductory questions of sources and methodology for our reconstruction and interpretation of the teaching of Jesus, we then turned to the content of that teaching. We began where Jesus began—by concentrating our attention first on the activity of God.

3. THE KINGDOM OF GOD

In the phrase "kingdom of God," the emphasis is on God acting as king. God is irrupting into human history and human experience, acting decisively and eschatologically to visit and to redeem. God is manifesting kingly activity toward responsive and obedient children.

Jesus used "kingdom of God" in two ways. The first usage was as in the Kaddish prayer, a prayer of the Jewish synagogue at the time of Jesus. In the Kaddish, we have a prayer that was certainly known to Jesus and to his contemporaries and frequently used by them. Jesus uses "kingdom of God" in a future sense, as does the Kaddish prayer. Second, Jesus uses "kingdom of God" with emphasis on the decisive intervention of God in human history and human experience. This is illustrated in the sayings about exorcisms, and casting out of demons, and the forgiveness of sins.

Jesus challenges people to recognize that now is the time for God to act decisively, just as they have prayed God would act in their Kaddish prayer. Jesus challenges them to recognize that God is acting in his own ministry and through him in the experience of individuals. He teaches that this activity is leading to a final blessed state of the redeemed, a perfect relationship with God, which sin cannot harm and death cannot end.

Having called attention to the activity of God manifest as king, we then turned to the major aspect of this activity in the teaching of Jesus—the forgiveness of sins.

4. THE FORGIVENESS OF SINS

In Judaism in the first century there was a very strong consciousness of sin, an expectation of hope for the messianic forgiveness of sins, and the hope that the Messiah would come with the final, eschatological forgiveness of sins. This hope excluded the gentiles because the contemporaries of Jesus believed that the gentiles had no hope. They also believed that Jews who had made themselves as gentiles—such as tax collectors—could not hope for the forgiveness of God.

In his own teaching, Jesus claims to bring the messianic forgiveness of sins; and he refuses to acknowledge the boundaries set by his contemporaries to the forgiveness. This attitude is illustrated in the call of Levi (Mark 2:13–17), the incident of the woman who was a sinner in the house of Simon the Pharisee (Luke 7:36–50), and the parable of the prodigal son (Luke 15:11–32).

5. THE FATHERLINESS OF GOD

The teaching of Jesus about the fatherliness of God is not the commonplace statement that we hear so often today. That is, Jesus is not concerned with the idea of the fatherhood of God and the brotherhood of man. He teaches about a new kind of relationship with God that is now possible for humankind. This new kind of relationship is possible because God is acting decisively as king, because of the coming of the kingdom, and because of the final forgiveness of sins.

God as Father in Greek thought has as its main feature the concept of God as physical progenitor. In Greek thought, God is Father because he has begotten humankind. But in Jewish thought the emphasis is on God as creator and God as Father—acting in a fatherly manner toward humankind. The corollary is that Israel should respond to God by acting as children toward God, honoring and obeying. But the prophets cry out that this is precisely what Israel has not done, and they point to a future period when God will so act that Israel will be able to respond as children. This was the hope for an eschatological parent-child relationship with God, a hope for the activity of God as king in human experience, enabling persons to enter into the true parent-child relationship.

Jesus teaches that he himself has this relationship with God. This is shown by the audacity of his addressing God as *abba* in prayer, a thing no other Jew would have done. Not only does Jesus address God as *abba* in his prayers, but he also teaches his disciples to do so in the Lord's Prayer. Thus he claims not only that he himself enjoys this eschatological father-son relationship with God, but that his disciples can also enter into it as they respond to what God is doing for them through him.

This is what God has done for us as we find it in the teaching of Jesus. God has manifested kingly activity, has forgiven us eschatologically, and has made possible a new kind of relationship—the true parent-child relationship. The question then is, "What do we do for God?" And the answer is that we respond to what God has done for us.

6. ETHICS AS RESPONSE

The dynamic of the ethical teaching of Jesus is response. In the Lord's Prayer we have the central petition, "forgive us our sins as we also forgive those who have sinned against us." This indicates the main concern of the ethical teaching of Jesus—we are to respond to what God has done and is doing for us. We respond to God's forgiveness by forgiving and to God's love by loving. Throughout the teaching of Jesus there is given to us consistently a series of examples of the way we can and should respond to God. This is the dynamic of the ethical teaching of Jesus—what gives it its form, its power, and what relates it to the activity of God.

7. ETHICS AND THE WILL OF GOD

The central concern of the ethical teaching of Jesus is the will of God. Jesus is regarded by his contemporaries as a rabbi, as one who interprets the will of God. But his method of interpretation is different from that of his contemporaries. For example, he has a contempt for tradition because the time for tradition is past. He has no concern for ritual cleanliness because the new relationship with God makes it unnecessary. He even rejects the specific law of Moses because the new relationship with God brings a new understanding of the will of God. This new understanding of the will of God is possible as persons seek to imitate God, to be as much like God as possible in their everyday experience.

Having discussed the activity of God, the response of humankind, and the central concern of the ethical teaching of Jesus, we turned to Christian discipleship.

8. DISCIPLESHIP

The practice of religious teachers taking disciples is widely known in Jesus' time. Thre are many rabbis and their disciples (pupils); John the Baptist and his disciples were such a group. Jesus calls out certain individuals from the group that surrounds him so that they may follow him. Not only does he call them out, he names them, not as the rabbis called their disciples, *talmid*, but he calls them *shewilya*, or "apprentice," because they are persons who will carry on and extend his ministry.

Concerning discipleship, Jesus teaches that the challenge to discipleship has a sense of immediacy and urgency. And, further, this challenge must not be answered heedlessly. The call to discipleship is also a call to conflict. Jesus called twelve disciples; this number symbolizes that the disciples are the new and true people of God.

9. JESUS AND THE FUTURE

Jesus looked toward the future. He was concerned not only with what was happening in his ministry and in the experience of those confronted by his ministry, but he was also concerned with what this would lead to. He was concerned with the Consummation of that which began in his ministry and in the experience of those confronted by his ministry.

This is revealed in the teaching about the kingdom of God. For Jesus, the kingdom of God is both present and future. He looks forward to a climax, a culmination, a Consummation of that which begins in his ministry. He does not teach how, when, or where concerning this Consummation—he simply teaches that it will come. He teaches that this future Consummation can reverse the present situation because it will be an establishment of the values of God. He teaches that the Consummation will be like a Temple not made with hands—a perfect sacral relationship with God. He teaches that the future will be a Messianic Banquet, an eternal sharing of and a participation in the blessings of God. The company of the saints of all the ages will participate in these blessings. He teaches that the Consummation is sure—as sure as the harvest time that follows the sowing of seeds. He teaches that the Consummation is the climax of discipleship. His disciples must think of themselves as being caught up in the tension between the now of the first confrontation with God and the then of the Consummation.

10. JESUS' UNDERSTANDING OF HIMSELF

New Testament scholars have moved away from the idea that Jesus claimed specifically to be the Messiah, the Son of man, or the Son of God. Instead, scholars are concerned with what is implied in his teaching on other subjects. The teaching of Jesus about the kingdom of God and the forgiveness of sins, added to his attitude toward the Jewish Law, imply very high claims. The claims were so strong that the response, "Thou art the Christ [Messiah], the son of the living God," was and is an appropriate response to make to him.

11. THE FIRST CENTURY AND THE TWENTIETH

There is a relationship between the historical Jesus and the risen Lord of our personal experience, the Christ of the church's *kerygma*. There is a continuity between these two figures. Because of this continuity, our knowledge of the teaching of Jesus constantly and consistently offers us new possibilities for faith and understanding. We do not study the teaching of Jesus simply out of academic curiosity. We study it because knowledge of the teaching of the historical

Jesus can add depth to our faith in the risen Lord of our personal experience; and, further, it reinforces our expression and living out of that faith.

B. Main Topics in the Teaching of Jesus

1. THE ACTIVITY OF GOD

First and foremost in the teaching of Jesus is his emphasis on God as active. We can see this when we compare his use of "kingdom of God" with the use his contemporaries made of this phrase. The activity of God is a major concern in first-century Jewish hope—the hope for God acting as king. But the Jews tend to use this phrase rather rarely, mainly in the Kaddish prayer and in apocalyptic literature. The contemporaries of Jesus used "kingdom of God" rarely, whereas he used it frequently.

His contemporaries spoke of the End, the days of the End, the Last Days, the Consummation, and so on. But Jesus speaks of the kingdom of God, the kingdom of God, the kingdom of God. Why? Because by using this phrase consistently, he calls attention to God's kingly activity.

Of course, to speak of the End, the days of the End, the Consummation, or the Last Days, is also to speak of God acting as king. Jesus emphasizes the kingdom of God directly and constantly, God acting as king. The hope of the Jews is based on the hope that God will act. The main claim of the teaching of Jesus is that God is acting in the exorcisms, acting to forgive sins, acting to relieve men and women of their burdens, acting to confront and to challenge them— acting as king.

One of the characteristics of biblical Hebrew is that it is almost impossible to speak of God in the abstract. Thus it is almost impossible to talk about the "love of God" in Hebrew. What one has to talk about is "God loving." In "kingdom of God," the emphasis is not on "kingship," but on God acting as king. In Jewish thought about God, God's activity is the concept expressed. The Jews thought of God as father because God acted in fatherly fashion. They were not concerned with the abstract idea of fatherhood.

The emphasis Jesus constantly makes about God's activity is a characteristic of the Old Testament. In this respect, Jesus stands firmly in the Old Testament tradition. He challenges people to come back to a true understanding of God, to realize anew the significance of their faith in God as the one who acts. But there is a new emphasis: that the hope of the Jews for God's final, decisive, eschatological activity is now realized. In the ministry of Jesus, God is acting eschatologically and decisively.

2. GOD AND HUMAN EXPERIENCE

In a careful study of Jews and Judaism at the time of Jesus, especially Jewish apocalyptic literature, one senses major contrasts between Jesus and his contemporaries. We have seen the emphasis he puts on God and God's activity. In the teaching of Jesus, this activity is particularly and peculiarly related to human experience. In Jewish apocalyptic literature there is an emphasis on the activity of God, but conceived of in numerous ways—stars falling from heaven, earthquakes, all kinds of astrological and astronomical phenomena. In apocalyptic literature there are also wars and rumors of wars, uprisings of men similar to the uprisings of nature. In other words, there is the idea that the decisive activity of God would be accompanied by suitable cosmic and terrestrial phenomena.

In the teaching of Jesus, all this has disappeared. It is remarkable that he never does talk about stars falling, earthquakes, or wars. So strangely absent is all of this from the teaching of Jesus that his disciples put it back in; so sure were they and their contemporaries that when God acted decisively, the action would be accompanied by external phenomena. They compose Mark 13 (Matthew 24, Luke 21) to make Jesus say the same thing. Mark 13 apparently represents an attempt by his disciples to describe something they feel is lacking from that teaching—the idea of God acting cosmically with external wonders and signs. There is nothing of this in the teaching of Jesus. And the absence of such things is absolutely remarkable.

If you look at Luke 17:20, 21 you find that this saying is concerned with external phenomena. The Pharisees asked Jesus for a sign that the kingdom of God was coming. In other words, they were asking him to point out the falling stars, the earthquakes, the wars and rumors of war—where are the phenomena expected to be associated with the coming of God's decisive activity? According to Luke, Jesus roundly rejects all of this: "The kingdom of God is not coming with signs to be observed." It cannot be said more plainly than that. There are to be no external phenomena—no falling stars, erupting volcanoes, no wars and rumors of wars—to be associated with the coming of God's decisive activity. It is not a matter of being able to say, "It's over there" or "Look, it's over here!" Instead of being able to point to such external phenomena, Jesus says, "the kingdom of God is in the midst of you." In other words, it is a matter of human discernment. You have to have eyes to see and ears to hear—eyes to see God acting and ears to hear God's voice. God's activity is not something you can photograph; it is not something you can put on a tape recorder, but a matter of human experience.

Not only does Jesus specifically reject the idea of external phenomena associated with the coming of the kingdom of God, he also teaches that the kingdom of God is revealed in other ways open to personal experience. God is acting as king in casting out demons, restoring shattered individuals to wholeness of mind and life. God acts as king in the forgiveness of sins—the restoration of the sinner to full personal relationship with God, the removal of the barrier between the individual and God. God acts as king in making possible the new parent-child relationship. The activity of God as king is always related to human experience in the teaching of Jesus. There is nothing external to which one can point. One has to be able to recognize God acting in human lives. In other words, one needs faith—a living relationship with the living God.

3. THE FORGIVENESS OF SINS

The activity of God related to human experience appears in two ways: the forgiveness of sins and the privilege of enjoying the eschatological parent-child relationship. The major challenge of the teaching of Jesus is the forgiveness of sins—the main thrust of his message. Many of his parables relate to this theme. They also relate to a parallel theme—the difficulty caused by his refusal to acknowledge the boundaries to the love and forgiveness of God set by his contemporaries.

There can be no doubt that Jesus accepts the Jewish understanding of sin as real, leading to estrangement from God. Jesus begins where his contemporaries are—separated from God by their sin. God is announcing through Jesus the messianic and eschatological forgiveness of sins for those who will accept his authority to make this announcement, to those who will accept the glorious good news that God is acting as king to visit and redeem people. God is now forgiving sins.

Whatever else we may say about the teaching of Jesus, whatever other help we may draw from it, we must always do justice to the fact that he is concerned above all with announcing and proclaiming and challenging his contemporaries to accept God's regal forgiveness of their sins. There can be no Christian gospel that does not begin where the preaching of Jesus began—with sin. There can be no Christian gospel that does not announce, as the preaching of Jesus announced, forgiveness. There can also be no Christian gospel that does not stress the new kind of relationship with God now possible because of this forgiveness of sins.

4. THE NEW RELATIONSHIP

The relationship that arises out of the recognition of sin and forgiveness is the eschatological parent-child relationship. Jesus uses this emphasis from the Old Testament. God acts fatherly; persons who respond as children enter into a true relationship with God. This emphasis in the teaching of Jesus is clear. He is concerned with bringing persons into that relationship with God, typified by the *abba* addressed to God in prayer. This can be characterized by the trust that can be put in God. It must be characterized by the obedience now to be shown to God.

Jesus is concerned in his teaching to stress the new relationship with God that now becomes possible. We must always do justice to this in our thinking about the teaching of Jesus. It is true that Jesus also has other concerns, such as ethics and the challenge to discipleship. But running through it all like a golden thread, always to be seen and never to be overlooked, is his constant emphasis on the relationship with God, which persons may now enjoy as they respond to the challenge of the forgiveness of sins that he announces.

Jesus emphasizes the activity of God as it is particularly and peculiarly related to human experience. The central aspect of this teaching is on the forgiveness of sins and the possibility of entering into the true parent-child relationship with God.

C. Response to the Teaching of Jesus

We turn now to the means by which persons enter into the experience of the love and forgiveness of God acting as father and as king. What are we to do in response to the teaching of Jesus?

1. RECOGNIZE WHAT IS HAPPENING

We must learn to recognize that God is indeed acting in our own personal experience. Our eyes must become opened to God and our ears tuned to hear God's voice. When we are confronted, we must learn to understand that it is God who acts. Above all, we must never let our presuppositions hinder us from hearing God's voice. Some Jewish contemporaries of Jesus were sure they knew exactly how God would act. They were good and pious men, strong in their faith. They would have died rather than deny their Lord. In many respects they were admirable and worthy of emulation, but they were overly sure of their faith and certain that they knew how God would act. They were confident that God would acknowledge the division they maintained between the faithful Jew and the Jew who had made himself as a gentile. They were sure that God would forgive the Jew, but not the Jew who had made himself as a gentile. It was probably their preconceived notion of God that prevented them from recognizing Jesus.

This human attitude always exists. Those who learn of God and learn to recognize God also tend to build up presuppositions, as others have done before them. We should not be so sure we know who God is and what God is doing that we do not recognize God in the most decisive moment of activity—self-revelation. No, we must constantly test our presuppositions, constantly stand humbly before God and ask to be taught. We must learn to seek God's presence and seek to understand our own experience in relationship to God. But we can never be sure that we know God absolutely. We can never know exactly what God will do.

2. RESPOND TO THE ACTIVITY OF GOD

As we learn to recognize the activity of God in our personal lives, we must learn to respond to that activity. This is the main thrust of the ethical teaching of Jesus. We learn to recognize God acting to forgive us; we must learn to respond by forgiving. We learn to recognize God acting toward us in love; we must learn to respond by loving. And as the parable of the good Samaritan shows, we must learn to respond by loving in accordance with the specific needs of men and women with whom we are confronted from day to day. The forgiveness and love that we know must be shown to other persons who surround us. We must learn to respond, in other words, in the immediacy of our experience, in the specific situations of our every-day lives. It is today that we must love, today that we must give to the person next door, like or dislike, love or hate. The love and forgiveness we feel from God must be expressed toward others. We enter ever more deeply into an experience of love and forgiveness by responding to it in the world in which we live and toward the persons with whom we live.

3. BE LIKE GOD

We must accept the challenge of seeking to be like God. This is the audacity of the teaching of Jesus—that we should seek to be like God as revealed to us, who is being continually revealed to us. As we experience God, we can learn what God is like. This is why we respond to forgiveness by forgiving, to love by loving, and to gifts by giving. The more we know what God is like, the more we know what we must seek to become. We experience God; we must learn to be like God. This is the supreme challenge of the teaching of Jesus. This is the way we determine what the will of God is in our specific situation. If we truly have recognized God, if we truly come to know what God is like, above all in Jesus himself, we will learn what we must do as we seek to be like God in our everyday lives, as we seek to manifest God's spirit as we live.

4. ACCEPT THE CHALLENGE OF DISCIPLESHIP

We must accept the challenge of specific discipleship. This is the parallel between the disciples of Jesus and ourselves. "Follow me," he said to them, "and I will make you fishers of men." They were to do something specific. If there is a real parallel between the ministry of Jesus and confrontation by the risen Lord of our personal experience, if there is a real parallel between discipleship in Galilee in the first century and discipleship here and now in the twentieth century, there is for us as there was for those first twelve disciples a specific challenge: the challenge to do something for our Lord.

We must seek the will of God for ourselves. We must learn what it is that we should do, where we must walk, what we must say, what God has for us to do. We must accept the challenge to be like God and accept the challenge of specific discipleship; these two are always to be held together. We must learn what it is God would have us to do and the spirit that we are to manifest as we do it. For us, the means can never justify the end. Both the means and the end must reflect God. The means must reflect God's spirit as we seek to be like God. The end that we must follow is God's will and purpose for us as revealed to us in our confrontation with God. This is the teaching of Jesus.

D. Resource Material

SCRIPTURE REFERENCES

Mark 2:13–17	Mark 13	Luke 17:20, 21
Luke 7:36–50	(Matthew 24,	Mark 3
Luke 15:11–32	Luke 21)	Mark 2

BIBLIOGRAPHY

Boers, Hendrickus. *What Is New Testament Theology? The Rise of Criticism and the Problem of a Theology of the New Testament.* Philadelphia: Fortress, 1979.

Braun, Herbert. *Jesus of Nazareth: The Man and His Time.* Philadelphia: Fortress, 1979.

Carpenter, Humphrey. *Jesus.* New York: Hill & Wang, 1980.

Davies, W. D. *The Setting of the Sermon on the Mount.* Cambridge: Cambridge University Press, 1964.

Fuller, Reginald H. *The Foundations of the New Testament Christology.* London: Lutterworth Press, 1965.

Grant, Michael. *Jesus: An Historian's Review of the Gospels.* New York: Scribner, 1977.

Jeremias, Joachim. *Jesus' Promise to the Nations.* London: SCM, 1958.

_____. *New Testament Theology: The Proclamation of Jesus.* New York: Scribner, 1971.

Martyn, J. Louis. *History and Theology in the Fourth Gospel.* New York: Harper & Row, 1968.

Marxsen, Willi. *The Resurrection of Jesus of Nazareth.* Philadelphia: Fortress, 1970.

Moltmann, Jürgen. *The Crucified God.* New York: Harper & Row, 1974.

Pannenberg, Wolfhart. *Jesus: God and Man.* Philadelphia: Westminster, 1979.

Perrin, Norman. *Jesus and the Language of the Kingdom.* Philadelphia: Fortress, 1976.

_____. *The Kingdom of God in the Teaching of Jesus.* Philadelphia: Westminster, 1963.

_____. *Rediscovering the Teaching of Jesus.* New York: Harper & Row, 1967.
Schillebeeckx, Edward. *Jesus: An Experiment in Christology.* New York: Seabury, 1979.
Tillich, Paul. *The New Being.* New York: Scribner, 1955 (esp. chaps. 10, 11, 12).

QUESTIONS

Chapter 1 What are the sources for our knowledge of the teaching of Jesus? How are the sources used to reconstruct the teaching?

Chapter 2 What are the sources for our knowledge of Jews and Judaism at the time of Jesus? How do we use our knowledge of first-century Judaism in studying the teaching of Jesus?

Chapter 3 What does "kingdom of God" mean in the teaching of Jesus?

Chapter 4 In what aspects of the teaching of Jesus do we find him claiming to bring the forgiveness of sins?

Chapter 5 Jesus taught his disciples to pray the Lord's Prayer using *abba* ("Father") to address God. What is the implication of the use of *abba*?

Chapter 6 "The ethical teaching of Jesus is designed to illustrate the response by means of which we enter ever more deeply into the experience of that which is offered to us by God." This is a statement from the chapter; illustrate what the statement means, using the teaching of Jesus from the synoptic gospels.

Chapter 7 "In his ethical teaching, Jesus was more concerned with the 'attitude' and less concerned with external activity than were his contemporaries." This is a statement from the chapter. Does the statement do justice to the difference between the ethical teaching of Jesus and his contemporaries?

Chapter 8 According to the teaching of Jesus, what is the particular responsibility of a Christian disciple?

Chapter 9 Do you believe that there is a future element in the teaching of Jesus based on the kingdom of God? If your answer is yes, how would you interpret the teaching?

Chapter 10 To what extent and in what ways did Jesus claim to be the Messiah?

Chapter 11 Does knowledge of the teaching of the historical Jesus have any relevance to Christian faith in the twentieth century? Explain.

Chapter 12 What are the major themes in the teaching of Jesus?

AFTERWORD

Norman Perrin died before this book was written. His death was most unfortunate, because his stature as a scholar and his vitality as a person would have contributed a great deal to the writing of this book. Because Norman died nearly six years before the completion of this book, he cannot be held responsible for its final form, since he had no opportunity to read any of the manuscript. The world of New Testament scholarship has been prematurely deprived of his future contributions to biblical knowledge.

Norman is important to me because I was his student, friend, and colleague. He and I became very close when he came to Emory University just after finishing his doctoral studies at Göttingen University in Germany. At Emory he made a strong impression on the students, and his courses were extremely popular. He delivered forceful and entrancing lectures. He especially entertained himself and his students when his research had uncovered something important to him. At such times he would prance around at the front of his classroom, limping slightly on his lame leg, often speaking in several different languages without realizing it.

He was not a meek person, although he was gentle in spirit and compassionate. When he was involved in an argument about something new he had learned, he could hold his own in an academic debate. Fellow students in London, Manchester, and especially at Göttingen set up fierce arguments with him to see how long his knowledge would last. These exercises trained his brain well, but they also made an academic animal out of him. At times, he could really be arrogant.

We had had many similar experiences on each side of the Atlantic. Each of us had spent about the same amount of time in military service. Because he was more than a decade older than I, his time in the Royal Air Force had taken him to North Africa in World War II, while my service in the U.S. Air Force had taken me to the Far East during the Korean War—called the Korean "conflict" back then.

Since both of us had bumped up against rough times early in our lives, we had many, many things in common, including being shot at, wounded, and scared half to death. Norm had spent much of his military time in the desert, sitting on a footlocker learning languages—German, French, Syriac, Coptic—and brushing up on his knowledge of Aramaic, Hebrew, Latin, and Greek. I had spent my spare time in the military teaching English, studying religion, and absorbing Oriental culture, which I found a pleasant contrast to my Western ways.

Becoming a naturalized citizen in the United States was a major thrill for Norman. He was proud of his citizenship and told me that next to his ordination service, the naturalization ceremony was the highlight of his life. These feelings came from a passionate love for America that was pure and unashamed, old-fashioned patriotism.

Actually, he was a citizen of the world, at home in any country, especially in the major cities of the world. He liked Chicago, where he was living and teaching at the time he died. He visited often in New York while I was doing graduate studies at Union Theological Seminary and Columbia University. A perfect day for him on vacation in New York would be to study and read for several hours, soak up art in a museum downtown, see a Broadway production, then relish a leisurely seven-course dinner. He was a great teller of stories. His British accent was hypnotizing, and after-dinner stories rolled from his memory like a flowing stream of water. I often wondered if his sensitivity to religion, which caused him to appreciate intricacies of the human predicament, had given him his unusual powers as a raconteur. I should have asked him about that while I had the chance.

Neither Norm nor I was particularly interested in what Jesus said or what he meant for purely academic reasons. Although much of this work employs historical and critical methodology, its writing was motivated by a commitment to the Christ of faith. Both of us will confess—I will say it now on Norm's behalf—we believe in Jesus Christ. If that belief colored our convictions, obscured our necessary scholastic detachment, or prejudged the outcome of this study, we cannot apologize.

Subject matter at this level of personal sensitivity cannot be approached merely as information. The teaching of Jesus is a special kind of information, not to be tampered with or entered into lightly. For this reason we wrote from conviction, from our own personal experience, and with a desire to analyze what we believe and why. In short, Christians study, organize, and write from within the community of faith.

In this community, it is understood that to be a Christian implies a great deal. If you call yourself "Christian," that adjective qualifies your existence. That label does not mean you are limited, but that you have drawn some boundaries around your life and accepted some commitments and conditions on how you will live your life. It also means that there comes a time in your reflective thinking when you decide whether you are truly a Christian—truly believe—or not. The Christian faith won't let us take ultimate reality lightly. And the more knowledge we develop, the more meaningful the Christian faith becomes to us. Anselm called this process "faith seeking understanding." I believe he was right.

I would be ungrateful not to thank everyone who helped me to get this book into its final form. Many persons assisted me in the shaping and development of the research materials. Close friends read the manuscript and helped with many suggestions. Many of these people gave their time to show their appreciation of Norman Perrin, their respect for him, and because of their fond memories of him. They also willingly gave their abilities, time, and energy because of Jesus Christ.

David Abernathy
Connelly Springs, North Carolina
June 27, 1982

AUTHENTIC SAYINGS
OF JESUS

by David Abernathy

Introduction

The sayings of Jesus presented in the gospels are a portion of the narrative format the evangelists used in presenting the story of Jesus and his teaching. The synoptic gospels represent not only at least twenty or thirty years of oral tradition before their appearance in written form as teaching and preaching documents; they also present the theology and literary orientation of the evangelists who wrote them. Matthew, Mark, and Luke are teaching and preaching documents produced by the early Christian believers for interpreting the faith, defending doctrine, and evangelizing new members.

The discovery of the Coptic gospel of Thomas, showing sayings of Jesus without any connecting narratives, revealed the starkness of the sayings themselves. Any reader accustomed to Western civilization, literature, and thought forms, readily sees in the 114 sayings of the gospel of Thomas a foreign quality of expression. Without the familiar narrative format of the canonical gospels, the individual sayings of Jesus take on their natural, Eastern quality. Except for the major parables, the sayings leave the reader with an empty feeling because the barren and isolated teachings create a feeling of mystery about their meaning.

Some of that same quality of the gospel of Thomas is felt in reading the teaching of Jesus as the evangelists present it after it is stripped of connecting narrative and reduced to the brevity the collection of authentic sayings displays. The sayings then are like unstrung pearls. They are not at all self-explanatory, appearing to be more like riddles

203

than disclosures of great truth through teaching. One needs to have a proper orientation for these statements of Jesus—in first-century Palestine. The sayings were originally spoken in Galilean Aramaic (most likely), written in Greek, then translated into English. Also, the sayings probably represent only a portion of the oral teaching given to disciples by Jesus of Nazareth, who uttered them in the first century of our era.

It is quite likely that the teachings contained in the canonical gospels are not all the teachings Jesus offered. However, there is little doubt that the teaching presented in the three forms by Matthew, Mark, and Luke do represent what the early Christian church considered significant enough to preserve and use for purposes of instruction and preaching. No one will likely ever say with absolute certainty what sayings included in the gospels are the *ipsissima verba,* or "actual words," that issued forth from the lips of Jesus. Unfortunately, there are no eyewitness accounts of the teaching of Jesus, just as there are no audiotapes of his sayings or videotapes of his ministry in Galilee. So, in the absence of any literal recordings, we must be content to deal with what the early church chose to preserve in the form in which the gospel writers elected to present the teaching of Jesus. The gospels are, of course, postresurrection documents— written in the setting of faith in Jesus as Messiah, as Christ, and as Lord. They are faith documents, witnessing to the meaning of the teaching of the historical Jesus, accepted as holy and sacred history with the saving power of the God of Abraham, Isaac, and Jacob.

The criteria for determining the authentic teaching of Jesus are fully stated earlier in this book; they have also been stated before by Norman Perrin in his other works. Here is a brief summary of the criteria, commonly understood to be the result of the redaction-critical approach to interpreting the scriptures. This approach builds on the results of more than a century of New Testament scholarship and interpretation.

After following procedures of form criticism as set out by Rudolf Bultmann in *The History of the Synoptic Tradition* and Joachim Jeremias in *The Parables of Jesus,* the principles of redaction criticism as devised by Norman Perrin, Willi Marxsen, and Reginald Fuller are followed.

The criteria used for determining authentic sayings are: first, the criterion of *dissimilarity,* meaning that a saying must be known to be dissimilar to Judaism before Jesus and the early Christian church formed after his death. The second criterion is that of *multiple attestation,* which means that material is accepted as authentic if it appears in multiple forms or sources, unless that material has not been unduly influenced by practices of the early church. The third criterion is that of *coherence*, or material consistent with authentic material clearly established by the other criteria (for further explanation, see Perrin, *What is Redaction Criticism?*, or Fuller, *A Critical Introduction to the New Testament*).

In addition to my own paraphrase in contemporary American English, I have included in parentheses the relevant Old Testament passages related to the sayings of Jesus. Jesus quoted scripture extensively; in some cases, the references indicate a new interpretation of the Law of Moses, or Torah, and in other cases the scripture is somewhat related and merely informative. No attempt is made to differentiate, since the purpose of reproducing the sayings in this format is primarily to allow the reader to encounter the teaching in as direct a manner as possible. The gospel-of-Thomas parallels have been included, not as an attestation as to their authenticity, but because of their unfamiliarity for many readers. These parallels with their similarities and differences are, of course, an interesting study in themselves.

The authentic sayings fall into four general categories. The first, singularly important, is the Lukan version of the Lord's Prayer. As professor Jeremias has pointed out, the uncharacteristic use of *abba* in addressing God is unparallelled in the Judaism of the first century. Compared with prayers taught their disciples by other rabbis, this one characteristic sets this prayer apart so distinctively that one can and should draw major theological implications from it, especially the relationship with God implied by Jesus in the use of *abba*. The audacity of the teaching of Jesus lies in his using *abba* to address God in prayer and implying that we may do the same.

The three Kingdom of God sayings in the second category are not the only kingdom sayings in Jesus' teaching, but they are indisputably authentic as Norman Perrin points out in *The Kingdom of God in the Teaching of Jesus*.

The third category of proverbial sayings includes many references to the kingdom of God, but are slightly different from the sayings devoted to the kingdom only. References to the kingdom are numerous: both in the authentic sayings and in the various levels of tradition preserved in the gospels it represents by volume the largest element in Jesus' teaching. It appears that teaching about the kingdom of God was a primary part of his message and was perceived as such by his hearers. The overall teaching as we have it could be summarized succinctly: Jesus came proclaiming the kingdom of God, announcing the messianic forgiveness of sins in his ministry, and claiming that a new relationship with God did in fact exist in the present and would continue in the future.

The fourth category of sayings is the major parables of Jesus. Joachim Jeremias has made a most important contribution to understanding these parables in their historical setting in first century Judaism. His pioneering efforts have enabled numerous scholars to deal with their interpretation in a remarkably fresh way, as well as leading us to understand them as they were presented historically. So, a study of Jeremias' *Parables of Jesus* is indispensable. In addition, there are two other directions indicated for the serious student of parabolic sayings, including those apparently uttered by Jesus. In the one direction, the work of such scholars as Dan Via and others should be investigated—work by serious theologians dealing with the typology and form of parables, the kind of sayings these utterances are and come to represent. In the other and broader direction, theologians, philosophers, and biblical scholars deal with the kind of reality involved in communicating about God in human language. To mention a few names at random, one would include the eminent biblical New Testament scholar James M. Robinson, along with Amos N. Wilder and William Baird, and other hermeneutical specialists such as Edgar V. McKnight, and John Macquarrie.

Read these sayings and let the words of Jesus speak directly to you. Imagine for a moment that you are in first-century Palestine, hearing them for the first time from this teacher.

I
The Lord's Prayer

When you pray, say: Father, hallowed be your name. May your kingdom come. Give us each day our daily bread. And forgive us our sins as we ourselves forgive every one who is indebted to us. And lead us not into temptation. Luke 11:2–4 (cf. Matthew 6:9)

II
The Kingdom of God

1. From the days of John the Baptist until now, the kingdom of heaven has suffered violence, and men of violence take it by force. Matthew 11:12 (see also Malachi 3:1)

2. But if it is by the finger (power) of God that I cast out demons, then the kingdom of God has come upon you. Luke 11:20 (see also Ezekiel 8:19, 31:8)

3. The kingdom of God is not coming with signs to be observed; nor will people say "Lo, here it is!" or "There!" The kingdom of God is in your midst. Luke 17:20, 21

III
Proverbs

1. Do not resist one who is evil. If any one strikes you on the right cheek, turn the other to him also. If any one would sue you and take your coat, let him have your cloak as well. If any one forces you to go one mile, go with him two miles. Matthew 5:39b–41

2. Love your enemies and pray for those who persecute you so that you may be sons of your heavenly father. God makes the sun rise on the evil and the good, and sends rain on the just and on the unjust.

If you love only those who love you, what reward have you? Do not even the tax collectors do the same?

And if you greet only people like yourself, what more are you doing than others? Do not even the gentiles do the same?

You, therefore, must be perfect, as your heavenly father is perfect. Matthew 5:44–48 (see also Leviticus 11:44, 45; 19:2; 20:26)

3. Enter by the narrow gate. The wide gate and the easy way lead to destruction and those who enter by it are many. The narrow gate and the hard way lead to life, and few people find it. Matthew 7:13, 14

4. If a kingdom is divided against itself, that kingdom cannot stand.

And if a house is divided against itself, that house will not be able to stand.

And if Satan has risen up against himself and is divided, he cannot stand, but is coming to an end. Mark 3:24–26

5. No one can enter a strong man's house and plunder his goods unless he first binds the strong man; then indeed he may plunder his house. Mark 3:27 (see also Isaiah 49:24)

6. There is nothing outside a person which by going into that person can make him/her ritually unclean. The things which come out of a person are what make that person ritually unclean. Mark 7:15

7. Whoever would save his/her life will lose it. Whoever loses his/her life for my sake and for the sake of the gospel will save it. Mark 8:35

8. Whoever does not receive the kingdom of God like a child will not enter it. Mark 10:15

9. How hard it will be for those who have riches to enter the kingdom of God. Mark 10:23b

10. It is easier for a camel to go through the eye of a needle than for a rich person to enter the kingdom of God. Mark 10:25

11. Many who are now first will be last, and the last, first. Mark 10:31

12. Leave the dead to bury their own dead. As for you, go and proclaim the kingdom of God. Luke 9:60

13. People who put their hands to the plow and look back are not fit for the kingdom of God. Luke 9:62

14. Those who exalt themselves will be humbled. Those who humble themselves will be exalted. Luke 14:11

15. You are included among those who justify yourselves before people, but God knows your hearts. What is exalted among people is an abomination in the sight of God. Luke 16:15 (see also 1 Samuel 16:7; 1 Chronicles 28:9; Proverbs 21:2, 24:12)

IV
Parables

1. THE CHILDREN IN THE MARKETPLACE

But to what shall I compare this generation? It is like children sitting in the market places and calling to their playmates:

"We played music for you, but you did not dance;
We sang sad songs but you did not cry."

John came neither eating nor drinking and they say, "He is possessed." The Son of man came eating and drinking and they say, "Behold, a glutton and a drunkard, a friend of tax collectors and sinners!"

The truth speaks for itself. Matthew 11:16–19 (see also Luke 7:31–35)

2. THE HIDDEN TREASURE AND THE PEARL OF GREAT PRICE

The kingdom of heaven is like treasure hidden in a field which a man found and covered up. Then—in his joy—he goes and sells all he has and buys that field.

Likewise, the kingdom of heaven is like a merchant in search of fine pearls, who, on finding one pearl of great value, went and sold all that he had and bought it. Matthew 13:44–46 (see also Proverbs 2:4)

3. THE UNMERCIFUL SERVANT

The kingdom of heaven may be compared to a king who wished to settle accounts with his servants. When he began counting, one servant was brought to him who owed him a million dollars. Since the servant could not pay, the king ordered him to be sold with his wife and children and all he had in order to make the payment. So the servant fell on his knees, imploring him, "Lord, have patience with me and I will pay you everything." And out of pity for him the lord of that servant released him and forgave him the debt.

But that same servant, as he was leaving, came upon one of his fellow servants who owed him several hundred dollars. Grabbing him by the throat he said, "Pay me what you owe me." So his fellow servant fell down and begged him, "Have patience with me and I will pay you." He refused and had him put in prison until he paid the debt.

When his fellow servants saw what had happened, they were greatly distressed and they went and reported to their lord all that had taken place.

Then the lord summoned him and said to him, "You wicked servant! I forgave you all that debt because you begged me. Should you not have had mercy on your fellow servant, just as I had mercy on you?"

And in anger his lord delivered him to the jailers until he paid all his debt.

So my heavenly father will be to every one of you if you do not forgive your brother from your heart. Matthew 18:23–35

4. THE WORKERS IN THE VINEYARD

The kingdom of heaven is like a landowner who went out early in the morning to hire laborers for his vineyard. After agreeing with the laborers for a silver coin a day, he sent them into his vineyard.

Going out again about 9 A.M., he saw others standing idle in the market place. To them he said, "You go into the vineyard too and whatever is right I will give you." So they went. Going out again about noon and 3 P.M., he did the same.

And about 5 P.M. he went out and found others standing around. He said to them, "Why do you stand here idle all day?" They said to him, "Because no one has hired us." He said to them, "You go into the vineyard too."

When evening came the owner of the vineyard said to his steward, "Call the laborers and pay them their wages, beginning with the last, up to the first."

And when those hired about 5 P.M. came, each of them received a silver coin. When the first ones to be hired came, they thought they would receive more, but each of them also received a silver coin. And on receiving it, they grumbled at the landowner, saying, "These last worked only one hour and you have made them equal to us who have borne the burden of the day and the scorching heat."

But he replied to one of them, "Friend, I am doing you no wrong; did you not agree with me for a silver coin? Take what belongs to you and go. I choose to give to these last ones as I give to you. Am I not allowed to do what I choose with what belongs to me? Or do you begrudge my generosity?"

So the last will be first, and the first, last. Matthew 20:1–16 (Note: A *denarius*, translated here by "silver coin," was the customary wage for a day's labor.)

5. THE TWO SONS

What do you think?

A man had two sons. He went to the first and said, "Son, go and work in the vineyard today." And he answered, "I will not." But later he changed his mind and went.

And the man went to the second son and said the same. He answered, "I go, sir." But he did not go.

Which of the two sons did the will of his father?

The first son.

Truly, I say to you, the tax collectors and prostitutes go into the kingdom of God before you. John came to you to show you how to live and you did not believe him. But the tax collectors and the harlots believed him. And even when you saw the way of righteousness, you did not later change and believe him. Matthew 21:28–32

6. THE GREAT SUPPER

The kingdom of heaven may be compared to a king who gave a marriage feast for his son and sent his servants to call those who were invited to the marriage feast. But the invited guests would not come.

He sent other servants, saying, "Tell those who are invited I have made ready my dinner, my oxen and my fat calves are killed, and everything is ready; come to the marriage feast."

But they paid no attention and went off, one to his farm, another to his business, while the rest seized his servants, treated them brutally, and killed them.

The king was angry. He sent his troops and destroyed those murderers and burned their city.

Then he said to his servants, "The wedding is ready, but those invited were not worthy. Go therefore to the thoroughfares and invite to the marriage feast as many as you find." And those servants went out into the streets and gathered all they found, both bad and good; so the wedding hall was filled with guests.

But when the king came in to look at the guests, he saw one man who had no wedding garment. He said to him, "Friend, how did you get in here without a wedding garment?" And he was speechless. Then the king said to the attendants, "Bind him hand and foot and throw him outside into the darkness; there people will weep and gnash their teeth."

Many are called but few are chosen. Matthew 22:1–14

Compare with:

A man once gave a great banquet and invited many guests. When the time came for the banquet he sent his servant to say to those who had been invited, "Come, for all is now ready." But they all began to make excuses. The first said to him, "I have bought a field and I must go out and see it; I pray you, have me excused." Another said, "I have bought five yoke of oxen and I must go to examine them; I pray you, have me excused." And another said, "I have married a wife and therefore I cannot come." So the servant came and reported this to his master.

Then the householder in anger said to his servant, "Go out quickly to the streets and lanes of the city and bring in the poor and maimed and blind and lame." And the servant said, "Sir, what you commanded has already been done and there is still room."

And the master said to the servant, "Go out to the highways and hedges and compel people to come in so that my house may be filled. For I tell you, none of those who were invited shall taste my banquet." Luke 14:16–24

Compare with:

A man had received visitors. When he had prepared the dinner, he sent his servant to invite the guests.

The servant went to the first one and said, "My master invites you." The guest said, "I have claims against some merchants. They are coming to me this evening. I must go and give them my orders. I ask to be excused from the dinner."

The servant went to another guest and said, "My master has invited you." The guest replied, "I have just bought a house and am required for the day. I shall not have any spare time."

The servant went to another guest and said, "My master invites you." The guest answered, "My friend is going to get married and I am to prepare the banquet. I will not be able to come. I ask to be excused from the dinner."

The servant went to another guest and said, "My master invites you." The guest replied, "I have just bought a farm and I am on my way to collect the rent. I shall not be able to come. I ask to be excused."

The servant returned and said to his master, "Those whom you invited to the dinner have asked to be excused."

The master said to his servant, "Go outside to the streets and bring back those whom you happen to meet so that they may dine."

Businessmen and merchants will not enter the places of my Father. Thomas 64

7. THE SOWER

Listen!

A sower went out to sow. And as he sowed, some seed fell along the path and the birds came and ate it.

Other seed fell on rocky ground without much soil, and immediately it sprang up since it had no depth of soil. When the sun rose, it was scorched, and since it had no root, it withered away.

Other seed fell among thorns; the thorns grew up and choked it and it yielded no grain.

And other seeds fell into good soil and brought forth grain, growing up, increasing and yielding thirtyfold, sixtyfold, and a hundredfold. Mark 4:3–8 (see also Matthew 13:3–9; Luke 8:5–8)

Compare with:

A sower went out, took a handful of seeds, and scattered them. Some fell on the road and the birds came and gathered them up.

Others fell on rock and did not take root in the soil and did not produce ears.

And others fell on thorns which choked the seeds and worms ate them.

And others fell on the good soil and produced good fruit; it bore sixty per measure and a hundred and twenty per measure. Thomas 9

8. THE SEED GROWING BY ITSELF

The kingdom of God is like a person scattering seed on the ground, sleeping and rising night and day; the seed sprouts and grows without the person knowing how.

The earth produces by itself—first the blade, then the ear; then the full grain in the ear. When the grain is ripe the person reaps because the harvest has come. Mark 4:26–29

9. THE MUSTARD SEED

With what can we compare the kingdom of God, or what parable shall we use for it?

It is like a grain of mustard seed which, when sown on the ground, is the smallest of all the seeds on earth. Yet, when it is sown, it grows up and becomes the largest of all shrubs and puts forth such large branches that the birds can make nests in its shade. Mark 4:30–32 (see also Matthew 13:31, 32; Luke 13:18, 19)

Compare with:

(The kingdom of Heaven) is like a mustard seed, the smallest of all seeds. But when it falls on tilled soil, it produces a great plant and becomes a shelter for birds. Thomas 20

10. THE WICKED TENANTS

A man planted a vineyard, put a hedge around it, dug a pit for the wine press, built a tower, let the vineyard out to tenants, and went to another country.

When harvest time came, he sent a servant to the tenants to get some of the fruit of the vineyard from them. The tenants took the servant, beat him, and sent him away empty handed.

Again, he sent another servant to the tenants. They wounded him in the head and treated him shamefully. He sent another servant and the tenants killed him. And he sent many others, some of which they beat and some of which they killed.

The owner of the vineyard then had only one person left to send, a beloved son. Finally he sent him to the tenants, saying, "They will respect my son." But those tenants said to one another, "This is the heir. Come, let us kill him and the inheritance will be ours." And they took the son and killed him, throwing him out of the vineyard.

What will the owner of the vineyard do? He will come and destroy the tenants and give the vineyard to others. Have you not read this scripture: "The very stone which the builders rejected has become the cornerstone; this was the Lord's doing and it is marvelous in our eyes." Mark 12:1–12 (see also Psalm 118:22, 23; Matthew 21:33; Luke 20:9; Isaiah 5:1, 2)

Compare with:

There was a good man who owned a vineyard. He leased it to tenant farmers so they could work it and he would be able to collect the produce from them.

He sent his servant so the tenants could give him the produce from the vineyard. The tenants seized his servant and beat him, almost killing him. The servant went back and told his master. The master said, "Perhaps they did not recognize him."

He sent another servant. The tenants beat this one as well.

Then the owner sent his son and said, "Perhaps they will show respect to my son." Because the tenants knew the son was the heir to the vineyard, they seized him and killed him.

Let those who have ears hear. Thomas 65

11. THE GOOD SAMARITAN

A man was going down from Jerusalem to Jericho and he fell among robbers who stripped him, beat him, and left him half dead.

By chance a priest was going down that road. When he saw him he passed by on the other side.

Likewise a Levite, when he came to the place and saw him, passed by on the other side.

But a Samaritan, as he traveled, came to where he was. When he saw him he had compassion and went to him and bound up his wounds, pouring on oil and wine. Then he sat him back on his own beast and brought him to an inn and took care of him. The next day he took out two silver coins and gave them to the innkeeper, saying, "Take care of him. Whatever else you spend I will repay you when I come back."

Which of these three, do you think, proved neighbor to the man who fell among the robbers?

"The one who showed mercy on him."

Go and do likewise. Luke 10:29–37

12. THE FRIEND AT MIDNIGHT

Which of you who has a friend will go to this friend at midnight and say, "Friend, lend me some bread; a friend of mine has arrived on a journey and I have nothing to set before him." The friend will answer from inside, "Do not bother me; the door is now shut and my children are with me in bed. I cannot get up and give you anything."

I tell you, though he will not get up and give him anything because he is his friend, yet because of his persistence he will rise and give him whatever he needs. Luke 11:5–8

13. THE LEAVEN

To what shall I compare the kingdom of God? It is like leaven which a woman took and put into a bushel of flour until all of it was leavened. Luke 13:20, 21 (see also Matthew 13:33; Daniel 4:21)

Compare with:

The kingdom of the father is like a certain woman. She took a little bit of leaven, put it in some dough, and made it into large loaves. Let those who have ears hear. Thomas 96

14. THE TOWER BUILDER AND THE KING GOING TO WAR

Which of you, wanting to build a tower, does not first sit down and count the cost—whether you have enough to complete it? Otherwise, when you have laid a foundation and are not able to finish, all who see it will begin to mock you, saying, "This man began to build and was not able to finish."

Or what king, going to encounter another king in war, will not first sit down and decide whether he is able with ten thousand to meet one who comes against him with twenty thousand? And if not, while the other is still a great way off, he sends an ambassador and asks for terms of peace.

So therefore, those of you who do not give up all that you have cannot be my disciple. Luke 14:28–34 (see also Matthew 10:37, 38; 16:24; 8:34; Luke 9:23)

15. THE LOST SHEEP and THE LOST COIN

What person among you with a hundred sheep, if you have lost one of them, would not leave the ninety-nine in the wilderness and go after the one that is lost until you find it? And when you have found it, lay it on your shoulders, rejoicing. And when you come home, call together your friends and neighbors, saying to them, "Rejoice with me, for I have found my sheep which was lost."

Just so, I tell you, there will be more joy in heaven over one sinner who repents than over ninety-nine righteous persons who need no repentance.

Or what woman, having ten silver pieces, if she loses one coin, does not light a lamp and sweep the house and seek diligently until she finds it? And when she has found it, she calls together her friends and neighbors, saying, "Rejoice with me, for I have found the coin which I had lost."

Just so, I tell you, there is joy before the angels of God over one sinner who repents. Luke 15:4–10

16. THE PRODIGAL SON

There was a man who had two sons. The younger of them said to his father, "Father, give me the share of property that falls to me."

And the father divided his possessions between the two sons.

Not many days later, the younger son gathered all he had and went to a far country where he squandered his property in loose living.

When he had spent everything, there was a great famine in that country and he began to be in want. So he went and joined himself to one of the citizens of that country who sent him into the fields to feed swine. He would gladly have fed on the pods that the swine ate; no one gave him anything.

But when he came to himself he said, "How many of my father's hired servants have bread enough and some to spare, but I am here, starving from hunger! I will rise and go to my father and I will say to him, 'Father, I have sinned against heaven and against you. I am no longer worthy to be called your son; treat me as one of your hired servants.'"

He returned home. While he was still at a distance, his father saw him and had compassion, and ran and embraced him and kissed him. And the son said to him, "Father, I have sinned against heaven and against you; I am no longer worthy to be your son."

But the father said to his servants, "Bring quickly the best robe and put it on him; put a ring on his hand and shoes on his feet; bring the fatted calf and kill it and let us eat and make merry; for my son was dead and is alive again; he was lost and is found."

And they began to make merry.

His elder son was in the fields. As he came near to the house he heard music and dancing. He called one of his servants and asked what this meant. And he said to him, "Your brother has come and your father has killed the fatted calf because he has received him safe and sound." But he was angry and refused to go in.

His father came out and begged him, but he answered his father, "For many years I have served you and never disobeyed you. Yet you never gave me a kid so I could make merry with my friends. But when this son of yours came who has squandered your money with harlots, you killed the fatted calf for him!"

And he said to him, "Son, you are always with me and all that is mine is yours. It was fitting to make merry and be glad, because your brother was dead and is now alive; he was lost and now is found." Luke 15:11–32 (see also Genesis 41:42; Deuteronomy 21:16; Proverbs 29:3)

17. THE UNJUST STEWARD

There was a rich man who had a manager; charges were brought to him that this man was wasting his goods. And he called him and said to him, "What is this that I hear about you? Give me a final report on your management of my affairs; you can no longer be manager."

And the manager said to himself, "What will I do, since my master is taking the management away from me? I am not strong enough to dig and I am ashamed to beg. I have decided what to do so that people may receive me into their houses after I am put out of my position."

Summoning his master's debtors one by one, he said to the first, "How much do you owe my master?" He said, "A hundred measures of oil." And he said to him, "Take your bill, and sit down quickly and write fifty." Then he said to another, "And how much do you owe?" He said, "A hundred measures of wheat." He said to him, "Take your bill, and write eighty."

The master commended the dishonest manager for his shrewdness because the children of this world are more shrewd in dealing with their own kind than the children of light.

And I tell you, make friends for yourself by means of unrighteous money so that when it fails, they may receive you into the eternal habitations. Luke 16:1–9

18. THE UNJUST JUDGE

In a certain city there was a judge who neither feared God nor respected man. There was a widow in that city who kept coming to him and saying, "Help me against my adversary."

For a while he refused. But afterward he said to himself, "Though I neither fear God nor respect man, yet because this widow bothers me I will help her or she will wear me out by her continual coming."

Hear what the unrighteous judge says. And will not God help people who cry for help day and night? Will God be slow to help them? I tell you, God will judge in their favor speedily. But when the son of man comes, will he find faith on earth? Luke 18:1–8

19. THE PHARISEE AND THE TAX COLLECTOR

Two men went up into the temple to pray, one a pharisee and the other a tax collector.

The pharisee stood and prayed, "God, I thank you that I am not like other men—extortioners, unjust, adulterers, or even like this tax collector. I fast twice a week, I give tithes of all that I get."

But the tax collector, standing far off, would not even lift up his eyes to heaven, but beat his chest, saying, "God, be merciful to me, a sinner!"

I tell you, this man went down to his house right with God rather than the pharisee.

Every one who exalts himself will be humbled, but he who humbles himself will be exalted. Luke 18:9–14 (see also Ezra 9:6)

BIBLIOGRAPHY

Baird, William. *The Quest of the Christ of Faith.* Waco, Tex.: Word Books, 1977.

Bultmann, Rudolf. *The History of the Synoptic Tradition.* New York: Harper & Row, 1963.

Fuller, Reginald. *A Critical Introduction to the New Testament.* Naperville, Ill.: Allenson, 1966.

Jeremias, Joachim. *The Parables of Jesus.* London: SCM, 1958.

Lapide, Pinchas. *Israelis, Jews and Jesus.* New York: Doubleday, 1979.

May, Herbert G., and Metzger, Bruce M., eds. *The New Oxford Annotated Bible with the Apocrypha.* New York: Oxford University Press, 1977.

McKnight, Edgar V. *Meaning in Texts: The Historical Shaping of a Narrative Hermeneutics.* Philadelphia: Fortress, 1978.

Nickle, Keith F. *The Synoptic Gospels.* Atlanta: John Knox, 1980.

Perrin, Norman. *Jesus and the Language of the Kingdom.* Philadelphia: Fortress, 1976.

_____. *The Kingdom of God in the Teaching of Jesus.* Philadelphia: Westminster, 1963.

_____. *A Modern Pilgrimage in New Testament Christology.* Philadelphia: Fortress, 1974.

_____. *The New Testament: An Introduction.* New York: Harcourt Brace Jovanovich, 1974.

_____. *The Promise of Bultmann.* Philadelphia: Fortress, 1979.

_____. *Rediscovering the Teaching of Jesus.* New York: Harper & Row, 1967.

_____. *The Resurrection According to Matthew, Mark and Luke.* Philadelphia: Fortress, 1977.

_____. *What is Redaction Criticism?* Rev. ed. Philadelphia: Fortress, 1970.

Talbert, Charles H. *What is a Gospel?* Philadelphia: Fortress, 1977.

Vermès, Géza. *Jesus the Jew: A Historian's Reading of the Gospels.* New York: Macmillan, 1974.

GLOSSARY INDEX

The numbers in parentheses refer to chapters.

INDEX OF
SCRIPTURE REFERENCES

Each passage that has been discussed in the text is listed below. The numbers in parentheses refer to the chapter in which the scripture was mentioned.

The Old Testament

The New Testament

The Apocrypha

Other Writings

BIBLIOGRAPHY

Anderson, Charles C. *The Historical Jesus: A Continuing Quest.* Grand Rapids: Eerdmans, 1972.

Aulen, Gustaf. *Jesus in Contemporary Historical Research.* Philadelphia: Fortress, 1976.

Baird, William. *The Quest of the Christ of Faith.* Waco: Word Books, 1977.

Barrett, C. K. *The New Testament Background: Selected Documents.* New York: Harper & Row, Torchbooks, 1961.

Beardslee, William A. *Literary Criticism of the New Testament.* Philadelphia: Fortress, 1975.

Boers, Hendrickus. *What is New Testament Theology? The Rise of Criticism and the Problem of a Theology of the New Testament.* Philadelphia: Fortress, 1979.

Bornkamm, Günther. *Jesus of Nazareth.* 3rd ed. New York: Harper & Brothers, 1960.

_____. *The New Testament: A Guide to its Writings.* Philadelphia: Fortress, 1973.

Braun, Herbert. *Jesus of Nazareth: The Man and His Time.* Philadelphia: Fortress, 1979.

Bruce, F. F. *History of the Bible in English.* New York: Oxford University Press, 1978.

Bultmann, Rudolf. *The History of the Synoptic Tradition.* New York: Harper & Row, 1963.

_____. *Jesus and the Word.* New York: Scribner, 1958.

Cameron, Ron. *The Other Gospels.* Philadelphia: Westminster Press, 1982.

Carpenter, Humphrey. *Jesus.* New York: Hill & Wang, 1980.

Cartlidge, David R., and Dungan, David L. *Documents for the Study of the Gospels.* Philadelphia: Fortress, 1980.

Connick, C. Milo. *Jesus: The Man, the Mission and the Message.* 2d ed. Englewood Cliffs, N.J.: Prentice-Hall, 1974.

Cross, Frank M., Jr. *Ancient Library of Qumran and Modern Biblical Studies.* New York: Doubleday, Anchor, 1961.

Crossan, John Dominic. *Cliffs of Fall: Paradox and Polyvalence in the Parables of Jesus.* New York: Seabury, 1980.

_____. *Finding Is the First Act.* Philadelphia: Fortress, 1979.

_____. *In Parables.* New York: Harper & Row, 1973.

228

Danby, Herbert, ed. and trans. *The Mishnah.* London: Oxford University Press, 1958.

Davies, W. D. *The Setting of the Sermon on the Mount.* Cambridge: Cambridge University Press, 1964.

De Lange, Nicholas. *Apocrypha: Jewish Literature of the Hellenistic Age.* New York: Viking Press, 1978.

Detwiler, Robert. *Story, Sign and Self: Phenomenology and Structuralism as Literary-Critical Methods.* Philadelphia: Fortress, 1978.

Dodd, C. H. *The Parables of the Kingdom.* Rev. ed. New York: Scribner, 1961.

Drane, John. *Jesus and the Four Gospels.* New York: Harper & Row, 1979.

Dupont-Sommer, André. *The Essene Writings from Qumran.* New York: World, 1967.

Ebeling, Gerhard. *On Prayer: The Lord's Prayer in Today's World.* Philadelphia: Fortress, 1978.

Farmer, William R. *Jesus and the Gospel.* Philadelphia: Fortress, 1982.

Frye, Northrop. *The Great Code: The Bible and Literature.* New York: Harcourt Brace Jovanovich, 1982.

Fuller, Reginald H. *A Critical Introduction to the New Testament.* Naperville, Ill.: Allenson, 1966.

_____. *The Foundations of New Testament Christology.* London: Lutterworth Press, 1965.

Gaster, Theodore H., trans. *The Dead Sea Scriptures.* New York: Doubleday, Anchor, 1964.

Gerhardsson, Birger. *The Origins of the Gospel Traditions.* Philadelphia: Fortress, 1979.

Goodspeed, E. J. *The Apocrypha.* New York: Modern Library, 1959.

Grant, Michael. *Jesus: An Historian's Review of the Gospels.* New York: Scribner, 1977.

Grant, Robert M. *Early Christianity and Society.* New York: Harper & Row, 1977.

Guillaumont, A. et al. *The Gospel according to Thomas.* New York: Harper & Row, 1959.

Hamerton-Kelly, Robert. *God the Father.* Philadelphia: Fortress, 1979.

Harner, Philip B. *Understanding the Lord's Prayer.* Philadelphia: Fortress, 1975.

Henry, Patrick. *New Directions in New Testament Study.* Philadelphia: Westminster, 1980.

Hultgren, Arland J. *Jesus and His Adversaries: The Form and Function of the Conflict Stories in the Synoptic Tradition.* Minneapolis: Augsburg, 1979.

Jeremias, Joachim. *The Central Message of the New Testament.* New York: Scribner, 1965.

_____. *The Eucharistic Words of Jesus.* New York: Scribner, 1966.

_____. *Jerusalem in the Time of Jesus.* Philadelphia: Fortress, 1978.

_____. *Jesus' Promise to the Nations.* London: SCM, 1958.

_____. *The Lord's Prayer.* Philadelphia: Fortress, 1964.

_____. *New Testament Theology: The Proclamation of Jesus.* New York: Scribner, 1971.

_____. *The Parables of Jesus.* London: SCM, 1958.

_____. *The Prayers of Jesus.* Philadelphia: Fortress, 1978.

_____. *The Problem of the Historical Jesus.* Philadelphia: Fortress, 1964.
_____. *Rediscovering the Parables.* London: SCM, 1966.
_____. *The Sermon on the Mount.* Philadelphia: Fortress, 1963.
_____. *Unknown Sayings of Jesus.* New York: Scribner, 1959.
Jonas, Hans. *The Gnostic Religion.* 2d ed. Boston: Beacon Press, 1963.
Josephus, Flavius. *The Great Roman-Jewish War.* New York: Harper, 1960.
Kähler, Martin. *The So-Called Historical Jesus and the Historic Biblical Christ.* Philadelphia: Fortress, 1964.
Keck, Leander E. *A Future for the Historical Jesus.* Nashville: Abingdon, 1972.
Kee, Howard Clark. *The Origins of Christianity: Sources and Documents.* Englewood Cliffs, N.J.: Prentice-Hall, 1973.
Keller, Werner. *The Bible as History.* New York: Morrow, 1981.
Krentz, Edgar. *The Historical Critical Method.* Philadelphia: Fortress Press, 1975.
Kummel, W. G. *Promise and Fulfillment.* London: SCM, 1957.
Küng, Hans. *On Being a Christian.* New York: Doubleday, 1978.
_____. *Signposts for the Future.* New York: Doubleday, 1978.
Lapide, Pinchas. *Israelis, Jews and Jesus.* New York: Doubleday, 1979.
Lattimore, Richard. *The Four Gospels and the Revelation.* New York: Farrar, Straus & Giroux, 1979.
Lewis, C. S. *The Four Loves.* Philadelphia: Westminster, 1978.
Lipman, Eugene J., ed. and trans. *Mishnah: Oral Traditions of Judaism.* New York: Schocken, 1974.
Lohse, Eduard. *The New Testament Environment.* Nashville: Abingdon, 1976.
MacArthur, Harvey K. *Understanding the Sermon on the Mount.* New York: Harper & Brothers, 1960.
McKnight, Edgar V. *Meaning in Texts: The Historical Shaping of a Narrative Hermeneutics.* Philadelphia: Fortress, 1978.
_____. *What Is Form Criticism.* Philadelphia: Fortress, 1965.
Macquarrie, John. *The Humility of God.* Philadelphia: Westminster, 1978.
Manson, T. W. *The Teaching of Jesus: Studies of Its Form and Content.* 2d ed. Cambridge: Cambridge University Press, 1959.
Martyn, J. Louis. *History and Theology in the Fourth Gospel.* New York: Harper & Row, 1968.
Marxsen, Willi. *Introduction to the New Testament: An Approach to Its Problems.* Philadelphia: Fortress, 1968.
_____. *Mark, the Evangelist.* Nashville: Abingdon, 1968.
_____. *The Resurrection of Jesus of Nazareth.* Philadelphia: Fortress, 1970.
May, Herbert G., and Metzger, Bruce M. *The New Oxford Annotated Bible with the Apocrypha.* New York: Oxford University Press, 1977.
Metzger, Bruce M. *The Early Versions of the New Testament: Their Origin, Transmission, Limitations.* Oxford: Clarendon Press, 1977.
_____, gen. ed., *The Reader's Digest Bible.* New York: Reader's Digest Association, 1982.
Moltmann, Jürgen. *The Crucified God.* New York: Harper & Row, 1974.
_____. *The Passion for Life: A Messianic Lifestyle.* Philadelphia: Fortress, 1978.
Mowry, Lucetta. *The Dead Sea Scrolls and the Early Christian Church.* Notre Dame: University of Notre Dame Press, 1966.

Nickle, Keith F. *The Synoptic Gospels*. Atlanta: John Knox, 1980.

Pannenberg, Wolfhart. *Jesus: God and Man*. Philadelphia: Westminster, 1979.

Pagels, Elaine. *The Gnostic Gospels*. New York: Random, 1979.

Patte, Daniel. *What Is Structural Exegesis?* Philadelphia: Fortress, 1976.

Perrin, Norman. *Jesus and the Language of the Kingdom*. Philadelphia: Fortress, 1976.

_____. *The Kingdom of God in the Teaching of Jesus*. Philadelphia: Westminster, 1963.

_____. *A Modern Pilgrimage in New Testament Christology*. Philadelphia: Fortress, 1974.

_____. *The New Testament: An Introduction*. New York: Harcourt Brace Jovanovich, 1974.

_____. *The Promise of Bultmann*. Philadelphia: Fortress, 1979.

_____. *Rediscovering the Teaching of Jesus*. New York: Harper & Row, 1967.

_____. *The Resurrection according to Matthew, Mark and Luke*. Philadelphia: Fortress, 1977.

_____. *What Is Redaction Criticism?* Rev. ed. Philadelphia: Fortress, 1971.

Rabin, Chaim. *Qumran Studies*. New York: Schocken, 1975.

Reicke, Bo. *The New Testament Era: The World of the Bible From 500 B.C. to A.D. 100*. Philadelphia: Fortress, 1979.

Reumann, John. *Jesus in the Church's Gospels*. Philadelphia: Fortress, 1977.

Robïnson, James M., ed. *The Nag Hammadi Library*. New York: Harper & Row, 1977.

_____. *The New Quest of the Historical Jesus*. London: SCM, 1959.

_____. *The Problem of History in Mark and Other Marcan Studies*. Philadelphia: Fortress Press, 1982.

The Sayings of the Fathers. New York: Schocken, 1962 (Hebrew and English).

Russell, D. S. *The Method and Message of Jewish Apocalyptic*. Philadelphia: Westminster, 1964.

Sanders, Jack T. *Ethics in the New Testament*. Philadelphia: Fortress, 1975.

Schillebeeckx, Edward. *Jesus: An Experiment in Christology*. New York: Seabury, 1979.

Schweitzer, Albert. *The Quest of the Historical Jesus*. New York: Macmillan, 1968.

Simon, Marcel. *Jewish Sects at the Time of Jesus*. Philadelphia: Fortress, 1980.

Smith, Morton. *Jesus the Magician*. New York: Harper & Row, 1978.

Spivey, Robert A., and Smith, D. Moody, Jr. *Anatomy of the New Testament: A Guide to Its Structure and Meaning*. New York: Macmillan, 1969.

Stoldt, Hans Herbert. *History and Criticism of the Marcan Hypothesis*. Macon: Mercer University Press, 1980.

Talbert, Charles H. *What Is a Gospel?* Philadelphia: Fortress, 1977.

Tatum, Barnes. *In Quest of Jesus*. Atlanta: John Knox Press, 1982.

Throckmorton, Burton H., Jr., ed. *Gospel Parallels: A Synopsis of the First Three Gospels*. 4th rev. ed. Nashville: Nelson, 1979.

Tillich, Paul. *The New Being*. New York: Scribner, 1955.

Tödt, H. E. *The Son of Man in the Synoptic Tradition*. Philadelphia: Westminster, 1965.

Vermès, Géza. *The Dead Sea Scrolls in English*. 2d ed. New York: Penguin, 1977.

_____. *Jesus the Jew: A Historian's Reading of the Gospels*. New York: Macmillan, 1974.

Wilder, Amos N. *Early Christian Rhetoric: The Language of the Gospel*. Rev. ed. Cambridge: Harvard University Press, 1978.

Wrede, William. *The Messianic Secret*. London: J. Clarke, 1971.

ANSWERS TO
CHAPTER QUESTIONS

Sources and Methodology—Chapter 1

1. In order to distinguish between the authentic sayings of Jesus and interpretations by the writers of the gospels.
2. The four gospels; the nonsynoptic sayings of Jesus; the Coptic gospel of Thomas.
3. It is known as the "spiritual gospel"; its main purpose is to bring out Christ's significance to the believer; the teachings of Jesus have been filtered through the thinking of John; it offers little help in reconstructing the actual historical teaching of Jesus.
4. Everyone speaks with the same voice; there is too much interpretation by the evangelist; the vocabulary is different; the form of the gospel in John is different from the other three gospels; the illustrations in the synoptic gospels that are parables become allegories in John.
5. The parable is a story in which the characters are characters only and the story has only one major point. An allegory is a story in which the characters represent something else, and an allegory may have several major points.
6. The mistake has been made of interpreting parables as allegories in which the elements of the parable take on meanings that Jesus likely did not intend.
7. The Jesus of the first three gospels is reticent about making claims. But the Jesus of the fourth gospel, John, makes sweeping claims that seem to have been interpretations by John that the historical Jesus did not make, but that are true of the Christ of the Christian experience.
8. The Lord's Prayer, the parables, and the teaching concerning the kingdom of God.

9. The synoptic gospels.
10. Because they are similar in that they summarize the life of Jesus, are fairly parallel, and not always contradictory. These gospels are known as the "historical" gospels, while John is known as the "spiritual" gospel.
11. Mark.
12. Q.
13. M.
14. L.
15. No. They represent the way the teachings were understood and interpreted at a later date. These gospels were not written down until at least thirty years after Jesus died.
16. The noncanonical teachings of Jesus, some of which are found in portions of the Bible other than the gospels; others are found in Mohammedan sayings.
17. The Coptic gospel of Thomas.
18. There are sayings in Thomas that are parallel with those in the synoptics. There are also previously unknown sayings in the Coptic gospels that bear the mark of authenticity.
19. We compare the forms of the sayings from various sources; discover which is the earliest saying; discover the kinds of changes made in later forms; retranslate into Aramaic. In doing this we become aware of the reasons for some of the changes made in the early church as the sayings were translated from Aramaic to Greek; look for places in which there are elements in the teaching of Jesus that are different from the common teachings of Judaism of his day; concentrate on the actual teaching of Jesus and use these to discover consistencies in other supposed teaching of Jesus.

First-Century Judaism—Chapter 2

1. It helps to interpret the sayings of Jesus that are authentic according to the methods outlined in the first chapter. It also helps to understand the reinterpretations of the authentic sayings of Jesus made by the early church.
2. Palestinian Judaism and Hellenistic Judaism.
3. Palestinian Judaism.
4. The Old Testament, the Apocrypha, apocalyptic literature, the Dead Sea Scrolls, the writings of Flavius Josephus, rabbinical literature.

5. The Apocrypha.
6. Yes.
7. The Roman Catholic church.
8. It contains historical books, wisdom literature, novels, and apocalyptic literature.
9. "To reveal" or "to uncover."
10. The book of Daniel in the Old Testament and the book of Revelation in the New Testament.
11. It was written in symbols to confuse Syrians, but it was understood by Jews.
12. Qumran Texts.
13. The Dead Sea Scrolls consist of Old Testament texts, church "orders," devotional literature, apocalyptic literature, commentaries on Old Testament books, and passages from these books.
14. The children of light.
15. The children of darkness.
16. *The Wars of the Jews* and *The Antiquities of the Jews.*
17. Exposition of the Law, commentaries on scriptures, translations of Hebrew scriptures into Aramaic. (These are highly interpretative.)
18. Mishnah—interprets the Law of Moses in the Torah; Talmud—seeks to apply the interpretations to a way of life.
19. Midrashim.
20. Targums.
21. Shammai, Hillel, Akiba.
22. No. Not until his father has died.
23. It makes him as a gentile; he is associated with unclean animals; it puts him outside the mercy of God because Jews thought of gentiles as outside the mercy of God.
24. Jews were reluctant to use the name of God.
25. Puts a robe on him; puts a ring on his finger; puts shoes on his feet.
26. It means that his son is the guest of honor.
27. The ring signifies authority. It gives the son the authority to enter into contracts for his father.
28. Shoes are the mark of a free man.
29. God would accept only penitent Jewish sinners; God would not accept penitent gentiles; God would not accept penitent Jews who had made themselves as gentiles.
30. God did not limit his mercy only to Jews; Jesus was saying the scope of God's mercy reached out to all persons.

The Kingdom of God—Chapter 3

1. One hundred times.
2. Twelve times.
3. The Christian gospel, the Christian way of life, the Christian church.
4. No.
5. No.
6. Matthew 4:23; Luke 9:27.
7. Determining what he meant.
8. The era of Pentecost in the Christian church; a moral reformation of society; the rule of God to be established by moral and spiritual reform; the catastrophic activity of God in which God breaks into history, moving stars, transforming the earth, and destroying evil.
9. Palestinian Judaism.
10. Jesus used the term "kingdom of God" without explaining what he meant. Therefore, his hearers must have understood his meaning. If we reach an understanding of what his hearers would have understood the meaning to be, we will then know what Jesus meant by the term.
11. The two terms mean the same thing.
12. Because they were reluctant to use the actual name of God. They would find a substitute that would communicate the same meaning.
13. He uses "kingdom of heaven" because he is a conservative Jew and does not want to say God.
14. He uses "kingdom of God" because he is gentile and has no prejudice against using the term that communicates best.
15. Both terms because he is a Jew who has lived a long time in the gentile world.
16. Power, mighty deeds.
17. Area of rule; kingship.
18. *Malkuth*.
19. It meant what the king does or the kingly activity.
20. They looked toward the future.
21. The time when God would act decisively and visit to redeem people; the time when God would intervene in human history to save people; the time when God would change everything, destroy evil, forgive sins, and establish the blessing of the End Time.
22. The eschatological hope.

23. It is in connection with this eschatological hope that the term kingdom of God is used.
24. It is speaking of that precise moment in human history when the kingly activity of God would become known in human experience.
25. They are prayers asking God to act in behalf of people, to visit and redeem; to destroy evil; to forgive sins and bring salvation; to establish a perfect relationship with people that will last forever. In other words, it is a prayer that God will act speedily in people's behalf.
26. The intervention of God into human history at some precise moment; the final blessed state which this intervention will bring about.
27. No. It is a new note in apocalyptic literature and the Dead Sea Scrolls.
28. To refer to the activity of God; the end to which this activity of God is directed, that final blessed state. ·
29. He used it in the same way it was used in the Kaddish prayer—to refer to God's kingly activity.
30. It was in reference to a decisive intervention into history and human experience similar to the decisive intervention expected by the people of the Dead Sea Scrolls in the war between the children of light and the children of darkness, except it is broader in scope than this.
31. The individual is the arena of conflict between good and evil; it is through Jesus and his ministry that God is manifesting kingly activity.
32. It is saying that Jesus is manifesting the kingly activity of God by entering in the struggle of good and evil.
33. John the Baptist.
34. This is taken to mean that evil will counterattack against the forces of good and that they will have temporary victories. This is also taken to be an implication of the coming death of John the Baptist.
35. They believed God's intervention would be accompanied by signs such as falling stars, earthquakes, etc.
36. He says that it does not show up in signs such as earthquakes and stars falling, but it is known in the experience of the believer; it is present in the individual who is confronted by the ministry of Jesus.
37. The activity of God will lead to a final state in which the values of God will be established and not the values of humankind.

38. It is used to symbolize that final sharing of the eternal blessings of God that will happen at some time in the future.
39. Jesus says, "How can the guests fast when the bridegroom is still with them?" He is saying that the feast is in the present and claims that people in his ministry are now sharing in the blessings of God.
40. Both a present and a future time.
41. Persons will receive or enter into the kingdom, or this final blessed state, through his ministry.

The Forgiveness of Sins—Chapter 4

1. He thought God looked with favor toward him.
2. He thought God looked with disfavor toward him, a consequence of his sins.
3. God would look with disfavor upon the nation and would cause it to be unhappy and meet with misfortune.
4. He had committed a small sin without knowing it.
5. They must have done some good things without knowing about it.
6. Temple sacrifices; works of special virtue; the suffering and death of righteous individuals; the High Priest, coming from the Holy of Holies, could give atonement simply by touching a person. Also, the death of a High Priest atoned for sin. For instance, all murderers were set free when the High Priest died; the people of the Dead Sea Scrolls thought the suffering and death of the High Priest would atone for the sin of the land.
7. It was not seen as a burden but as a means of grace and as a gift of God, and a means through which the Jew could earn God's favor.
8. No; in fact there was a sort of 10 percent "breakage allowance."
9. He earned special favor.
10. Isaiah 53, the story of the suffering servant who suffers for the sins of many. Also, from the Maccabean Revolt, in which many Jews were subject to persecution. In an attempt to force them to renounce God, they did not renounce God, but kept their faith. It was thought that this atoned for the sins of the people.
11. The coming of the Messiah, who would pardon their sins.
12. A gentile was a person who lived beyond or outside the law and therefore was "beyond the pale" or beyond the scope of God's forgiveness.

13. The sinner or gentile who lived beyond the law and scope of God's mercy; the Jews—people who lived within the Law yet failed.
14. Only destruction because they lived beyond the scope of God's mercy.
15. If he made himself as a gentile. For instance, to become a swineherd or to become a tax collector.
16. If she accepted only Jewish clientele, she was only a sinner and still had hope; but if she accepted gentile clientele, she became as a gentile and was beyond the scope of God's mercy.
17. It means tax collectors and other Jews who have made themselves as gentiles and hence have put themselves beyond the scope of God's mercy.
18. No; he was to be a Messiah only to the Jews. Gentiles and Jews who had made themselves as gentiles were to be excluded.
19. No; Jesus taught that the mercy of God extended to gentiles as well as Jews.
20. By claiming to forgive sins and also by healing.
21. No; the Jews would have seen the paralysis as a result of this man's sins. If Jesus had not been able to heal this man's paralysis, the Jews would not have considered his sins forgiven.
22. The treasure and pearl are symbols of Jesus' offer of forgiveness.
23. He would be cut off from the forgiveness of God.
24. He forgave sins through his actions and not through words; he implicitly claimed to be the Messiah. Second, he healed people in the context of forgiveness of sins. Third, he claimed that God forgave the sins of those who had made themselves as gentiles if they responded to the challenge of his forgiveness.
25. Levi was a tax collector, a Jew who had made himself as a gentile.
26. Table fellowship for the Jews was a most intimate fellowship; to eat at the same table with a gentile was to make yourself as a gentile.
27. They reject the idea that Jesus is a man of God because if he were, they assumed, he would know that the woman was a sinner; since God rejected a person who had made herself as a gentile, he would not allow her to do this.
28. The Jews had no word for "thank you"; to shows thanks, they expressed it through some act. To kiss a person's feet was the supreme way of saying "thank you."
29. He is offering to bring the challenge of the forgiveness of sins to all who will repent. This would include gentiles.
30. The Christian gospel is for all the world.

The Fatherliness of God—Chapter 5

1. The child's word *daddy*.
2. *Abba*.
3. "Maker and Father of this universe."
4. Aratus of Soli.
5. Cleanthes (300–220 B.C.).
6. Because God is Creator.
7. There is a vast difference between Old Testament thought and Greek thought.
8. Because God acts in a fatherly way toward children.
9. God redeems children; guiding and helping them; disciplining them.
10. We should act as children of God, acting in the way children should act toward their parent.
11. With love and obedience.
12. God is parent to those who respond as children who are God-fearing.
13. It carries with it privileges and responsibilities.
14. God will visit and act decisively in the End Time to redeem people and to form a new relationship with them.
15. Yes.
16. Because *abba* is the same as the English word *daddy*, which they felt is not dignified enough.
17. To stress the new relationship that Jesus enjoys with God, the eschatological parent-child relationship.
18. Yes, he teaches the disciples they also enjoy this new relationship, this eschatological relationship with God. He shows this by teaching them to use *abba* in the Lord's Prayer.
19. By forgiving others.

Ethics As Response—Chapter 6

1. The Sermon on the Mount.
2. Augustine; Francis of Assisi; Leo Tolstoy; the Anabaptists.
3. The phrase "without a cause."
4. The teaching of Jesus found in the New Testament should be interpreted literally.
5. The teaching of Jesus should be taken literally, but not absolutely so.

6. The ethical teaching of Jesus contains hyperbole, which are over-statements made to get the point across; the teaching need not be followed strictly or drastically.

7. Jesus' teachings are merely illustrations used to communicate principles of conduct, which we must understand and apply accordingly, rather than literally.

8. Jesus is talking about attitudes in many places rather than teaching us the literal act of which he is speaking; also, Jesus apparently means that if we have the right attitude, we will naturally act appropriately.

9. We are to distinguish between precepts and counsels in the teaching of Jesus. Precepts are those teachings absolutely essential for us to follow for salvation. Counsels are those teachings that are not absolutely essential, but which give added insurance for those who wish to be saved and wish to follow them.

10. The perfect class, which attempts to fulfill both precepts and the counsels; the second class, which attempts to fulfill only the precepts.

11. The two-realms view.

12. Martin Luther said that human activity can be divided into two spheres, the spiritual and the temporal, or worldly sphere. The spiritual sphere is the Christian obligation to obey all the commandments of the Sermon on the Mount. The temporal, or secular sphere, says that man should follow the dictates of natural law or conclusions which are based on common sense or logic.

13. No. There are no distinctions in the teaching of Jesus that would substantiate these views.

14. That Jesus proclaimed the kingdom of God as imminent; that God is about to act and persons should make a superhuman effort ethically to conform to the teachings of Jesus before the coming of the kingdom in the future. It is only in this interim period between the proclamation of Jesus and the coming of the kingdom in the future that the ethical teachings of Jesus are proclaimed.

15. Albert Schweitzer.

16. Johannes Weiss.

17. That the teaching of Jesus expresses impossible ideals, which are designed to drive people to despair so they may be prepared for the good news of the gospel.

18. The absolutist view; the modification view; the hyperbole view; the general-principles view; the attitude-not-acts view; the double-standard view; the two-realms view; the interim-ethics view; the preparation-for-the-gospel view.

19. The proclamation of the kingdom.
20. God is active in the world.
21. That the proclamation of the kingdom has been understood.
22. That the disciples have already found the light of the world in Jesus himself.
23. The commandment to forgive trespasses presupposes the offer of forgiveness.
24. He presupposes the proclamation that the time of the Law has run out because the time of salvation is beginning, and the paradise will of God is now valid.
25. It presupposes the dynamic of the boundless goodness of God experienced in the intervention in our history and experience.
26. No. It refers to the formal persecution of the followers of Jesus as heretics.
27. That the Christian has already responded to the activity of God experientially.
28. The key to understanding the ethical teaching of Jesus is that the ethical teaching follows after the proclamation.
29. It is designed to illustrate the response that persons must make to the kingly activity of God.
30. Jewish prayers tend to be unconditional; they simply ask for forgiveness. The Lord's Prayer is conditional; it is based on the condition that God forgives us as we ourselves forgive.
31. Because the same Aramaic word means both "sin" and "debt."
32. Luke, who says, ". . . as we ourselves forgive everyone who is indebted to us," which indicates something that is happening now in the present.
33. No. It happens at the same time as God's forgiveness.
34. It is another example of our response to the forgiveness of God or the proclamation of the kingdom.
35. No.
36. The Lord's Prayer is brief, personal, and direct; the Jewish prayers are long, involved, and indirect.
37. In the Dead Sea Scrolls, from the Manual of Discipline.
38. To the people of the Dead Sea Scrolls.
39. It is like the person who discovers the kingly activity of God and makes the appropriate response.
40. Because she has shown a willingness to respond to the forgiveness of God.
41. She has faith that Jesus has the right to forgive sins. She has shown faith in her willingness to respond to this forgiveness.

Ethics and the Will of God—Chapter 7

1. Because the Law of God was considered to be the Law of the community.
2. It was a trick question asked to trap Jesus into saying either that it is lawful, in which case they would have said he was being sacrilegious; or that it was not lawful, in which case they would have said to the Romans that "this man teaches sedition."
3. That he had public stature and recognition as a rabbi.
4. In Mark 12:18, where the Sadducees ask him about the woman who married seven brothers in succession; in Mark 12:28, where Jesus is asked which commandment is the first of all; Luke 12:13, where Jesus is asked by a man to make his brother share his inheritance with him.
5. Yes.
6. No.
7. He has a contempt for tradition because he says the time for tradition is past; he has no concern for ritual cleanliness; in his teaching, the new relationship with God makes it unnecessary; he rejects the specific Law of Moses; in his teaching, there is a new law for the new situation.
8. His saying "You do not sew a new patch on to old cloth" and the saying "You do not put new wine into old wineskins."
9. He rejects the practice of fasting because he says the time for this particular aspect of the Law is past; he rejects the traditional understanding of the sabbath and work; contempt for everyday law was interpreted and applied to life.
10. He says, "How can wedding guests fast when the bridegroom is still with them?"
11. If there were a wedding on a fasting day, the requirement for fasting would be lifted. Jesus was saying that his coming was like the wedding feast of God, the Messiah, and his community.
12. He points out that David ate the show bread when he was on a special mission with his army.
13. That he and his disciples are on a special mission for God that supersedes the requirement for not working on the sabbath.
14. That the sabbath was made for people, and not people for the sabbath.
15. Jesus says that it is not the things that go into a man, but those things that come out of him that defile him.

16. He is implying that it is the person's attitude, the way he approaches life, which is critical; by this saying, he banishes the distinction between the sacred and the secular.
17. He brushes the teaching of Moses aside almost contemptuously.
18. He refers to Genesis 1:27 and Genesis 2:24, in which the paradise understanding of marriage is indicated, in which man and woman become one flesh; he says that Moses gives his teaching because of our hardness of heart, which is the fallen state of humanity. He implies, then, that this is no longer applicable because of the new understanding of the will of God brought about by the proclamation of the kingdom.
19. More.
20. Concrete and specific situations.
21. He says, "He who is angry at his brother," etc., found in Matthew 5:21-26.
22. The implication that if the person simply has the wrong attitude, he is also in the wrong.
23. Jesus deliberately contrasts the new interpretation with the old Mosaic Law.
24. He says that he who lusts after a woman in his heart does the same as committing the act itself.
25. In the fact that he says, "The old law says, but *I* say," i.e., he contrasts his teaching with the old teaching.
26. Jesus said, "Resist not evil."
27. Jesus is saying to give the man your animal because you are exercising love in a concrete human situation. He does not say it as a practical matter of not being beaten.
28. The Christian is to do this out of love rather than self-consideration.
29. We must guard against legalizing the commandments of Jesus in the same way the Pharisees legalized the teachings of the Old Testament. Jesus' teaching is more of an attitude from which actions are a natural response.
30. He is suggesting that we imitate God in the sense that we try to attain the perfection of God by loving other persons.
31. No.
32. The nature of love reveals a unity here. God challenges us in the concreteness of our neighbor's situation.

Discipleship—Chapter 8

1. They were trained in exegesis and interpretation of the Law and oral tradition.
2. *Talmids.*
3. He was an interpreter of the Law; he settled legal disputes and was considered to be a lawyer; at times he functioned as a judge, teacher, and preacher.
4. No.
5. John the Baptist.
6. John and his disciples not only preach and teach, but John proclaims the imminent coming of the kingdom of God and conducts a ministry of preparation for the coming of the kingdom. He challenges men and women to repent and prepare themselves for the coming by being baptized; he asks them to live a special kind of life, following high moral standards.
7. The baptism of John was a purification for the preparation to receive the kingly activity of God. Jesus' baptism was the possession of the knowledge of the kingly activity of God, its gift and benefits as well as its challenge and responsibilities.
8. John prepares his followers for the kingdom to come; Jesus declares the kingdom to be present in his own ministry.
9. Jesus' disciples were those from among his followers whom he personally chose to call to discipleship.
10. *Shewilyas.*
11. The disciples of Jesus were called to be practical apprentices instead of academic apprentices. Jesus' disciples were to learn a task, as a carpenter or builder might, and then go out and perform this task. This can be contrasted with the role of the *talmid,* who simply learned theoretical teaching and then reproduced these teachings. Jesus' disciples were called upon to do something as well as teach something.
12. They are to go out and proclaim the presence of the kingdom, manifest the presence of the kingdom by exorcism or the casting out of demons, as well as teaching and doing good. They are to be "fishers," who are to go out and challenge others to participate in the kingly activity of God.
13. The call to discipleship is for anyone; God's forgiveness knows no bounds; anyone can be a disciple of Christ; there must be no delay in responding to the call to discipleship; the call must not be answered hastily, but must be considered well; the call to

discipleship is a call to conflict; Jesus said, "I come not to bring peace, but a sword."

14. It should read, "Cause me not to come into the power of temptation."

15. The Greek word *peirasmos* should be used. This word means much more than our word *temptation*. It means "temptation," "trial," "tribulation," "stress," and refers to anything that can bring doubt or difficulty or cause trouble or distress. It can also mean "to have doubt."

16. There were twelve tribes of Israel, the people of God; outside the Temple, as a part of every weekly worship, the Jews placed twelve loaves of bread, called the bread of the Presence, which symbolized that the people of God were in the presence of God. The twelve disciples of Jesus represent the formation of the new and true people of God.

Jesus and the Future—Chapter 9

1. Yes.
2. They believed that his message was one of moral and political reform and that his message was concerned with the transformation of society and of human relationships. They believed that the kingdom of God was to be the transformed society—that society which would be transformed by the spirit of God. They believed that transformation began with the ministry of Jesus and will continue until it is complete.
3. No. This is a basic misunderstanding of the phrase; the phrase does not refer to a community or society.
4. The kingly activity of God.
5. Schweitzer said that the "kingdom of God" means the activity of God breaking into world history. He thought of Jesus as a deluded fanatic who expected God's activity to irrupt into history sometime in the immediate future.
6. The importance of his view is that he exploded the liberal myth—the understanding of the term "kingdom of God" by the liberals. He emphasized the kingly activity of God rather than the kingdom of God being a community or society.
7. Dodd agrees that the kingdom of God refers to God's activity, but thinks this activity is wholly present, i.e., it refers to present rather than future. He says that it does not refer to the future at all.
8. The kingdom of God refers to both the present and the future activity of God.

9. It referred to the eschatological figure of the Messiah, who would shepherd the sheep of God.
10. Yes.
11. The presence of the kingdom is part of the message of the parables; Jesus continually speaks of himself and his work in eschatological imagery; Jesus applies to himself and to his ministry Old Testament prophecies referring to the joys of the messianic age that were understood by Jews of his day to be references to the End Time; Jesus speaks of himself and his ministry in a way that implies that the messianic times have begun.
12. Yes.
13. The Son of man depicts one who comes from God as a judge; this coming of the Son of man symbolizes the judgment of God. This was interpreted later by the church to mean a return of Jesus.
14. Agriculture was understood by the Jews at the time of Jesus, but not in the way we understand it, as a gradual growth, the blossoming and fulfilling of the natural process of plant life; they understood it as magic. The only connection seen was that the seeds were planted and the contrasting result was fruit.
15. The future state of things will reverse conditions of the present, i.e., the hidden will be revealed, things valuable will become valueless, etc. The values of God will be established. There will be a new Temple that is not made with hands; this symbolizes a future state in which there will be pure relationships with God. There is symbolism of the messianic banquet, the feast of the End Time. This means that people will enjoy the closest possible kind of fellowship with one another. The experience of the disciples of Jesus will come to an end, or climax. The teachings about the climax about discipleship in which the disciples were taught to expect a future climactic judgment. The teaching that people will be judged according to their response to the challenge of Jesus.

Jesus' Understanding of Himself—
Chapter 10

1. Jesus did not explicitly claim to be the Messiah; we do not know how he understood his own death; he may have never used the term *Son of man* in reference to himself.
2. No. Nowhere in the gospels is there anything that resembles a biographical account or autobiographical account of the experience of Jesus.

3. This is the understanding of the early church, which read back these expressions of faith onto the lips of Jesus. Jesus likely did not actually say them.

4. They are primarily proclamations of faith by the early church.

5. We cannot know anything directly because we simply do not have the resource material. The gospels represent the understanding and faith of the early church, rather than presenting a historical account of the teaching of Jesus.

6. We must learn about the messianic consciousness indirectly by studying the teaching of Jesus and by understanding what is implied by these teachings.

7. The implication of the claim of Jesus that the kingdom of God was present in his teaching is that he himself is a mediator between humankind and God. This claim is never directly stated by Jesus, only implied.

8. It would seem that in Jesus' claim to be able to forgive sins on his own authority there is the implied claim that he is a mediator between persons and God.

9. This implied claim shows that Jesus himself enjoyed the eschatological father-son relationship of the End Time. He also taught his disciples to address God as *abba*. By this, he implied the claim that he had the authority to include others in this relationship. This again demonstrates an authority similar to that expected by the Jews of his time of the expected Messiah.

10. Jesus had contempt for oral tradition and indicated that the time for oral tradition has passed. He reinterprets the law with authority. This implies that he himself supersedes Moses, and that he is the Messiah.

11. In Mark 8:38, Jesus claims that he who is ashamed of Jesus will find the Son of man ashamed of him when he comes in his glory. This indicates that a person will be judged in the eschatological End Time according to his reaction to the ministry of Jesus. This implies that Jesus is the Messiah.

12. Jesus did not claim directly that he was the Messiah, but certainly this claim was implicit in his actions and teachings.

13. He claimed implicitly to mediate between God and humankind; he proclaimed the eschatological forgiveness of sins; he claimed to enjoy the eschatological father-son relationship with God; he claimed the authority to supersede the Law of Moses; he claimed that one's response to him would be a criterion for judgment at the Consummation.

14. Direct experience of God.

15. A vision from God.
16. No.
17. He derived his authority from the chain of tradition in which he stood.
18. No.
19. Yes.
20. No; the Jews expected the Messiah to authenticate himself and his teaching.
21. The directness of the teaching itself.
22. This is the early church reading authentication back into the authority of Jesus.
23. Jesus made no claim of authority, but simply acted directly with authority with the people he dealt with; he healed the sick, called the disciples, cast out demons, and forgave sins.
24. He showed it indirectly and implicitly by acting and teaching with authority.
25. Because he apparently thought the Jews would become involved in an objective, legalistic inquiry over whether he was the Messiah or not, and would tend to look at his teaching and actions secondarily. Jesus wanted his actions and teaching to be the prime center of attention, not a legalistic claim to authority of being the Messiah, because "objectivity is death to faith."

The First Century and the Twentieth—
Chapter 11

1. The Christ of the *kerygma* and the risen Lord of our own personal experience.
2. Our faith is not directly concerned with the historical Jesus except insofar as the teachings of the historical Jesus find confirmation in the Christ of our experience.
3. Jesus was wrong about the Consummation.
4. They identified these as one and the same. The Christ of the *kerygma* was the risen historical Jesus.
5. The historical Jesus proclaimed the kingdom of God; he was a proclaimer. But the Christ of the *kerygma* is proclaimed by the church as the eschatological event. The proclaimer has become the proclaimed. The historical Jesus is the pre-cross-and-resurrection figure and the Christ of the *kerygma* is the post-cross-and-resurrection figure.

6. They are one and the same; the resurrection of Christ is God acting eschatologically and decisively.
7. It interpreted, modified, and added meanings to the teaching of the Jesus tradition.
8. It presents new possibilities for a deeper understanding of the Christian faith in addition to those possibilities open to an uncritical reader of the New Testament.
9. He gave examples that illustrate what we should do in a given general setting; from this we must take the meaning of these examples and apply them ourselves as love dictates.
10. The kingdom of God and Jesus are the same thing; both are the eschatological irruption of God into human activity.
11. Forgiveness of sins.
12. It has lost none of its meaning from the early church; it indicates the need for a dynamic expression of the intimacy of the relationship of God possible for humankind because of Jesus.
13. It may mean settling down in a community and supporting the local church. The disciple today is commissioned, like the disciples of Jesus' time, to do what Jesus could not do in places where he could not go; to carry the same message and have the same authority and power as the disciples of the first century.

GENERAL INDEX

ACKNOWLEDGMENTS

To each person for a special and meaningful contribution: James W. Sells, Jeanne H. Page, Phillip Prescott, Barbara Prosch Lloyed Perkins, Pat Shropshire, James W. Abernathy, Nolan B. Harmon, Paul Walter, Jonne Walter, Charles Preacher, Lorena Abernathy, William H. Danforth, June Alexander, William Greider, Oswald Bronson, Neil Kirschner, Ross Cox, Theodore Runyon, Ira L. Andrews III, Ben Abernathy, John E. Fellers, D. W. Alexander, Thomas Lane Butts, Emma Norris, Mike Anderson, Kathy Abernathy, Earl G. Hunt, Jr., Alice Lee, Jim Abernathy, John Hayes, Nancy Ergle, Ruth Elaine Miller, Marc Abernathy, J. W. Parker, Savannah Scarborough, Horace Maness, A. Glenn Lackey, Bev Jones, Diane Davis, Costen J. Harrell, Tricia Fordham, Chad Abernathy, Clay Lee, Bill Mallard, William R. Cannon, Bill Huie, Jim Lineberger, Leonard Gillingham, Bob Robertson, Barry Bailey, Merton Coulter, Jean Berry, Nan Day, Laura Lowman, Beverly Masters, Al Norris, Gene Carroll, Rosalynn Kirshner, Mildred Lyerly, David O'Keefe, Bill Asher, Jack Whelan, W. Kenneth Goodson, Yeshua bar Joseph, Joel D. McDavid, Ernest Fitzgerald, John Thomas, Amy Chadwick, Alton Fitzgerald, Kazuko Yamagichi, Larry Emard, Ross Freeman, Horace Tron, Fred Lefever, L. Scott Allen, Don Kraus, Marcia Tuttle, Al Weston, Paul Duffey, Keli Arwood, C.J. Lupo, Curtis Schofield, F.O. Foard, Dick Byrd, Beatrice Cobb, and Eugene J. Coltrane.

About the Author

DAVID ABERNATHY has taught at several colleges and universities in the United States and overseas. He was also a tutor at Union Theological Seminary in the city of New York and served as a visiting faculty member at Emory University for seven years.